Knowing Her Place:
Research Literacies
and Feminist Occasions

Lorri Neilsen

1

Knowing Her Place

Knowing Her Place:
Research Literacies and Feminist Occasions

By Lorri Neilsen

Copyright 1998 by Lorri Neilsen

Published jointly by
Caddo Gap Press
    3145 Geary Boulevard, Suite 275
    San Francisco, California 94118, U.S.A.
Backalong Books
    Great Tancook Island
    Nova Scotia B0J 3G0, Canada

Artwork by Lorri Neilsen
Cover photograph of Kaikoura Coast, Aotearoa New Zealand
    by Lorri Neilsen
Cover design and production by Punch Productions
    Alan Barbour and Ted McInnes
    Halifax, Nova Scotia, Canada

ISBN 1-880192-27-6
List Price $25.95 US; $28.95 Canada.

Library of Congress Cataloging-in-Publication Data

Neilsen, Lorri.
    Knowing her place : research literacies and feminist occasions /
  Lorri Neilsen.
        p.   cm.
    Includes bibliographical references.
    ISBN 1-880192-27-6 (alk. paper)
    1. Feminism and education. 2. Education--Research--Social
  aspects. 3. Literacy--Social aspects. 4. Neilsen, Lorri.
  5. English teachers--Canada--Biography.   I. Title.
LC197.N45   1998
370'.7'2--dc21   98-16745
                                                           CIP

Contents

Acknowledgments

I have many people to thank for reading and responding to this work in its various forms. These readers variously cajoled me, cautioned me, and pushed my understanding. Some gave unbridled praise, and strengthened my convictions; others simply refused to understand what I was on about, and, as a result, my struggle to explain to them produced much clearer text. I am privileged to live a life that indulges such conversations.

I thank Donna Alvermann, Elizabeth Cantafio, Ardra Cole, Elizabeth Chiseri, Carolyn Colvin, Bronwyn Davies, Vivian Gadsden, Roy Graham, Madeleine Grumet, Jane Hansen, David Jardine, Gary Knowles, Susan Lytle, Allan Neilsen, Steve Phelps, Gary Rasberry, Sharn Rocco, Bonnie Sunstein, Rob Tierney, Valerie Walkerdine, and John Willinsky for your observations on the ideas in this collection over the years: in conversations over e-mail, at professional gatherings, at conference sites, or at my kitchen table, each of you has shaped and informed this work in ways you may never know. I have been enriched by the good humor and support of colleagues and friends who help me keep

4

Acknowledgments

a sense of proportion about being a woman/writing: Lindsay Brown, Ardra Cole, Arlene Connell, Sheree Fitch, Ursula Kelly, Ann Vibert, Verlie Wile, and Helen Woodrow. I owe a particular debt of gratitude to Alan H. Jones who, with Gary Knowles, was quick to support this work: Alan's care and attention have proven to me the benefits of small presses. I also thank anonymous reviewers whose comments improved the text in its many incarnations. Above all, I thank the women and men with whom I've worked in courses, seminars and workshops over the years.

—Lorri Neilsen

Prolegomena

"I just cleaned out my office and threw out three paradigms," my partner and colleague quipped as he prepared for his sabbatical. Like most humorous comments, it had the ring of truth. If we are socially constructed, our individual scholarly history must be, in its unique way, part of a history of the profession itself. We are always participating, in Fleck's term, in a "thought collective"; we are always a pulse in Jung's vibrant collective unconscious, responding to the world in ways we believe are individual but which surprise us by their widespread commonality when we work with them in public. It's a rich paradox: How many times have we responded to an intellectual impulse to pursue a specific direction, only to find, like the wolf arriving at the market at dawn, that the pig had already been and gone? How often have we felt that, whether we like it or not, the river of ideas will simply carry us with it, as long as we learn how to paddle and negotiate the patches of rough water?

Maxine Greene writes of the tension of striving to be an individual within the shaping influence of contexts in which we do our work: "Conscious as I have tried to be, I have lived inside a whole variety of ideologies and discursive practices, in spite of trying—through resistance and critique—to liberate myself" (1995, p. 74).

These essays can be read as a researcher's journey, for they track my development as a individual researcher working in writing and reading education, and my learning to participate in that broader community of researchers and educators. This collection travels the path I began as a graduate student schooled in experimental research, who turned a corner into qualitative inquiry. Then, inspired by the women with whom I have worked and challenged by the androcentric assumptions and practices of inquiry in literacy research, I continued the journey, finding myself now writing and reading in the field of feminist inquiry. Early in my professional life, I learned methods and formulae as one would learn the alphabet; as the seasons passed, my research literacies, like my writing and reading, began to describe and to motivate me: I began to live inside the work that I do, just as a literate adult (Neilsen, 1989) uses her literacy to be at home in her world.

Inside such work, I hear the wisdom in Carolyn Heilbrun's caution about feminist work, and scholarly work in general: that we are in "danger of refining the theory and scholarship at the expense of the lives of women who need to experience the fruits of research" (1988, p. 20). And so, this book, which tracks the beliefs about teaching, literacy, and inquiry that have shaped me, invites the reader to the edge of further exploration, just as my inquiry has invited me into the possibilities of untethered imaginings. Research is not only the creation of products to market at the academic ideology fair; research is the process of learning through the words, actions, and revisionings of our daily life. Inquiry is praxis that cannot be boxed up and deliv-

8

ered; it is a story with no ending.

And inside this work, too, I realize that the fact this research autobiography is written by a woman announces it differently. Because male, public discourse has traditionally been valued more highly in academia, women who choose to speak, and speak intimately, have learned to be self-conscious about their desire to be authors of their own words and their own lives. We have learned to believe those fictions about femininity (Walkerdine, 1990) that have regulated us, so that when we speak, when our voice—finally—rises above the malestream, we, ourselves, tend not to hear it.

This collection of research reports, poetic notes, interviews, field notes, and reconsiderations makes public and explicit the problematic relationship I have had with language and scholarly identity. It also offers commentary on the need for us all, male and female, to make explicit who we are as researchers and the consequences of what we do. The field benefits from our disclosures and our revisions, and our willingness never to give up on either.

The choice to discuss research perspectives by describing my own research forays and dilemmas is a choice to make visible what most of us, as researchers, have kept invisible. Countless books on method and theory in educational research will give us protocols and procedures we can follow. But creating research products is a little like producing a grand meal from delectable-sounding recipes; few of us choose to take our guests through the kitchen area afterwards where the evidence of creation and adaptation appears in all its mess and hopefulness. Few of us talk of how our menus reveal our personalities, our demons, and our predilections. This book does not elevate narcissism or solipsism, a charge often leveled at scholars, especially women, who divulge the personal in the public arena. This book, instead, aims to illustrate two key issues facing literacy research today. One, that the growth and life of the researcher is written into the work—the body is in the text. And secondly, making the invisible processes visible is an act of responsible scholarship, the final push to remove the vestiges of Cartesian thought and Western scientism that have allowed us all to escape response-ability.

We have too long hidden behind the mask of researcher and the products we market. Not enough has been written about our motives, our locations, our vested personal and political interests. Feminist perspectives have shown us how the flesh of story embraces, disturbs, and connects more strongly than disembodied, neutralized text. If we aim to change our worlds in small ways by the work we do, we owe those worlds as authentic a presence as we can bring. Elliot Mishler's call to researchers to show how our work is done (Mishler, 1990, p. 423) echoes his earlier call for meaning in context. We are learning that we are no longer mere creators of text, we are texts ourselves.

The term "research literacies" is a useful term to explore. At our university in Nova Scotia, graduate students in education were faced with a choice of a course either in statistical, experimental research or in qualitative methods. By the 1980s, students wanted to learn more about the diverse perspectives between and beyond the overly simplistic quantitative/qualitative split that research journals and university coursework seemed only to reify. Andy Manning initiated the course for the education department; since then several members of our department, including Blye Frank, Anne MacCleave, Ann Manicom, Allan Neilsen, John Portelli, and I, among others, have developed their versions of the "research literacies" course. Because the graduate students enrolled in the course are typically classroom teachers, the course offers not only a much-needed overview of research perspectives in education (including, as it must,

teacher research), it also offers teachers a passport into understanding research as it is used and abused by policymakers, by
tenured academics, and by commercial educational ventures.
Becoming "research" literate gives classroom teachers the encouragement, and the courage, to resist the practices and to
challenge the agendas of the powerful systems, governing institutions, and economic forces which affect the day-to-day lives of
children and adults in schools. And teaching "research literacies"
provides us, as academic researchers and teacher educators,
with regular opportunities to revise our understandings as well.

● ● ● ● ●

Prolegomena. The word rolls around my tongue, circles in my
mind like ribbons in the air. Its gently rhythmic quality is
appealing. To Begin sounds ominous, throat-clearing. Prolegomena sounds like a dance. But prolegomena is also a word not
commonly used on the street or in classrooms; it is a scholarly,
pretentious word. And therein lies the tension.

For almost two decades now, conversations with colleagues
have ignited my beliefs about teaching, inquiry, reading, writing, and gender. What seduces me with its power to clarify, and
to educate me, however, has always been writing. Writing not
only lets me know what I know, writing leads me to what I need
to learn. Words entice me; they are hooks on which to hang
ideas, malleable clay to mold tentative thoughts into coherent
forms, matches struck to sear my consciousness, alarm my
senses. Words in the academy, however, can be deadening, dull.
They are the coin of discursive power, and for those outside the
circles of such power, words can sound pompous, block a door to
understanding and connection. Clarity, concrete details,
grounded description are often hard to find in universities, and

11

seldom valued. The tension writers in the academy often feel is the tension embodied in the word "prolegomena": dancing word, distancing word, both? And so, throughout these essays, I have aimed to explain my ideas in ways that connect with both the classroom and the common room, the porch and the library. The stylistic choice here, as the reader will see, is also a political one.

This collection of essays grew out of my recognition that my research travels in education have, indeed, been a long, strange trip. Along the way I have invented, revealed, and struggled with identities for which the only name I can use, contested as it might be, is "selves"; these selves have participated in the world of educational research as I have perceived and understood it. Now, at the present, as I look around my own office, I know that even if I boxed up and removed the texts, journals, and research reports comprising the methodological shifts and understandings of twenty years—even if I, too, threw out three paradigms— the influence of these works remains. From these years and these materials I have forged a dedication to feminist inquiry in literacy and learning, and become passionate about writing and the creation of alternative texts for teaching, knowing and telling. E.M. Forster's credo that we "only connect" urges me to fuse the particular with the universal. We are what we do each moment: we become what we have done in the lattice of stories we carry with us.

With the exception of the first chapter, these essays have been written in chronological order. The chapters are meant to be read in the order in which they appear, but the pieces also stand alone. Some include the poetry or prose that rose from experience. Some essays have been published in another form elsewhere. While the collection here describes a certain chronology in inquiry, the pieces themselves appear in different genres, as snippets, anecdotes, poems, prose poetry, commentary, academic report, and dialogue. The voices of hundreds of co-re-searchers appear solo and in chorus. This collection might best be sampled, rather than read in a linear fashion. Whatever else these pieces do, my wish is that they resonate in the reader's memory and experience: yes, I've been there. Yes, I know this story.

My aims, as a writer, are familiar: to understand and to question. This work is not a textbook, nor is it a how-to book on inquiry. It violates the academic precept that writing must offer solutions, serve as a polemic, or as a panacea. The impulse to write this collection—or to be more accurate, to revise, to gather, to ruminate about years of work—is not to proselytize. Yes (in answer to Patti Lather's recent, and timely, conversation with me about inquiry): yes, I claim the inquiry in which I engage as science. And yes, feminist theorists and researchers are rebodying science in our own terms. But the field is open and we must argue for keeping it that way. Can the conventionally scientistic research done in literacy aspire to the status of inquiry, or feminist inquiry to the status of science? Who must answer to whom here? If there is room for multiple subjectivities, there is room for multiple authorities. Nancy Mairs' words speak for me here. Her perspective, while I share it, still leaves us with the challenges and the consequences of power games—the privileging of certain ideas—in academic inquiry.

> *To be blunt...I have no intention of trying to persuade others to adopt precepts and ways of being with which I'm still struggling myself. Moreover, the endless replication of a single system for structuring beliefs and behaviors in relation to the whole complicated world...strikes me as a dangerous idea....We're human, after all.... Safer to recognize our fallibility, generate a number of different imaginative patterns, and share them freely. (Ordinary Time.* Boston, MA: Beacon Press, 1993, p. 8)

Knowing Her Place

The first chapter, written recently as a "prequel," describes my initiation into inquiry, and situates studies I completed during my two graduate degree programs. Subsequent essays describe research activities and projects as I completed them, and as I analyzed their influence in a shifting relationship with inquiry. Because the work is cumulative, threads are brought through each successive piece. The appearance of these threads will be redundant for some readers, necessary context and clarity for others. These pieces are assembled so that graduate students in education, particularly in their studies of research perspectives, might find the chapters useful both individually and collectively.

The writing of the final chapter, "Painting Ghosts and Writing the Poetry Report," proved to me again how necessary writing is to my learning. Although I have been working with certain assumptions and beliefs about research for the last several years, it is writing which forces them out into the open. This is not news. Writing as inquiry remains one of the few "truths" I cling to. Beside me always are Miss Fergus, who told me to "just write" and not to censor myself, and Donald Murray, who said "when you think you've gone too far, go farther." My inquiry has been informed by hundreds who have taught me about inquiring with passion and care—Joe Maxwell at Harvard School of Education, the students and faculty of the Reading/ Writing program at the University of New Hampshire during the 1980s, teachers and students in Alberta, Nova Scotia, Newfoundland, North York, New Zealand, and Australia. Each person has left her or his mark on my ideas, my words, these pages: writing in research communities, after all, writes the researcher.

—Lorri Neilsen, Hubbards, Nova Scotia

References

Heilbrun, C. (1988). *Writing a woman's life*. New York: Ballantine Books.

Greene, M. (1995). *Releasing the imagination: Essays on education, the arts and social change*. San Francisco, CA: Jossey-Bass.

Mairs, N. (1993). *Ordinary time*. Boston, MA: Beacon Press.

Mishler, E. (1990). Validation in inquiry-guided research: The role of exemplars in narrative studies. *Harvard Educational Review*, 60, 415-442.

Neilsen, L. (1989). *Literacy and living*. Portsmouth, NH: Heinemann Educational Books.

Walkerdine, V. (1990). *Schoolgirl fictions*. London, UK: Verso Books.

Part One:
Finding Her Place

—1—
Degrees of Freedom

Not a tree but the tree
we saw, it will never exist, split by the wind
and bending down
like that again. What will push out of the earth
later, making it summer, will not be
grass, leaves, repetition, there will
have to be other words. When my
eyes close language vanishes.

—Margaret Atwood, *There is only one of everything*

Somewhere Out There

At the beginning of my adolescence, my family moved to a small northern Manitoba town, where my desire to know the world began to wax, mixed as it was with that inchoate adolescent longing to be Out There, wherever Out There happened to be. Late at night, I pretended to do homework while I turned the knob on the radio searching for signals from down south, usually American stations, carrying snippets of the newest songs. I strained to listen to the chatter of disc jockeys such as Wolfman Jack, and hear advertisements for products I knew would never reach the store shelves of a northern Canadian town. My longing, I realize now, was heavy with the desire for identity, any identity, and the recognition of all that I was not: not American, not mature, not knowledgeable, not in the center of the action of what I sensed, even then, to be the most influential generation, for good or ill, of the twentieth century. I ached to be free of that small town, to be somewhere other than on the edge of life, a restive, shy teenage girl grasping at scatterings of rock lyrics arcing over the earth's atmosphere in the night.

Had I been pressed for an answer about where Out There might be, I likely could not have said. New York? Motown? The beaches of California? or closer to home: Winnipeg? Montreal? The irony of my situation, of course, is rich: as the eldest daughter of a white working class family, as a healthy child born into one of the safest and wealthiest nations on the planet, and as a young student whose intellectual curiosity was recognized early and nourished by many teachers, I had no sense of my positioning as privileged, as being, in many respects, already in the mainstream of North American culture. The older girls at the back of the room, seemingly worldly and disinterested girls from the Métis reservation across the river from my home, drifted in and out of my awareness as they drifted in and out of class, sometimes for days at a time. I envied their insouciance, marvelled at their self-containment, giggled with them in the washroom during breaks. While I did not share my white classmates' derision and suspicion about Indian ways, I nevertheless saw little connection between these girls and me, understood nothing about the relationship between the centers and borders marking my life and theirs. They, too, were simply Out There.

To quell the confusion, like many adolescent girls whose

yearnings had no name, I wrote and I drew. Words, pencil lines, became my solace and my strength. If I was especially bored, I made up my own crossword puzzles or factoring problems to calculate: I loved patterns. I enjoyed mastering details as well, especially in school where it brought me approval and status. History and Latin appealed to me because the knowledge boundaries of those subjects, at least as presented by my teachers, were the boundaries of the textbook: facts could be memorized. English class engaged me because I enjoyed words and writing and, although I could not master the subject in the way I mastered a Latin verb list, I was attracted to the creative frontier that working in words represented.

More than twenty years later I found myself in a graduate program at the University of Minnesota. As a former junior high English, art, and drama teacher, now married to a Ph.D. student in education, I had come along to Minnesota because, well, that's what wives did. I never thought to do otherwise. The decision to spend my time there studying was similar, in many respects, to my decision to enter teaching years before. I was not nurse material; I loved language and the arts. Jobs were abundant. And so, like many women of my generation, I shifted from a degree in arts to one in education, landed a job, and was married. Six years later, at the time my husband applied for graduate school, I was teaching in a junior high school where the principal, an inflexible autocrat, was unsympathetic to the cause of the arts, and repressive in his treatment of adolescents. His assistant, who also believed in "running a tight ship," patrolled the hallways and found a certain delight in slipping his yardstick up the skirts of the girls who gathered in the hall when they ought to have been in class. My novice teacher idealism eroded quickly in that climate, and I knew full well I was powerless to change much. Someplace better, more humane had to be Out There. If

21

Finding Her Place

I knew more, perhaps I could help create such a place. If I knew more, perhaps I could name this unease. I was good at studying: why not try graduate school?

Although my passion for prose and poetry drew me to coursework about the Bloomsbury group, modern world drama, and contemporary poetry, the lure of the work of Levi-Strauss, the Russian formalists, and Noam Chomsky was irresistible. Here were ways to describe not only this moment, but this time, the ways we produce and use language to move the world. Theories of language, of literature? Imagine. My naivete about the world of ideas astonishes me now, but memories of the excitement I felt at the swelling of this awareness are clear. People created patterns out of ideas, latticework for the universe. Out There could be described, and people were doing just that. I had come to the place where could I peer through a keyhole, put my ear to the wall, listen to the conversation, and learn.

What I did not know then was that induction into the world of ideas about what reading, writing, and research are and can do would be a journey as much embodied as cerebral, and as much about being a woman socialized into communities, as an individual choosing to participate in the scholarly life. Somewhere out there is, in so many ways, in here, but I did not know it then; it takes years of experience to realize that life goes through us as much as we go through life, that we are trapped as much as we are free, and that those notions of liberty and constraint are constructs we create together. What follows here, in this chapter, is a description of the beginnings of the end of the foundationalism upon which I was raised. Chronologically, the story begins with my masters program in English education, and ends at the time of my doctoral studies ten years later. Epistemologically, I mark this time as the journey from positivist to post-positivist perspectives (Denzin & Lincoln, 1994). Since then,

22

another ten years have passed, and perhaps those years will tell another story. The journey in literacy research I describe here focuses on the ways in which a well-schooled academic becomes intellectually troubled; when the stone in my shoe at the beginning of my academic career brought me, finally, to an understanding of my need to engage in work that is artful, connected, and consistent with my emerging feminist sensibilities. This is a description not only of how and why an experimental researcher turned to qualitative research, but also how the personal and professional contexts conflate to create the researcher herself.

The Influence
of Headed Nominal Complexity

...statistics is a method of pursuing truth. If it is not your inclination to think that it can reveal "eternal truth," put it this way: it can least tell you the likelihood that your hunch is true in this time and place, with these sorts of people. This pursuit of truth...is the essence of psychology, of science and of human evolution. (Aron & Aron, 1994, pp. 1-2)

The act of research itself pleased and soothed me. Researching the work of Anton Chekhov or Vanessa Bell for English literature seminars, I could lose myself in the stacks of the library for hours. Only nightfall, and the flicking of the overhead lights, alerted me to the outside world again. The world of words, an expanding universe holding the promise of clarity and understanding, was documented in texts, in letters, in theoretical conversations to which all of us who could read and write had access. It was late in the day for the New Critical belief that meaning resides solely in the text, and a time of immense curiosity about universals.

Finding Her Place

Structuralist theory offered form, access to a code: skeletal structures for these fleshy texts, global melodies using universal notes. The weight of all I did not know was reassuring now, not daunting. Like a string saver, I began to gather.

But to complete my graduate program in English education, I would have to conduct research in education, not in English; this meant I would have to study inferential statistics. In the culture of the English department, research did not involve statistics: it was the task of putting together, often from the texts of centuries, a jigsaw puzzle of a million pieces, many of them sky or trees, either creating a theory or using a prevailing one in which to frame the pieces. Ironically, my close readings of E.M. Forster's *Howard's End* and C.P. Snow's *Two Cultures* offered the timely provocation I needed to alert me to the disjunctures ahead between research in the two communities of English and English education.

In the early days of statistics, in the 17th and 18th Centuries, it was popular to use the new methods to prove the existence of God. For example, John Arbuthnot discovered that more male than female babies were born in London between 1629 and 1710. In what is considered the first use of a statistical test, he proved that the male birthrate was higher than could be expected by chance, concluding that there was a plan operating, since males face more danger to obtain food for their families, and such planning, he said, could only be done by God. (Aron & Aron, 1994, p. 3)

Cognitive psychology and structural linguistics were the lenses through which most researchers approached the study of reading and writing in the mid-Seventies. Chomsky's work in transformational grammar not only served as an underlying model for research in reading and writing, but seemed to promise a structuralist agenda for the study of other human activity as well. The hope was that an understanding of the workings of linguistic variables in the text might tap into an understanding of cognition itself, of the way we think and we learn. Researchers' attempts to locate, identify, and name the building blocks of reading and writing in order to manipulate them and test their effect on comprehension seemed to comprise much of the field's research activities at the time. While my husband, working in a nearby building where "reading" was housed, used schema theory to look at the effects of macro structures and linguistic connectors on children's reading comprehension, I explored the structuralist promises of an understanding of syntactic complexity and composition instruction. Words together created sentences; sentences were syntactically different, and yet shared common features, or to use Chomsky's terms, deep structures, structures for which the writer may, like the speaker, be "prewired." Perhaps more sophisticated writers wrote more syntactically complex sentences, and perhaps the acquisition or development of this skill had a pattern, and could be taught. The logic was compelling, and the interlocking nature of parts, like the algebraic equations I loved to tackle in high school, created a satisfying challenge: like fixing a clock, solving a Mensa question, making a ledger add up. If structuralist notions applied to the text held a key, and if statistical analysis turned that key, perhaps there might be answers to the questions which grew in my mind: what is good writing? what can teachers do to foster the production of good writing among their students?

Janet Emig's monograph (1971) on the composing process of twelfth graders was an intriguing anomaly in the work of composition research at the time: it focused on process, not product. Although Emig had dropped a stone which would send ever-widening ripples through the profession about composing as a process in the years ahead, most researchers and theorists continued to use psycholinguistics as a foothold for examining the writer's product. The combined forces of psychology, linguistics, cognitive science (and the expanding computer metaphor), and statistics seemed a powerful alliance for unlocking the secrets of text. Structuralism was a movement which aimed to understand and articulate the systems which make an integral whole (systems of words, meanings, linguistic patterns, and so on); participating disciplines in this worldwide movement gathered at the level of text (encoding and decoding it) to search for universal patterns, and integrative strategies. As the French critic Barthes described it: "the structuralist activity involves two typical operations: dissection and articulation" (1964, p. 85). In their oft-quoted summary of the state of the science of written composition, Braddock, Lloyd-Jones, and Schoer (1963) wrote:

> ...the further we get away from the particularities of the sentence, the less stable our research becomes...some terms are being defined usefully, a number of procedures are being refined, but the field as a whole is laced with dreams, prejudices, and makeshift operations. (5)

Calling for research in composition isolating the writer variable, the assignment variable, the rater variable and the colleague variable, and lamenting the lack of research done "with the knowledge and care of the physical sciences" (5), Braddock *et al* set a course for research in composition that wanted a description of product as a function of variables, writing as a teachable set of behaviors, and teaching as a cause-effect activity. Although the structuralist goals of dissection and articulation were paramount, Braddock *et al* nevertheless commented on "the primacy of the writer's own experiences" (29) and the fact that the "student is inextricably intertwined with his [sic] environment" (33), including in their agenda for future research the very question that Janet Emig had begun to explore: what is involved in the act of writing? It seemed as though the elusive nature of composing, like a butterfly in flight, held certain mysteries: could we, at least, capture and dissect it?

My desire to work inside words was growing. I read poetry, attempted to write it. I spent hours at the Guthrie Theater in Minneapolis soaking up the words of contemporary dramatists. The seductive power of creating people and place with words mesmerized me; my engagement with words was as much "laced with dreams and prejudices" as it was informed by analysis and a facility for parsing sentences. As a teacher, I had taken great delight in the art of writing and the skill of wordplay, searching always for ways to entice school-worn adolescents back into the magic of language. I knew good writing when I read it; but what made some writing good, and elevated other writing into art, eluded me.

At the time I worked in writing research and linguistics in the education department, I studied the personal essay in the English department. Where the challenge of statistics and linguistic analysis engaged my logical, pragmatic side, locking me into difficult, but satisfying intellectual work, writing the personal essay gave me a freedom I had never before experienced. Writing gave shape to my experience, and the process of writing allowed me to plumb stories and recollections from places I had forgotten existed. For the first time in my schooling, I was given permission to write about my life in ways of my choosing, to allow my emotions, my whole being, to talk on the page. "We tell ourselves stories in order to live," Joan Didion wrote. In this, the first line of Didion's *The White Album*, I heard a voice I did not know was sanctioned by publishing houses, and which told stories resonating with my own life. Literary journalism, material essayed and filtered through an author's sensibility, recreated a time and place; this "personal" journey into society and culture, this was both research and art. The universe, was not only Out There, it was In Here too, and the further I explored the domain of writing about experience, the more liberated I felt.

Over in the education department, I would put away such stories. My advisor, a brilliant man, seemed to attract brilliant male doctoral students as well, all of whom were statistically literate. I was one of only a few master's students in the group and only one of a few women. The culture of our workplace created conversations about how to solve statistical problems, about the complexities of syntax, and about the relative virtues and the interplay of the various methodological debates at the time. It seemed a culture dedicated to solutions to micropuzzles. As a new graduate student, I found the conversation heady; as a woman, I believed I had little to say, and when I did have a contribution to make, often stumbled to say it. Frequently silent in seminars, I immersed myself in the language of the discipline and began to use the tool with which I felt most comfortable: the written word. During a sociolinguistics course, I encountered the work of Robin Lakoff and Cheris Kramerae: I was stunned to learn how my day-to-day language was constructing me as female. Lakoff's monograph, *Language and Woman's Place* (1975), sparked an awareness that speech, language in general, was not neutral: it was marked. Whether the context was a graduate student seminar or a family gathering, I was unwittingly the exemplar of the woman whose tentative speech marked her cultural role as relational and subject to approval of others. As a female graduate student, I was doubly marked.

Although as a researcher I was interested in the factors that account for what I called "good" writing, I followed the conventions of academic writing to gain participation in the culture of graduate school in education. And so, while my writing professor in the English department gently schooled me out of the use of the passive voice and lengthy subordinate clauses in my reflective essays, the research journals in education provided another discourse model: I learned that writing must be "distant," free of bias, or, as my fellow graduates students said, "objective and authoritative." By the time my thesis proposal was due, I had learned the discourse.

> Studies investigating the influence of textual variables in the evaluation of student writing have focused largely on syntactic criteria, using the sentence, the t-unit, and the clause as basic grammatical units in analysis and interpretation of differences. These studies inform a body of research in writing that has attempted not only to outline objective, normative criteria for "mature" or "syntactically complex" writing, but also to identify syntactic characteristics which are common to writing judged qualitatively superior. But where decisions about overall quality are made, syntactic criteria alone cannot suffice; the ingenuities of a writing sample, whether a single paragraph or an entire "essay," include semantic considerations as well. Lexical choice, or vocabulary, an essential element in communicating meaning in text, has traditionally received considerable attention by teachers who evaluate writing; to date, however, it has received little attention in the area of composition research.

I had also learned enough about linguistics and statistics, enjoying the manipulation of both syntax and numbers, to believe this kind of research would be challenging, and to want to succeed in the exercise. And it was an exercise, like a large school project which warranted one's full attention to detail: another hurdle for a well-schooled girl to jump. I had learned to enjoy such hurdles, and to invite them; my self-esteem as a student had always depended on their satisfactory completion. Determining whether or not the issues surrounding the exercise mattered to me as an individual or to the world at large was never a question: within that culture, these issues were deemed important, and so I took them on.

To study the factors accounting for teachers' decisions about quality in student writing, it was necessary for me, as the researcher, to hypothesize which variables might be the most salient in the minds of teachers. I isolated two: syntax (simple or complex noun heads, to be specific); and semantics (which I aimed to tap by looking at vocabulary, or what I called lexical choice). To conduct the experiment controlling for each of two levels of the variables without any threats to validity, I constructed the "student" passages myself. It would have been impossible to glean from students' samples enough passages which clearly isolated two levels of syntactic complexity (simple and complex) and two levels of maturity ("simple" and mature) in vocabulary choice. I needed four clean samples: "real" student writing was too messy to use for this experiment.

To measure syntactic complexity, I used a popular measure at the time, Hunt's t-unit, a basic grammatical unit (a subject and a verb) which was widely considered to be an objective and normative baseline for complexity. To measure maturity of vocabulary, I relied on measures of word frequency, using word frequency norms (the same norms used at the time to construct reading comprehension passages) for synonymous word pairs (hid/concealed, for example). Four passages, representing two treatment versions of each of the variables, were randomly assigned for grading to a total of 80 raters, in-service and pre-service English teachers attending summer school at the time. I chose a two-way fixed analysis of variance to test the difference between the ratings of the passages. Like the other graduate students, I agonized over the details of the statistical treatment, the "cleanliness" of the design, and the construct validity of the whole enterprise. I began to ask how I got here, engrossed in work I could never have imagined a year before. It was as though I had been driving in the open countryside, had decided to take a side road suggested by others, doggedly pursued the road until I had found myself in a dense maze of narrow alleys in a small town, each alley closing off options behind me. Now I was trapped, far from the open landscape where the promise of writing had first beckoned, reduced to tinkering with minutiae, waiting patiently for the result which would break the gridlock and set me moving again. Everything depended, it seemed, on statistical significance.

> For the usual highly motivated researcher the nonconfirmation of a cherished hypothesis is actively painful. As a biological and psychological animal, the experimenter is subject to the laws of learning which lead him [sic] inevitably to associate this pain with the contiguous stimuli and events. These stimuli are apt to be the experimental process itself, more vividly and directly than the "true" source of frustration, *i.e.*, the inadequate theory. This can lead, perhaps unconsciously, to the avoidance or rejection of the experimental process...we must...justify experimentation...as the only available route to cumulative progress. (Campbell & Stanley, 1963, p. 3)

Running the statistics for the study was nerve-wracking and cumbersome. The computer room (for, of course, a computer required an entire room at the time), was always crowded with graduate students, carefully guarding their sorted boxes of data cards, feeding the cards and waiting patiently for the print-out at the end of the process. Tension was high. Months of work was reduced to a verdict revealed in the number at the bottom of the wide, unwieldy printout. It did not matter that the statistics professor had reminded us frequently that a result of "no significant difference" did not mean the study was a failure; for me, a woman who was not "one of the boys," a significant difference at the .05 level or better would mean success in that culture of researchers. When my advisor and all the fellow graduate students around the table asked "was it significant?" I wanted to be able to say "yes."

The results, as the research report would read later, indicated that "mature" word choice with simple syntax appealed most to the raters of the passages. To use a comparison from literature, the teachers preferred a style closer to the spare and colorful prose of Hemingway than the denser and more lengthy prose associated with Faulkner. And these teachers preferred that style at a significance level of .05 or better. The study, it seems, was a success. I was elated.

My advisor asked if I was interested in staying to pursue doctoral studies, and although I was, I declined. My husband had a university position waiting for him in Alberta; I had prospects of teaching writing part-time in a community college. Besides, Allan and I were both aware that, whether as a result of our wishes or societal pressure, we had begun to think about having children. At the time, my decision to put my academic career on hold seemed "natural"; years later, I would read Bateson's (1989) words about women's lives of discontinuity, and recognize myself: biologically and socially constructed as female, I had little choice but to follow life where it took me, and make do. And I left graduate school feeling conflicted: I had contributed successfully to a larger project of wrestling with observable phenomena in order to identify a larger truth; but I also carried a vague feeling of having given up a freedom, of having tainted something of value to me. In the cause of science, I had dissected and articulated one more butterfly, pinning it for display with the other dead specimens.

As I drafted the article for publication more than a year later, I struggled with the writing. The syntax was knotted, tangled, and the prescriptive formula for writing up research results forced dry and lifeless words out of my pen. Although I was proud of having done the thesis work, I could not imagine taking the article back to the junior high school in Winnipeg where I had taught in order to share it with my English teaching colleagues. Although the work was putatively for the advancement of knowledge in English education, I knew headed nominal complexity and lexical choice would not connect with teachers' experience about writing. But, as graduate student colleagues reminded me, a master's level publication was a coup in the research community. And so, like other graduate students before me, I wrote the article myself and submitted it for review. Following the courtesy which apprenticing researchers apparently owed their masters, I added my advisor's name as second author. That fall, I became one of thirteen women hired as sessional instructors in writing at a local community college with a rapidly-growing student body. The few full time jobs available, and for which many of us had applied, had gone to men with doctoral degrees.

Reading People, Writing Lives

On the bus home to New Hampshire from Cambridge seven years later, I curled up with one of the recommended readings for the ethnography in education course I had begun at Harvard that day. From what I had heard about qualitative research, and as a result of my growing disenchantment with the detailed preoccupations of experimental research, I was eager to learn about methods and perspectives offering different pathways to truth. There was truth out there, I was certain; but other paths to it must be available. As I listened to Joe Maxwell's overview about ethnography, humbled by the realization that the world of anthropological research was vast and I was, once again, illiterate in a new culture, my fears grew with my curiosity. How would I know, as a researcher using these approaches, that I had, after all, got it right? There seemed to be so many pitfalls, so many areas of dispute. I headed directly for the catacombs of the nearest second-hand bookstore and loaded up my backpack with readings for the week ahead.

Under the dim overhead light of the Trailways bus, I read:

> Doc was born on Norton Street in 1908. His mother and father, who came from the province of Abruzzi, were the first non-Genoese Italians to settle on the street. In a large family, Doc was the youngest and his mother's favourite. His father died when he was a small boy. (Whyte, 1943, p. 3)

This was research? Where were the bibliographic references? By the time the bus pulled up to Young's restaurant in Durham over an hour later, I had read the first hundred pages, waiting in anticipation, as a reader will, for the other shoe to drop. I was engaged with the story of the Street Corner Society, an observer living vicariously with Whyte on the streets of Boston, or what Whyte called "an Eastern City." This so-called research read more like the journalism of Joan Didion and Tom Wolfe or a novel than the traditional research report. So, this, too, was legitimate? Where were the summary statements? Where were the hypotheses?

Elsewhere in my doctoral program, I was reading the work of Yvonna Lincoln and Egon Guba, who contrasted the assumptions of "naturalist" researchers with those of researchers they variously described as "rationalists," "scientific inquirers," and "positivists." For the positivist researchers, there is a real world which is "fragmentable into discrete or independent subsystems that can be dealt with a few variables at a time" (1981, p. 57). Inquiry can converge onto this reality until finally it can be predicted and controlled, moving us closer to converging on the truth (1981, p. 57). Their words articulated what I had learned to believe about writing in my graduate work in syntactic complexity: divide the written product into syntactic fragments, manipulate them, and add to the cumulative work of scientific knowledge. Their words also spoke to what seemed to be the prevailing approach to the study of reading.

But by now I was the mother of a five-year-old son, a boy who was attending to the signs in his environment and "reading" his world, as children do, in ways that astonished and taught his parents. Knowing the complexity, the unevenness, the some-times predictable but also random nature of David's induction into literacy, could I believe the results of a study which isolated factors in reading, determined a sample, and then applied a one-hour or three-day treatment during school hours? Would I want any curricular decision to be made about reading comprehension based on the results of such a study? Two of these studies? Six? Certainly there are factors in reading and writing we can isolate and manipulate, but what are the limits of these kinds of studies in understanding the complexities of literacy and literacy learn-ing? I began to explore qualitative research fully: what if we used words, scenes, artifacts, aspects, stories, metaphors, critical incidents to explain the processes of reading and writing, instead of reducing our findings to isolable variables and numbers? What if we looked for the complexities of meaning in a situation, rather than seek simplicity in generalizations for all readers?

My doctoral program, the first of its kind in reading and

writing instruction in North America, afforded me a wealth of opportunities: to continue to write, to study literary journalism and essay writing, to study development from childhood to adult, to learn about research from a range of perspectives, and most importantly, to research and write as part of a community which valued these processes highly. The University of New Hampshire was nationally known for its "Writing Process Lab," which "lab," in fact, was simply an average-sized room in Morrill Hall with a few desks, a rudimentary word processor, a highly competent secretary, and an enormous Rolodex with the names and addresses of key researchers and writers across the world. The work of Donald Murray, Donald Graves, Jane Hansen, and Thomas Newkirk had attracted students into the doctoral program, and the community itself was the "lab"; the research in "the writing process," which was gathering widespread interest in a number of countries, and the encouragement to write about our research in ways that honored writing and writers, kept us there.

The mid-Eighties were spirited and heady times for writing and reading research everywhere. The word "literacy" replaced the words "reading and writing" in the professional literature, reflecting the growing recognition of the interconnections between the processes. Researchers and theorists looked now to anthropology and sociology, as well as history and literary theory, for perspectives to inform literacy research. Reading and writing education began to meet literary theory in the works of Louise Rosenblatt, Stanley Fish, and Jane Tompkins, among others, bridging worlds which I saw as separate in the days of my first graduate degree program. Heartened by the support in this new community for research itself, and fascinated by the possibilities of using ethnographic approaches in education to study literacy, I embarked on two research studies simultaneously: a case study of a young writer in a rural New Hampshire school;

and a study of a writing course in a military setting. Out There were truths, and with ethnographic approaches, I had new tools to describe them.

> I propose an alternative formulation of the task or goal of the behavioral sciences. Rather than searching for general laws which are assumed to hold independent of context, the task is to specify the conditions under which a relationship of the form $Y=f(X)$ holds. Such laws have always contained an implicit assumption that the law holds under the condition of "all other things being equal".... Other things are never equal, however elegant and rigorous the design. The experimental situation, even the aseptic laboratory, is not neutral.... How can we formulate generalizations that make explicit the context dependence of relationships? How can we develop methods of observation, measurement, and analysis appropriate to the study of such context-dependent laws? (Mishler, 1979)

Both studies I undertook seemed to feed my emerging constructivist sensibilities. In the years between my masters and doctoral programs, I had taught basic writing in a community college, creative writing in a university, and business and technical writing in the workplace. I had sold several freelance journalism pieces to newspapers and magazines. Widening my focus, and apprenticing myself to diverse groups of writers and multiple purposes for writing in a number of settings, I was learning how school-centric my notions of literacy and of learning had been. An engineer must write accurate and dependable instructions for repairing the pump in a machine on an oil rig; he or she must have a clear understanding of the audience and purpose for the writing. A "basic" writer in a community college struggles simply to find the words and attempts to read the culture of school even as she is learning to put sentences together. No longer did I believe that there was only one way to divide reality into objects, properties, and relations. What I saw as "the real world" I believed was observable, but from a number of perspectives. I compared my shift in understanding as a move from the "one truth" model toward the "the traffic accident" model: ask enough witnesses, vary your detective work as necessary, and you will find out what really happened. The truth will be a construction among all participants. *What is going on here?* became the question that propelled my research. Both the study of the young writer and of the writing course offered me settings in which I might test my revised notions of what research is and does. And equally important, given my passion for writing, both studies afforded me the freedom to write about phenomena "close up," in the active voice, drawing on detail to bring to the page the people and places I observed. Although I was unable to see it then, the shift from passive to active voice in writing about others' lives was a shift more ideological than grammatical.

I framed the study of Jennifer, which I titled "A Teacher's Joy: the Schooling of a Writer," in the following way:

> *But I have been told, my dear Socrates, that what a budding orator needs to know is not what is really right, but what is likely to seem right in the eyes of the mass of people who are going to pass judgment.* —Phaedrus to Socrates
>
> Studying a writer without reference to her social, family, and instructional context is like studying a fish without reference to water. As a result, when I undertook a descriptive study of seven-year-old Jennifer Taylor with the question, "As a writer, what does Jennifer know?" I drew upon several sources of information: Jennifer; her teachers, friends, and parents; Jennifer's writing process and products; and my observations. As the amount of data grew with my on-going

collection and analysis, however, the picture that emerged became more than a descriptive composite of Jennifer, the writer. It became a picture of how one writer has reflected the values of her family and the school, and most particularly, those of the teacher. The results of the study, therefore, helped to clarify not only what Jennifer knew as a writer, but what forces and influences shaped that knowledge.

The Writer

At the time of the study, Jennifer Taylor was a second-grade student at a rural school in New Hampshire. Her mother is a school bus driver; her father works in the family business; her brother, Michael, who is a year older than Jennifer, attends the same school. Jennifer is known throughout the school, by teachers and students alike, as "a top student." She is a quiet person, whose school demeanour is always poised and attentive. She is articulate, and well-liked by both teachers and peers.

I chose to study Jennifer for two reasons: First, her reputation as a prolific and competent writer reassured me that I would be studying someone whom the educational system considers to be its successful "product"; and secondly, Jennifer's writing and verbal fluency suggested that she would have the metalinguistic awareness to both know and tell about herself as a writer.

The Research Question

To frame the question, "As a writer, what does Jennifer know?" it was necessary first to define what it means to know something, particularly to "know how to write." Jennifer, like all writers, "knows" in many ways and in many contexts.

Almost seven years of encoding and decoding language

has given Jennifer a reservoir of tacit knowledge about language—syntactic, lexical, and pragmatic knowledge so integrated that it has become natural and automatic (Halliday, 1978). The recursive process of translating thought to language, building the knowing on the known, has prepared Jennifer for the writer's task, "to engage in deliberate structure of the web of meaning" (Vygotsky, 1962, p. 100). Through writing, as she does through speaking, Jennifer makes explicit some of her tacit knowledge about language.

When a writer writes, she is making meaning from her personal knowledge and the cultural and contextual frames in which she moves. The words that come from the end of Jennifer's pencil are the artifacts of a dynamic process, the writer herself: a member of a family, a community, a school, and a peer group. To function within those roles successfully, Jennifer must learn to "know" and to read her personal and social contexts and to act within them.

The family is a society in itself, a potent force in a child's growth and attitudes toward literacy (Heath, 1983; Taylor, 1983; Ferreiro & Teberosky, 1982). Although socio-economic status (SES) may be a factor in language learning (Cazden, John, & Hymes, 1972; Ferreiro & Teberosky, 1982), it seems the most salient factor in a child's language development can cut across SES: it is simply an environment where literacy is embedded in the family fabric.

When a child such as Jennifer arrives at school, her thinking and language is embedded in the family and the community. Once she enters the school doors, however, she enters another community with its own assumptions, expectations, rules, and conventions (Cazden, John, & Hymes, 1972). Here again, she is expected to "know," this time not only as a daughter and sister, but a student and classmate as well.

Jennifer, the student, will learn school-appropriate language behaviors as well as the assumptions about language and learning held by the school. She will be exposed, for example, to what DeStefano (1980) refers to as the Language Instruction Register which can include "basalese" (such as the use of "Mother" and "Father" instead of "mom" and "dad"), but more often includes such lexical terms such as "sentence," "chapter," and "paragraph." For many students, even ones raised in language-rich environments such as Jennifer's, this recontextualizing of language can violate the beginning student's expectation of a contextually meaningful language event. Further, in many school contexts, language becomes an object of study, a product to be evaluated, and an atomistically-developed set of skills built by acquiring sub-skills (Emig, 1983). Such an approach to language learning can widen the gap between home and school language.

Because teaching is a theoretical activity (DeFord, 1978), a child is educated not only according to the educational belief system in society at that time, but also according to the teacher's beliefs about how we acquire knowledge (Harste *et al*, 1984). A teacher may see language, for example, not as a mode of learning and discovery or a tool for thought, but rather "a tube down which knowledge can be sent" (Barnes, 1976, p.142). The view of writing as a component skill which is taught, not learned, and which is a linear, conscious process capable of being "done swiftly and on order" (Emig, 1983, p. 140) is very commonly held by teachers of writing (Harste, Woodward, & Burke, 1984). The degree to which such assumptions—for good or bad—influence a writer such as Jennifer is, in part, the question this study addresses.

The influences of society, the school, and the teachers on the values a child holds about literacy have been studied over the last decade (Heath, 1983; Harste, Woodward, & Burke, 1984). Case studies of writers in process have broadened our knowledge of the forces that influence writers, the decisions they make and the contextual juggling act they regularly perform (Emig, 1971; Graves, 1973; Bissex, 1980; Calkins, 1980). Descriptive studies of writers in schools show that writing is used to participate in a community, to know oneself and others, to occupy free time, and to demonstrate academic competence (Florio & Clark, 1982; Britton *et al*, 1975). It is clear that the young writer knows a great deal more about

> writing and writerly behaviors than what appears on the page, and definitely more than research can tap.
>
> This study looks at a writer from a perspective different from those studies that have examined primarily the process, the product or the instructional setting. This research examines the writer as a prism, as the locus of several socializing forces—the home, the school, the teacher, and the classroom community. As a writer, Jennifer Taylor both assimilates and reflects the attitudes and beliefs about writing that surround her.

And so, embracing the notion of contextual understanding, of looking for meaningful truth "in context," I used data from participant observation, interviews with parents, teachers, and other students, writing samples from a variety of sources, surveys, protocol analyses of Jennifer's writing process, as well as standardized test scores, all in an attempt to render a composite picture—a freeze-frame—of Jennifer, the writer. Organizing my findings under several categories (social/personal context, writing concepts, metalinguistic context, and classroom context), I concluded:

> Jennifer is a child who was highly influenced from the beginning of her school years by the attitudes and expectations of her family and her teacher. The degree to which she has internalized their beliefs and attitudes or simply taken them on, knowing they make her "a teacher's joy," remain unclear. Nevertheless, reading others' expectations, and for the most part, meeting them, has made Jennifer Taylor what her observers describe as "a good writer, a good student, and a good girl."

As a writer, I had taken to the task of describing another writer, a young girl, with enthusiasm. Here I could place all of Jennifer's activities in categories and continua and still capture the range and complexity of her writing and her life. This was the "thick description" which Geertz (1973) talked about and which, from an observer's standpoint, seemed to be more authentic an account of the nature of writing than I had undertaken as an experimental researcher. This was the way, then, to do research.

But as a researcher, engaged in observation of the classroom with the permission of Jennifer's teacher, Mrs. Johnson, I was blindsided by my own arrogance. When I began to write about Mrs. Johnson's teaching practices, I hit a block: I believed the woman was teaching writing the wrong way, certainly not according to "writing process" principles, and yet I found it difficult to put that in words, knowing she might read them some day. In fact, my opinion about her teaching was consistent with the general climate of evangelical purism which we, as graduate students, were creating in our program. Within our community, we shared a meaning of "good research" and "process teaching," finding ourselves more likely to be critical of individuals than of social systems, and seeing social construction in children's literacy processes more readily than in the beliefs we and our colleagues held. In the larger research community, arguments had begun to erupt between the "flaming positivists" and the "crunchy-granola naturalists," between experimentalists and ethnographers, loosely, and inaccurately, categorized as quantitative versus qualitative researchers. At a pedagogical level, the "writing process" movement, supported by the emerging "naturalistic" classroom research on writing, had a dangerously zealous corps of proselytizers. Similarly, the parallel movement in reading, the "whole language" movement, left little room in its growing band of supporters for diversity of opinion or of practice. Further, neither writing process proselytizers nor whole language advocates seemed willing to address persistent pedagogical and research problems in their perspectives, side-stepping attacks with the "apples and oranges" argument that the assumptions of one perspective or paradigm cannot be used to judge the effectiveness of another. Such claims to epistemological incompatibility notwithstanding, the methodolatry was difficult to ignore. As a researcher and educator, I aligned myself with the qualitative, "process" camp, engaging, as the newly-converted and insecure always do, in dismissing or condemning other approaches.

Faced with the realization that I was the researcher, the one with the pen, and I was about to use that position to judge another human being—indeed, to write the teacher in a way she might not write herself—I stopped short. The evaluation and assessment I had done in my role as a teacher was a form of judgment, too; but (inexplicably) it seemed somehow more palatable to judge a child than an adult. Was it my assumption that judgment in teaching was for an educative purpose, which made it acceptable while judgment in research was not? Research was a human relationship in an educational environment, a relationship with different stakes for the parties, and some would say, unequal power among them. I was uncomfortable about being a doctoral student in a classroom: in part because that status caused Mrs. Johnson to look to me for knowledge about writing pedagogy; and in part because I knew, as a former classroom teacher, that this woman had twenty years of experience with teaching and managing children in classrooms. Who was I to judge her teaching; why ought she to defer to me? Research as an objective enterprise bound by rule-ordered expectations was becoming personal. My advisor gently reminded me that Jennifer's teacher, just like Jennifer herself, came from differing contexts, and her practices were informed by a number of often discrepant beliefs and influences, as were mine. In the teacher's mind, and in her words, she was "doing writing process as best as (I) can": who was I to judge her harshly?

Degrees of Freedom

The reader has already realized I was more like my infor- mants than I would have cared to admit. Trapped in the expec- tations of others, striving to learn socially-sanctioned research methods, and to be the "best" researcher and writer I could possibly be, I became Jennifer: "good writer, good student, good girl." Aiming for research practice consonant with the prevailing paradigm (wanting to do what seemed right in the "eyes of the mass of people" who would pass judgment), I was also like Mrs. Johnson, hoping to comply with the expectations of the "writing process experts" and "naturalistic researchers."

In the writing of that study, and the careful analysis of my own ethical dilemma and my contextual embeddedness, I began to understand my role as a woman as well, composing myself according to the expectations and formulae of the systems of contexts in which I lived and worked. Reading the work of Carol Gilligan and Nel Noddings, I searched for an understanding of what being female means.

> At the positions of received knowledge and procedural knowl- edge, other voices and external truths prevail....for women in our society this typically means adherence to sex-role stereo- types or second-rung status as a woman with a man's mind...these women seek gratification in pleasing others or in measuring up to external standards—in being "the good woman" or "the good student" or "the successful woman who made it in a man's world." A sense of authority arises primarily through identification with the power of a group and its agreed-upon ways for knowing. (Belenky *et al*, 1986, p. 134)

I felt humility and shame about my intentions to write criti- cally about the teacher, and was increasingly ambivalent about my rights and responsibilities as a researcher and an educator. The academic hierarchy positioned me as the "knowing observer"

45

with the pen. Was there an issue here I was not recognizing, or was I simply being the well-socialized and tentative woman again? That year, I completed the second of my ethnographic studies, a study which would cause me to come face to face, finally, with my incipient, but unarticulated, feminist beliefs.

Learning to Freefall
Context for the Study

Site

The education building at the air force base is a barracks-turned-offices with low ceilings, fluorescent lights, government-green-and-white painted walls, linoleum floors, metal doors, and a toilet and sink in every room. The writing course took place in two rooms: a spartan and uncluttered second-floor classroom with six large tables which was used for instruction; and the instructor's office, one of several small offices on the first floor, which was used for conferences and as a study skills centre. Several colleges and schools kept offices in the education building, each representing a different educational offering for military personnel. As Adam, one of the participants in the study, said: "A lot of guys are (in the military) to get an education. The military pays about 75 percent of the cost to go."

The course in which the study took place was offered by an educational organization known for its flexible and responsive programs especially suited to the needs of adults returning to school. One of its course offerings, a requirement for many of the students, is the course in which the study took place: Communication 500: The Writing Process. Billed as a course that "approaches writing as a process involving a sequence of stages including pre-writing, initial drafting, and re-writing," the course met for a ten-week semester twice a week for two hours a session.

Participants

Thirteen of the sixteen participants (five of whom were women) who attended the course regularly were in the military or were military wives. All were working toward an associate's or bachelor's degree. For all but two students, it was the first writing course they had taken since high school, except for a half-day course in effective writing required by the military upon entrance and before each promotion.

The participants' ages ranged from nineteen to approximately fifty, the majority being between twenty-five and thirty-five. Most of the military personnel had been in the service for less than five years—four, for ten years or more— and had home roots in places from Virginia to Maine to Oregon to Idaho. Many of the military wore fatigues to class; a few carried paging devices because they were on twelve-or twenty-four-hour shifts. During three of the sessions the base was "on alert" which meant that all personnel were to be at the ready for military action at any moment.

The instructor, Karen B., a thirty-five-year old woman who has a Master's Degree in English, has been a permanent part-time instructor with the adult education institution for several years. Her demeanor and her stylish "civilian" clothes set her appearance apart from the fatigues, crewcuts, and smoky and colorless institutional rooms. The faculty regard Karen as an approachable person whose teaching succeeds because she "treats these people like the adults they are."

As the researcher, I am both a writer and teacher of writing who has worked with adults in industry for several years. Because my doctoral work has been in adult writing and reading processes, researching writing was not a new experience for me. I was, however, introduced to two new cultures through this study: the non-traditional returning student and the military.

Theoretical Setting

Four influences were woven into the theoretical setting for the study. The first, the "Writing Process" course curricula from the adult education institution, described the course in a two-page list of behavioral objectives such as "the learner will identify and use appropriate intellectual strategies in selecting an organizing principle and designing a thesis statement" and "the learner will utilize both inductive and deductive reasoning in written communication."

The students' pre-course constructs about writing and learning to write formed a second thread in the theoretical setting. These constructs included the following: an expectation that writing would not be enjoyable; that the course would focus on grammar and punctuation); that the instructor would be harsh and unapproachable ("I expected some old bat in baggy nylons," John reported); that they would be told what to write and how to write it. (Two of the students had taken courses with Karen before and did not share these beliefs). In short, most students expected that the course would be a traditional writing course of the kind under which they were schooled years before. Most of the students wrote as part of their jobs in the military; as a result, many came to the course expecting a focus on "rules, regulations, and details" which guided their writing process at work.

The instructor, Karen B., was an influential theoretical force in the setting. She interpreted the course curricula loosely because she wanted to be "flexible and reasonable" and felt that adult students learned better when they were treated with respect and not required to follow a rigid set of expectations. Her own curricula were rigorous ("the only way to learn how to write is to write a lot") and her standards were high but she was, according to my observations and others' accounts, approachable and very fair.

Karen espoused learner-centred education and individualized teaching; however, this was the first course in which she "let the students take control," through more discussions, peer group conferences on writing, more opportunities for revision and for exploring their own topics. Up to now, Karen explained, she had always been flexible "as a person" but very structured in her preparation, "right down to the questions I wanted to ask—and the specific answer I wanted." Karen stated and the data corroborated that this course was a "tran-sition course" for her: she was "ready for a change" and caught between the old and the new approaches to teaching writing.

Finally, the text for the course and its author combined to be the fourth strong influence in the theoretical setting. *Write to Learn*, a college text written by Donald Murray, is meant to be primarily used by students rather than assigned by teachers. The book's emphasis on the writer's learning by trial-and-error through the process of writing illustrates a learner-centred approach to writing instruction:

> ...students do not learn to write, then write. Few students can listen to a lecture on writing or read a textbook on writing in advance of writing and understand the lessons they need to learn.... Each student should experience the same interaction between the act of writing and the process of learning about writing. (1984, p. xiii)

Karen chose the text, and because she had taken a course from Murray years before, she planned to have him visit the class mid-semester. Murray's upcoming visit was a topic of conversation for much of the early part of the course ("Let's wait and ask Donald Murray about that") and was discussed regularly afterwards. For the majority, Murray was the "first real writer" they had met; during the two and one-half hour question-and-answer session (only one hour was planned for)

> the students bombarded Murray with questions and hung on his every word. Murray had been in the military and, during the visit, described his reaction to combat. For the last half of the semester "I wonder what Murray would say about that" was the type of comment spoken regularly by both the instructor and the students.

During the course of this research, my intellectual life was becoming densely woven with continua and hierarchies. It seemed in whatever field I read, I found the world to be described in opposite pairs criss-crossing all aspects of human behavior. In adult learning, Kohlberg's (1984) levels of moral development differed from Gilligan's (1977) work in voicelessness/voice; Jane Loevinger (1976) described levels of ego development; John Naisbitt and Patricia Aburdene (1985) outlined global "megatrends" by describing shifts which echoed the earlier work of cultural observer Marilyn Ferguson (1980) whose own Aquarian conspiracy themes saw changes afoot for education, health, business, and politics. In business, Rosabeth Moss Kanter (1983) described shifts from segmented hierarchies toward networked, collaborative organizations. In writing education, the process-product continuum invited ongoing debate, and in reading, the text/the reader, and the bottom-up/top-down approaches were often pitted against one another. Constructivism seemed as much a consensus stance as it was ontological. In the search for some explicatory unity or coherence, sets of continua served as meridian lines stretched across language and behavior on which we might hook people and ideas, or seek ways in which we could not only describe, but perhaps resolve differences.

Beginning the study of a writing course in a military base, I saw the military organization as hierarchical and male-dominated, marked by rule-ordered activity, with little room for freedom of expression. Watching a female "writing process" teacher at work in such a setting, I hypothesized that a pedagogy which promoted risk-taking and the creation of one's own meaning on the page would be in direct contrast to the culture of the military. I saw Donald Murray's beliefs about writing at the other end of the spectrum from the student's incoming beliefs. Further, I saw Karen, the instructor, espousing a theory about writing which she did not, in fact, put in practice. I saw teacher-directed and student-centred approaches as incompatible; skill instruction and skill acquisition in process as either-or choices. Either-or seemed to be anywhere I wanted to stretch continua. The goal, at least in instruction, was to bring teachers and students from one end of the continuum toward enlightenment at the other end. I lived a contradiction as a researcher: while I believed meaning was constructed out of dialectical relationships, I imposed both continua and judgment on the phenomena I observed, silently cheering on both students and teacher to move from skill-oriented, top-down perspectives on learning to write toward holistic, process-driven understandings of writing.

I expected Karen to impose writing process principles on students, as well, rather than construct them within the work together. The notion that constructivism might be a viable stance for teaching and learning, as well as for research, seemed to be lost on this researcher committed to the latest version of the path to truth. Although I believed that the students in the writing course were learning to "freefall" as they learned about writing, and that, as the researcher observing the course, I was constructing my beliefs about inquiry and teaching as I worked, I constructed those meanings from the sidelines. These people in this setting were phenomena; my job, like an observer outside the glass wall of an aquarium, was to record, labelling people and

Finding Her Place

their practices according to whether they fit the continua and patterns I created to describe them. My version of a dialectical relationship in my interviews with informants was more akin to "fill in the blanks" reading instruction than it was to Mishler's "joint construction of meaning" (1986). It was more about my arm's length reading and recording the "text" of the field, more about following the map than walking the territory.

> Actually, no hard-and-fast line separates efferent—scientific and expository—reading on the one hand from aesthetic reading on the other. It is more accurate to think of a continuum, a series of gradations between the nonaesthetic and the aesthetic extremes. The reader's stance toward the text—what he [sic] focuses his attention on, what his "mental set" shuts out or permit to enter into the center of awareness—may vary in a multiplicity of ways between the two poles. (Rosenblatt, 1978, p. 35)

The military personnel who came into the course shared the following constructs about writing:

1. Writing ought to be easy, a one-shot effort.
2. Knowledge of grammar is the key to writing improvement.
3. Learning to write is first learning forms and rules.
4. Skills exercises are separate from the process of writing.
5. Non-work-related writing is "creative" writing done only by "creative" people.
6. Writing is organized and fully planned before the writer puts pen to paper.
7. Teachers and professional writers are the arbiters of writing quality.
8. Writing is a skill to be learned primarily for career advancement.
9. The goal of writing is a perfectly-formed product.
10. Writing is for communication only.

Degrees of Freedom

My research indicated that when the course was completed, the students and the teacher, Karen, shared these revised assumptions.

1. Writing can be hard, a process of revision.
2. Writing regularly with feedback results in greater improvement than grammar study.
3. Learning to write is first finding meaning/voice.
4. Skills are learned in context of the piece of writing.
5. Anyone can learn to write clearly with practice.
6. A writer can find form and meaning through the act of writing.
7. The writer learns to become his/her own critic, editor.
8. Writing can teach the writer about self.
9. The goal of writing is to discover the writer's own meaning.
10. Writing is for self-discovery as well as for communication.

In retrospect, had I replaced the words "writer" and "writing" with the words "research" or "researcher" in many of these assumptions, I might have learned more from the inquiry. I had been the dutiful and distant researcher, watching the "grammatical rules" of methods and data collection (Schatzman & Strauss, 1973), ensuring that I stayed with my plan for hypothesis creation and testing in several phases, and thinking ahead about how I would write up the results, what the product would look like. I knew that I had been reluctant throughout the research to share my notes and observations with Karen, but was unsure why; perhaps my experiences with Mrs. Johnson gave me pause. I finally agreed to a private meeting with Karen mid-way through the course, leaving her my fieldwork notebook ahead of time for her to read. When we talked, however, I knew that neither my professor nor my ethnography textbooks could stand in for me: I had to carry on the conversation myself.

What followed was an engaging discussion between two women about their struggles and their passion for writing and

teaching writing, stories about past courses and students, rev-
elations about insecurities and mistakes, observations about the
male in the military, confidences about working in institutions
dominated by men, and frustrations about working with other
women as sessionals who make do with whatever is left over in
institutions. In one hour-long meeting over coffee, Karen the
teacher in the field setting became Karen, the woman whose
perspective and experiences dovetailed with my own. When she
read my notebook, heard the tone of distanced recorder, saw her
own words in my handwriting, she was alarmed. Although she
claimed I had not written anything negative or particularly
critical, my question marks beside certain notes alerted her to
what she believed were inconsistencies in her practice. And, as
she read her own words, stark against the white page, she was
eager to explain why she said them, and was often puzzled
herself at what she might have meant by them at the time. Not
only did I begin to realize how the quantitative accumulation of
direct quotes can be a flawed practice, for it ignores the deep
chords from which a single statement can erupt (and ignores the
fact that not all statements are equally robust or substantive,
even if they are on the same topic); but the reduction of actual
people with rich and varied histories to the status of "informant"
and "participant"—objects of my research—belied the very
constructivism I espoused.

The more Karen explained her intention and the context for
her words and her behavior, the greater the number of cracks in
the glass wall separating us as researcher and informant. The
more I let the conversation take the direction she needed—which
was to share her perplexities, insecurities, and frustrations at
being a female in a male-dominated institution and a woman
writing instructor in a profession dominated by male theorists—
the more the clean categories of continua I had established by

this time did not hold their linear pattern. This woman, like me, was full of contradictions. To take her words as I had heard them and written them and to use them to create a research project seemed now to be appropriation of the worst sort, and yet I was still required to produce a product. My unease was deeper than a concern for method and the blurring of the lines between participant and participant observer, or between the "etic" and "emic" stances; it was the beginning of the end of my allegiance to prescribed method at all costs, and the recognition of my own fear of researching "out of step." I was the person who feared learning to freefall. My cherished assumption had always been that there was safety in wearing the suit of researcher, whatever label it sported, and that the suit inured me from the consequences of engaging in human interaction. With boundaries, a foundation, and a persona, whether these were the tight reins of isolated variables and statistical analysis, or the well-defined methods (Spradley, 1981; Schatzman & Strauss, 1973) that formed the core of qualitative research at the time, I could distance myself. I could "master" the work.

> [Naturalistic inquirers] focus upon the multiple realities that, like the layers of an onion, nest within or complement one another. Each layer provides a different perspective of reality, and none can be considered more "true" than any other. Phenomena do not converge into a single "truth," but diverge into many forms, multiple "truths"....the naturalistic inquirer tends to view the phenomena with which he deals as more likely to diverge than to converge as they are more fully explored. (Guba & Lincoln, 1981, p. 57)

And so I wrote about Karen and the students, discarding some of the neatly categorized data that kept leaking out of the categories to which I had assigned them; I ignored the fear that perhaps it was failure of my method, my hypotheses, or my analysis which made the data reluctant to behave for me. After all, weren't phenomena in the world manageable in some way, able to be harnessed by some method? I thought more about the more frightening prospect that the structuralist and positivist project of writing the world, whether it was in categories, continua, or truths of any stripe, might be an untenable one for the woman and the writer I was becoming. Not ready fully to accept this, however (and also having no other method on which to cling, nor the confidence to stray from what method I knew), I used the few categories and continua on which Karen and I seemed to agree, and wrote my final paper for the ethnography course. I mailed Karen a copy of the research report with a note, but did not hear from her again.

Returning to the data a few years later, I saw the words of the men and the women through a different lens. I had used the data from men, primarily, to construct my findings about the anti-thetical relationship between the writing process method and the culture of the military; when I looked at the data from the women students only, however, I saw parallels with the findings of Gilligan and Belenky *et al.*, among others, about women's ways of knowing and understanding the world. Many of the women made comments about writing consistent with the holis-tic, flexible, and recursive nature of the writing process, and they had made those comments from the beginning. Further, as students, these women were highly concerned with connection, relationship, and the wish to comply, to conform, to be "good" at what they do. But their comments, gendered as I now see them, did not fit with the either-or sets of continua I had constructed for hypothesizing the nature of learning in the writing course. Limited by my own understandings, both my research methods and my assumptions seemed now flawed, incomplete. At the time, however, they were all they could have been.

As I prepared to begin my doctoral research, I clung to one truth that seemed enduring. Qualitative approaches to educational research, approaches which relied on observation, description, and analysis, especially through writing and talking, seemed most consistent with my increasingly complex perspective on literacy and learning, my need as a researcher to tap into deeper social and political forces than I had to date, and my ongoing love for writing as a mode of learning, researching, and creating connection among people. The field of qualitative inquiry seemed to offer a measure of freedom in method that didn't chafe; open spaces were becoming more attractive than fences.

Pregnant now with my second child, I lobbied to complete my doctoral program by conducting my research near my home in Nova Scotia. I recognized that, in doing so, I would not be able to claim the distance required between researcher and researched, and I sensed, too, that my work might not, as a result, be taken as seriously as work done away from home. As Diane Bell (1993) will put into words for me many years later, working at home has many practical advantages, not the least of which is being with one's family; however, the work is also less public and performative, less "glamorous" (1993, p. 41). For a woman researcher this is double jeopardy: "one's biography, politics, and relationships become part of the fabric of the field" (41). I knew the complexities of overlapping my locations as female doctoral student and mother of children in a small community would be a challenge, but I wanted to try. I knew, like many women of child-bearing age, the responsibility to find ways of combining the exigencies of child-rearing and of an education was an individual or a family decision.

Most institutions in 1986 were dedicated to the continuous on-site four-to-six-year doctoral program, and were, by their organization, more consistent with the traditionally linear pattern of men's lives and careers than the discontinous pattern of women's lives. This institution was no different. I would not at the time have chosen to use the word "patriarchal" to describe the institutions in which I have studied over the years: everyone, after all, had been tremendously supportive. Nevertheless, each of us, male and female, graduate student and professor, were constructions of the same socio-political forces. I knew, as my female colleagues knew, that opportunities such as scholarships, flexible workloads, book publishing contracts, and mentoring by senior faculty, went primarily to male graduate students. I began to understand, too, not with bitterness, but with a new clarity, that within the institutions I studied, women graduate students were like the Métis girls at the back of my high school classroom over twenty years earlier. We knew we didn't fit somehow; the publicly-sanctioned patterns and issues were not the patterns and the issues of our day-to-day lives. And yet, on the surface, there were enough opportunities, and adequate, often generous attempts, to support our work. No one could say we weren't welcome; and in my case, no advisor nor administrator had ever been actively discriminatory. But then, the systemic and cultural practices which constrain women, and through which we have learned to allow ourselves to be constrained, are enough to hold us back. As Joanna Russ has written: "All of us accept perforce large chunks of our culture ready-made; there is not enough energy or time to do otherwise...to act in a way that is racist or sexist to maintain one's privilege it is only necessary to act in the customary, ordinary, usual even polite manner."

By this time, I wanted to be home, and I did not want to jeopardize my academic career. But because I knew that research and writing would remain at the center of my life, I fought fiercely for the right to combine work and family. My letters, meetings, and presentations were eventually able to overturn institutional concerns that, like so many academic women who want to bear children, I would became "ABD," lost in the land of maternity, spilled milk, and swimming lessons for toddlers.

By 1988, I had completed two graduate degrees, each of which offered experiences that changed my relationship to ideas and to the world Out There. I was no longer a student, and yet I recognized the ways in which I continued the patterns of the well-schooled girl. I looked to research theorists, to the methodologists, for current signposts for guiding my inquiry. I began to work in institutions whose hierarchical practices and demands kept me wary even as I strove to follow them. In the years ahead, work with women would deepen my commitment to understanding my own my place as a woman in writing and in inquiry.

References

Aron, A. & Aron, E. (1994). *Statistics for psychology*. Englewood Cliffs, NJ: Prentice-Hall, Inc.

Atwood, M. (1974). There is only one of everything. *You are happy.* Toronto, Ontario, Canada: Oxford University Press, p. 92.

Barnes, D. (1976). *From communication to curriculum*. New York: Penguin Books.

Barthes, R. (1964). The structuralist activity. In DeGeorge, Richard & DeGeorge, Fernande (eds). *The structuralists from Marx to Levi-Strauss*. (1972). New York: Doubleday, 148-154.

Bateson, M.C. (1989). *Composing a life*. New York: The Atlantic Monthly Press.

Belenky, M., Clinchy, B., Goldberger, N., & Tarule, J. (1986). *Women's ways of knowing: The development of self, voice, and mind*. New York: Basic Books.

Bell, D. (1993). Yes Virginia, there is a feminist ethnography: Reflections from three Australian fields. in Bell, D., Caplan, P, & Karim, J. (eds). *Gendered fields: Women, men and ethnography*. New York: Routledge.

Finding Her Place

Bissex, G. (1980). *Gnys at wrk*. Cambridge: Harvard University Press.

Braddock, R. Lloyd-Jones, R., & Schoer, L. (1963). *Research in written composition*. Champaign, IL: National Council of Teachers of English.

Britton, J., Burgess, T., Martin, N., McLeod, A., & Rosen, H. (1975). *The development of writing abilities 11-18*. London, United Kingdom: Macmillan.

Calkins, L. (1983). *Lessons from a child*. Exeter, NH: Heinemann Educational Books.

Campbell, D. & Stanley, J. (1963). *Experimental and quasi-experimental designs for research*. Chicago: Rand McNally College Publishing Company.

Cazden, C.B., John, V., & Hymes, D.H. (eds). (1972). *Functions of language in the classroom*. New York: Teachers College Press.

DeFord, D.E. (1978). A validation study of an instrument to determine a teacher's theoretical orientation to reading instruction. Unpublished doctoral dissertation. Indiana University.

Denzin, N., & Lincoln, Y. (1994). Competing paradigms in qualitative research. In Denzin. N. & Lincoln, Y. (1994). *Handbook of qualitative research*. Thousand Oaks, CA: Sage Publications, Inc.

DeStefano, J. (1980). Discourse rules for literacy learning in a classroom. Paper presented at the Conference on Communicating in the Classroom. Madison, WI.

Emig, J. (1983). *The web of meaning*. Upper Montclair, NJ: Boynton/Cook Publishers, Inc.

Emig, J. (1971). *The composing process of twelfth graders*. Urbana, IL: National Council of Teachers of English.

Ferguson, M. (1980). *The Aquarian conspiracy*. New York: Houghton Mifflin.

Ferreiro, C., & Teberosky, A. (1982). *Literacy before schooling*. Exeter, NH: Heinemann Educational Books.

Fish, S. (1980). *Is there a text in this class?* Cambridge, MA: Harvard University Press.

Florio, S., & Clark, C. (1982). The functions of writing in an elementary classroom. *Research in the Teaching of English* (16) 2:

Forster, E.M. (1921). *Howard's End*. New York: Vintage Books.

Geertz, C. (1973). *The interpretation of cultures*. New York: Basic Books.

Gilligan, C. (1977). In a different voice: Women's conceptions of the self

Degrees of Freedom

Degrees of Freedom

Degrees of Freedom

and morality. *Harvard Educational Review*, 47: 481-517.

Goetz, J. & LeCompte, M. (1984). *Ethnography and qualitative design in educational research*. New York: Academic Press.

Graves, D.H. (1973). Children's writing: Research directions and hypotheses based upon an examination of the writing processes of seven-year-old children. Dissertation submitted to the State University of New York at Buffalo.

Graves, D.H. (1973). Sex differences in children's writing. *Elementary English*, (50): October.

Guba, E. & Lincoln, Y. (1981). *Effective evaluation*. San Francisco, CA: Jossey-Bass.

Halliday, M.A.K. (1978). *Language as social semiotic*. Baltimore, MD: University Park Press.

Hawkes, T. (1977). *Structuralism and semiotics*. Berkeley, CA: University of California Press.

Harste, J., Woodward, V., & Burke, C. (1984). *Language stories and literacy lessons*. Portsmouth, NH: Heinemann Educational Books.

Heath, S.B. (1983). *Ways with words*. Cambridge, MA: Cambridge University Press.

Hillocks, G. (1986). *Research on written composition*. Urbana, IL: National Conference on Research in English and ERIC.

Hunt, K.W. (1970). *Syntactic maturity in school children and adults*. Monograph of Society in Child Development. Chicago, IL: University of Chicago Press.

Kanter, R.M. (1983). *The change masters*. New York: Simon and Schuster.

Kramerae, C. (1982). "Gender: How she speaks." In Ellen B. Ryan & H. Giles (eds), *Language and sex: Difference and dominance*. Rowley, MA: Newbury House.

Kohlberg, L. (1984). *The psychology of moral development: Essays on moral development, 2*. San Francisco, CA: Harper & Row.

Lakoff, R. (1975). *Language and women's place*. New York: Harper & Row.

Loevinger, J. (1976). *Ego development: Conceptions and theories*. San Francisco, CA: Jossey-Bass.

Mishler, E. (1986). *Research interviewing*. Cambridge, MA: Harvard University Press.

Mishler, E. (1979). Meaning in context: Is there any other kind?

Finding Her Place

Harvard Educational Review, 49 (1), February.

Murray, D. (1984). *Write to learn*. New York: Holt, Rinehart & Winston.

Naisbitt, J. & Aburdene, P. (1985). *Re-inventing the corporation*. New York: Warner Books.

Neilsen, L. (1985). A teacher's joy: The schooling of a writer. Paper presented at the Canadian Council of Teachers of English, Ottawa, Ontario, Canada.

Neilsen, L. (1985). Learning to freefall: A study of writing in a military setting. Unpublished paper. Harvard Graduate School of Education.

Neilsen, L., & Piche, G. (1981). The influence of headed nominal complexity and lexical choice on teachers' evaluation of writing. *Research in the Teaching of English*, (15) 1: 65-73.

Noddings, N. (1974). *Caring: A feminine approach to ethics and moral education*. Berkeley, CA: University of California Press.

Rosenblatt, L.M. (1978). *The reader, the text, the poem: The transactional theory of the literary work*. Carbondale, IL: Southern Illinois University Press.

Russ, J. (1983). *How to suppress women's writing*. Austin, TX: University of Texas Press.

Schatzman, L., & Strauss, A. (1973). *Field research: Strategies for a natural sociology*. Englewood Cliffs, NJ: Prentice-Hall.

Snow, C.P. (1959). *The two cultures and the scientific revolution*. New York: Cambridge University Press.

Tate, G. (Ed.). (1976). *Teaching composition: 10 bibliographical essays*. Fort Worth, TX: Texas Christian University.

Taylor, D. (1983). *Family literacy*. Exeter, NH: Heinemann Educational Books.

Tompkins, J. (Ed). (1980). *Reader response criticism*. Baltimore, MD: The Johns Hopkins University Press.

Vygotsky, L.S. (1962). *Thought and language*. Cambridge, MA: Harvard University Press.

Whyte, W.F. (1943). *Street corner society*. Chicago, IL: The University of Chicago Press.

A version of this essay previously appeared in Straw, S. and Bogdan, D. (Eds.). (1993) *Constructive reading: Teaching beyond communication*. Portsmouth, NH: Heinemann/Boynton-Cook. Written in 1990, it gives an account of an effort to use constructivist practices in inquiry with teachers. I wish to thank the teachers of Pictou County and Annapolis Valley who participated in these courses and who so willingly shared their journal reflections and insights into their growth.

—2—

Exploring Reading:
Mapping the Personal Text

Elbows on dry books, we dreamed
Past Miss Willow Bangs, and lessons, and windows,
to catch all day glimpses and guesses of the greening
woodlot,
Its secrets and and increases,
Its hidden nests and kind.
—Mary Oliver, Spring in the Classroom
(from *New and Selected Poems*, Boston, MA: Beacon Press, 1992, p. 230)

Because I believe, in literacy education and in life, that the unexamined text too often is oneself, I approached the planning of a graduate course in the foundations of reading and language instruction as a rich opportunity for exploring our own reading. Expeditions into understanding the act of reading in the last fifty years have given us reports on the mechanics of one second of reading, pictures of eye sweeps, accounts of prior knowledge (the reader's backpack, always carried separately), and, when computers became the dominant metaphor, megabytes of documentation on the human decoding software.

Finding Her Place

As each explorer returns, triumphant with the news of having found a theory to explain what reading is—and thus, of course, how to teach it—publishing companies, teachers, curriculum supervisors and the public have gathered to listen. And to pay, both financially and professionally. Millions of dollars have been spent to produce classroom materials based on the theories developed largely outside classrooms. And millions of students have been taught by teachers who borrowed maps of a territory explored by someone else.

Recent forays away from definition of the reading process into descriptions of it have caused us as educators to look beyond text to readers themselves. What happens as we read? What can we learn about what we do as we read so that we can help children as they begin the process? Our current explorations into understanding reading are marked by fundamental challenges: how do we map a dynamic process? How can we separate ourselves from the reading? How can we separate reading from the social and educational practices which shape it? Trying to describe reading is like trying to describe a fish swimming out of water. As Klinkenborg writes:

> A fish's colors fade rapidly when it's removed from water. You have one live instant in which to fix it with your gaze, to memorize the pattern and subtlety of its hues. In my experience, it cannot be done. (1990, p. 35)

And stopping to examine our own ways of reading, instead of getting on with teaching it, is time-consuming, challenging, and, for many teachers struggling with the demands of classroom life, impractical. How can navel-gazing with a book help me to teach students better? Why not simply use this "proven" approach—or that set of basal readers? I'm an adult reader; why should understanding my processes help a beginning reader?

Exploring Reading

The answers are neither easy nor obvious but, as this account of teachers' examination of their reading will show, they are extremely important to our understanding of our roles as teachers of literacy and participants in a larger institutional and cultural text. When we understand what shapes us as readers, we are better able to see our part in shaping or reproducing the instructional context. Our theoretical beliefs, played out in our classroom behavior, are always individually forming in dialectical relation to the ideas of others and to the culturally reproduced texts in which our own schooling is written. Each of us approaches our own reading uniquely and in diverse ways. And yet each of us has been "schooled" into literate behavior as a social practice that can privilege certain common patterns or beliefs. To paraphrase the playwright Arthur Miller, the fish and the water are in one another: the reader is part of a larger societal text which s/he both reads and is read by.

For more than two decades now, as educators had tried to approach the study of reading as more organic and less mechanistic in nature, we have found ourselves in rich, but messy territory. For what is "prior knowledge" after all, except a social construction of reality, neither objective nor value-free? What is a reader if not an individual always in the process of composing and recomposing herself as text in relation to the texts of others?

In this account of teachers' exploration of their own reading process, the teachers' journals show that those whose process is violated rather than validated by the institutional narratives for school reading gain understandings that invite recomposing not only of self, but of their teaching practices as well. Understanding reading is understanding ourselves: we, as educators, are part of a larger text which we must constantly revise.

Exploring reading: How we started

For the last few years, several teachers in rural areas have enrolled in the graduate program in reading and language instruction at our university. As "external" students, they meet off campus, often in school staffrooms or a borrowed college space. As practising teachers willing to devote most of their off-school time to professional growth, they typically come prepared to examine reading and writing with the endurance and enthusiasm of the experienced. As one of their instructors, I have learned from their classroom wisdom and have attempted to provide them with the support to continue to explore their teaching.

The first course in the program typically focusses on philosophical foundations of reading. Rather than assign a large reading list and require that everyone read and respond to the same articles or books, which is typically done, I see the course as an opportunity to fathom the depths of our own reading processes while we each read selectively from a variety of sources. My reasons for promoting this examination are both practical and pedagogical.

Practically, the teachers don't have ready access to a well-stocked library. And so weekly I must bring along a boxful of books and articles from which to choose, and which the teachers supplement with resources they find from curriculum libraries, other teachers, or trips to a local campus. And pedagogically, I am committed to our plumbing the depths of our own understanding about reading to counteract the tendency in our profession, as I mentioned earlier, to use without question the maps of reading drawn by others. I know from my experience as a graduate student, for example, that as provocative as I found the work of Vygotsky or Rosenblatt or Iser, I had no basis from which to assess my reaction to their theories. My experience before taking a course in reading was simply the experience of reading, not the opportunity to reflect on my process or to determine what my emerging theories may be. Further, the seminar-as-examination format typical of my graduate program presented fully-baked theories on a plateful of course requirements: who was I to say that my experiences or beliefs about reading differed from those of the oft-cited theorists? Were they not the experts? Now, as an instructor in a graduate program off campus, I see the need for a forum where teachers' ideas about reading are not silenced by deference to authorities, and where anomalies they feel in matching someone's theory with their own experience can be freely discussed.

This term I asked teachers to keep an extensive reading log, recording their attitudes, reactions, reading history and habits, concerns, quirks and questions as they read anything and everything. Their reading included popular novels, professional materials such as journals and newsletters, and seminal works by theorists such as Rosenblatt, Vygotsky, Piaget, and Polanyi. Occasionally two or three would read the same book or article; but for the most part, they chose their own reading according to interest or recommendation by another teacher. Not being able to amass and read a common body of books and articles was fortunate, as it turned out. Selfishly, I knew this approach would feed my strong aversion to a canon (at whatever educational level); but more importantly, it provided the opportunity for each teacher—without fear of having to compete for the "right" interpretation—to read and present the ideas s/he finds useful in her chosen readings and to offer her interpretation to others for discussion and for further reading. In other words, the teachers' journals and the reading selections they chose became their curriculum.

Finding Her Place

When the course ended three months later, no grand encompassing theory of reading had emerged from their individual and collective travels or from the discussion as a group. But neither had we expected one to emerge. What did develop, however, had as much to do with professional renewal as it did with understanding reading. For the teachers, the most striking development was the rediscovery of the humanity of reading, its connection to who we are as people. In doing so, they began to recognize and accept both diversity and anomaly in their reading process and in others' and to express these insights using their own metaphors and in their own voices. And, as one would expect, they began to translate these insights into changes in their understanding about learning and teaching. For many, it was a beginning step to freeing themselves from both curriculum and canon. And because most of the group were women (only two of twelve journals represented here are those of male teachers), the sense of relation and connectedness that the journals engendered among the group played a significant part in not only fathoming reading, but in gaining voice.

Reading begins at home but real reading is in school

Although many of the teachers were old enough to remember Tom and Betty and Dick and Jane, their earliest and most memorable reflections were not the white picket fence literacy of the early basal readers. Rather they were stories of beds, mothers, laps, books as treasures, and reading as a full-bodied experience.

Janice M. wrote:

Every weekend, Aunt Mary would read to me and my eight

Exploring Reading

cousins and no matter how tired she got, she'd keep reading as long as one of us was still listening. I was always the one who stayed to listen the longest.

Janice G. recalled a typically Canadian experience, the arrival of the encyclopaedia:

I remember gathering on my parents bed to listen to my mother read from a huge book of Bible stories which mom had bought from the same salesman who sold her our shiny new set of encyclopedias. I remember him in our tiny living room, two huge briefcases full of samples. I thought he had written all the books himself, until he brought out the Bible. I knew God had written that so figured this guy must be important.

John C. recalled his mother

clipping out stories for her scrapbook—songs, news items, deaths, births, marriages, interesting events. This was before television. She often read the scrapbook to me. I don't remember my father reading or writing.

Carol R. remembered the family had

a maid named Wilhelmina who told us all sorts of stories, the most memorable being one about the Boogie Man. I remember playing The Three Little Pigs at about age three, so I must have heard all the basic children's stories.

The early memories of reading and being read to, for the most part, were connected to maternity and to nurture and were sensual: the softness of a lap, the feel of a shiny new golden book from the grocery store, the redness of an apple on a book cover, the warmth of a bed. These are associations that many capable readers share. They are associations of reading as a full-bodied, intimate experience: reading as connection with those around

69

us, as though our ego had no margins, the words fusing with experience. But this denial of bodyreading, as Madeleine Grumet calls it, begins early in life. As Grumet describes it:

> Touch and the voice are the sensual passages between parent and child. Because these modes of contact are associated with the intimacy of familiar or erotic relations, they are barred from the classroom where sensuality in any form is anathema. (1988, p. 141)

In North American society, the chants and songs of early reading instruction soon give way to the distancing that makes reading a private act in schools. Reading in a story circle gives way to reading at a desk. The tears and human connection a poem evokes gives way to a study of iambic pentameter. Early reading for many is often associated with mother and with nurturing, and as Nancy Chodorow has reminded us, our ambivalence about that relationship in society causes us to vacillate and to feel guilty. Many, like Peter S., are apologetic about curling up with a book for pleasure. Even now, as adults, we need an excuse to engage fully with text (and even then, we resist it):

> On Monday, I was sick and took a day off school. I stretched out on my sofa, wrapped in a warm sleeping bag, and spent the day reading. Owen Meany is a 600 page book and I needed a day...the richer the story, the richer the world I become absorbed in. I slip away from the world I struggle with and become caught up in the book, until I finally give myself up to it, spending hours reading.

But "real" reading, as many teachers suggested in their journals, is not like this, not so full of passion, so embodied: "real" reading is disembodied, cerebral. Janice G.'s encyclopedia memory is a striking metaphor for the public (and patriarchal) text where we find real reading begins. And the place for that public text is in school.

Reading the school text

Most teachers recalled the ritual and the linearity of reading instruction in their early years at school. They recounted anecdotes of reading groups with animal names, of waiting in their long rows to read aloud and, in anticipation, rehearsing the paragraph that would be theirs to read. Janet V. enjoyed the ordered nature of her schooling:

> My formal reading commenced with the old Ginn series, "My little Red (Blue, Green, White) Story Book," and I recall taking great enjoyment and pride in reading them and progressing from one book to the next.

> I always looked forward to reading time in school, for I could get caught up in the experiences, personalities and adventures of the characters. I liked the poems, deciphering their meaning, enjoying the lilting flow of words, and memorizing them by heart. The first week of school, I would complete the entire year's text, curled up under a blanket in the fall evenings, enjoying the private freedom to be selective in the order of which stories I read first.

Janet's enjoyment of the "private freedom" underscores her sense that by "curling up" and reading ahead, she was deviating from the institutional narrative that shapes our expectations of what reading is and how it is taught and learned. She returned, if only briefly, to the situatedness of home where her reading began. But in order to survive in school, readers must not only master each basal in turn, she or he must participate in the larger institutional narrative, or school text. Dorothy Smith describes how such texts work:

> Our knowledge of contemporary society is to a large extent
> mediated to us by texts of various kinds. The result, an objecti-
> fied world-in-common vested in texts, coordinates the acts,
> decisions, policies and plans of actual subjects.... The realities to
> which action and decision are oriented are virtual realities
> vested in texts and accomplished in distinctive practices of
> reading and writing. We create these virtual realities through
> objectifying discourse; they are our own doing. (1990, pp. 61-62)

Many teachers described the "virtual reality" of reading
instruction in their school history as linear and sequential, with
accompanying routines, rules, and expectations. Everyone waited
until all readers could progress to the next reader. No one was
permitted to "read ahead." We all read the same books. Later,
reading became the search for the one "main idea" in a paragraph
or "theme" in a novel. The virtual reality of reading instruction,
cast in basals in the early years of school and in English courses
in later years, is a reality we seldom challenge as students and
which, because of its canonical nature, becomes tied to virtue.
Mike Rose describes the model of learning "implicit in the
canonical orientation (as seeming) at times, more religious than
cognitive or social" (1989, p. 237). In this way, both as students
and teachers, we participate in ways with words that seem
unimpeachable. We dare not challenge the canon. We learn to
read from the first line to the last and to find the main idea. Such
becomes the school text of reading itself.

Thus, response and connection, the vestiges of mother, are to
be cast aside in favor of what Kristeva has called the fathertongue,
the language of objectified knowledge, of rules and regulations,
of patriarchy. This patriarchal text, which wrote and shaped the
reading experiences of both boys and girls of twenty or more

years ago (and still does now, to a great degree), became the virtual reality that defined our conceptions as teachers of what learning is, what knowing must be. Carol R., who is now a principal, describes her first inkling as a young girl that what she knew was not valid; that there was, embodied outside of her, a text she ought to learn, to appropriate:

> I don't know why this memory is so vivid. In response to a test question for our Brownie badges, "how does a Brownie brush her teeth?" I eagerly offered: "with a toothbrush and tooth-paste." I was told no, that was wrong, that a Brownie brushes up and down. That moment initiated me into an understand-ing of how school worked. From then on, I lived from report card to report card.

As Dorothy Smith notes, institutions such as schools go a long way toward eradicating the messiness of personal knowing. Pure knowing is objective, and must transcend the local, historical settings to which the knower is necessarily bound. The pursuit of pure knowledge is impeded by what Smith calls the social and personal "detritus" dragged in by the knower. And, of course, from the perspective of women, whose knowing has been de-scribed by many as connected knowing (Belenky et al, 1986), marked by responsiveness and fidelity to care, learning to live inside the institutional texts that value objective knowledge can be particularly problematic. Learning to read then becomes learning to understand not only the Ginn readers or the Shakespearean play, but the larger cultural text which mediates the reality of the student.

For Janice G., this meant learning certain lessons, learning to read the rules:

> My science teacher always encouraged us to read everything

carefully and completely. I read through the first questions about stalagmites and stalactites on a test and figured I knew the difference, so I began writing the answers. When I got to the 25th question, the directions were not to put a mark on the paper. I was devastated. I now spend a lot of time going over questions first.

[My English teacher] always filled his room with posters of illustrated quotes. Each year, he gave us a few minutes our first day in his class to read them all. Then we weren't supposed to focus on them in class time again.
...In one university course, the mammoth reading assignments for each class were kept in large brown envelopes in the library and we could sign them out for two hours. For me, that meant photocopying each 30 to 40 page article, using student loan money that could be better spent. But if understanding the readings wasn't hard enough (the professor) added an element of anxiety. Each day one student on the hot seat had to paraphrase and explain the article for the rest of our relieved classmates. It was a nightmare. Sometimes this professor chose you two days in a row, just to keep you on your toes. I still feel anxious when someone asks me about something I have read.

Janice G. and Janice M. were among many who learned to live the institutional narrative. As they analyzed their own approach to reading as adults, they found they had so internalized ways of reading taught in school, they felt guilty doing otherwise. Both described their difficulties breaking away from reading as a linear, organized task; to deviate seemed to be a violation of "pure" reading. Janice M. talks about her reading of Maclean's magazine:

Last night, I tried starting at somewhere other than page one. I couldn't do it. I felt too guilty about skipping pages. This is a holdover from my school days when all textbooks and workbooks were done from page one and we never skipped a page.

Exploring Reading

I'm an avid magazine reader and I always read in exactly the same way. Even the newspaper—I couldn't possibly read section B or C before section A. I've decided to commit myself to varying my reading order. I wonder if I can re-program myself to do it?

Re-reading the school text: Revising a reader

As teachers compared notes about their reading experiences at school, discussed their personal histories and habits as readers, and read the work of theorists, they began to document their comparisons of their own reading process with others' and with their pre-conceived notions of themselves as readers. They began to broaden and deepen their understanding of reading, to chip away at perceptions of reading as a monolithic process. Diana G. realized her need to keep what she called a "goal-oriented" approach when she compared herself with a friend:

> This summer while my friend and I were picking blueberries and I glanced down at our two blueberries flats, I realized that those flats could tell quite a story about the two of us. The flats were in fact a representation of the way each of us approaches any task we have to do.

> My flat had full boxes. I concentrated on only one box at a time, topping it off before moving to the text. She was happily tossing handfuls of berries in the general direction of the flat and letting the berries land in whichever box they would.... When I read I generally use much the same approach. I read whole pieces of writing at a time.... My friend skips sections when she reads, endings here and chapters there.

John C. compared differences in readers to differences in choir members' approach to learning a new song:

Finding Her Place

I know from my own experience that if I understand the message of the song, everything else appears easier.... I'd say that people who do not read a great deal or realize the power of the printed word have less difficulty singing what they do not understand.... I'm surprised at the number of people who leave everything to the choir director. This person often supplies meaning for the choir, as well as background and expression. It's as if some choir members are doing little more than sentence surfing.

After a discussion in which I described my own reading process as often one of "snacking" (a comparison, I realized later, that bespeaks a consumption metaphor that doesn't please me), Linda M. wrote about her approach to reading Cazden's work:

As I began to read the book, I too found myself snacking. That is, I only had so much time to allot for reading so I tried to read the best first, to get a feel for the book. Usually, to warrant myself as a serious reader, I read a book from beginning to end. However, I have recently begun to make decisions as a reader based on my knowledge and understanding of reading.

Elsa B. talked about variations in approach she noted as her colleagues read articles by Halliday and Lefevre. Recognizing variation gave her confidence:

I'm amazed now at the panic I felt. Sharon said her ego wouldn't let her believe she was stupid. Judy and Susan laughed and said if they couldn't understand something they just read on and got the general idea. I couldn't do that then. But I'm now more confident.... Later, talking with (a colleague) about Wilkinson's work, I was floored to hear he found the reading difficult. I considered him to be super intelligent—how could he find it difficult when I found it easy?

Carol R., who had been reading Vygotsky, found herself

trying to solve a problem with the computer by talking herself through the process. She found not variation, but a validation of her process in Vygotsky's ideas.

> I suddenly realized I was in the act of egocentric speech to keep myself on task.... According to Vygotsky, the child's egocentric speech is the counterpart to inner speech, or verbal thought, before it has become entirely internal. The child produces such egocentric speech when he (sic) is planning or problem-solving.... As adults we probably revert to this externalized form of verbal thinking when we are having difficulty with a task. I had put Vygotsky away for awhile, but I am encouraged enough to go back.

Finding connections in Vygotsky's theory that described her reading behavior caused Carol to continue to pursue her reading of his theories. Ann C.'s reading of Rosenblatt gave her an insight into her memories of her schooling. The institutional text, she realized, denied her aesthetic response, and, by extension, denied her self:

> I found myself constantly reflecting on my in-school experience with literature. I enjoyed reading, but the teacher was always seeking the one, right answer and I seldom constructed it. I relied solely on note-taking, a good memory and regurgitation of someone else's ideas.... [Rosenblatt] has helped to focus on the reasons why I have such unpleasant memories and why learning environments like these stifled the development of my literary response. Did they also stifle the development of my personal voice?

Janice M. decided during the course to make it a personal goal to break away from reading from beginning to end:

> I'm teaching myself that it's okay to stop reading something, to pick and choose. For the first 37 of my years I have read all

of something because I felt it would be failure or admitting defeat if I didn't finish. I hope for the next 37 years, I can give myself some choice, and can feel less guilty.

Both Janice and Cathy commented that they are "learning to question what I read instead of accepting everything" just because it has been published in a book.

Objectified knowledge stands as "a product of an institutional order mediated by texts; what it knows can be known in no other way" (Smith, 1990, p. 80). Undertaking a critique of the school text—what we have believed about reading and hence how we must read and teach reading—requires that we inquire into the actualities of our own experiences as participants in reproducing that text. By digging deeply into an understanding of ourselves as readers, we can expose the broader cultural practices that regulate reading and readers. Critical theorists, who typically view such introspection as narcissistic and politically irresponsible, fail to accept that a free act, as Maxine Greene has described it, is a particularized one: "it is undertaken from the standpoint of a particular, situated person trying to bring into existence something contingent on his/her hopes, expectations, and capacities" (1988, p. 70). Or, as the feminist slogan has it, the personal is political.

By documenting their reading processes, comparing what they do with the descriptions of theorists, and by being surrounded by diversity in idea and approach, these teachers found themselves rejecting the roles the school text had written for them, both as students and as teachers. In fathoming their own reading, they began to think of ways to rewrite themselves and the school settings in which they play a key role.

Exploring Reading

Revising the reader: Revising the school text

As Heilbrun notes, "power is the ability to take one's place in whatever discourse is essential to action and the right to have one's part matter" (1988, p. 18). Without question, the fact that these teachers were able to meet regularly as a group and discuss issues gave them a discourse community that offered both support and challenge for their ideas. Nonetheless, as their revision of themselves as readers became apparent, their revisions of themselves as teachers were not far behind. Many described a new sense of, if not power, at least commitment to create different environments for students than those they had experienced.

Janice G. talked about her decision to weave into her Sunday School teaching what she realized had been important to her:

> My own warm memories of these (Bible) stories have made me somewhat of a radical. We follow a set curriculum but at the 3 and 4 year old level it has few tie-ins with Jesus or the well-known stories. I decided to ditch the curriculum and focus on story. Hopefully, some of these children will remember these first book experiences as fondly as I have.

Linda M. is rethinking the

> kind of reading experiences we offer the students in our classroom. Often I felt guilty about not opening the basal reader and going through the guide—am I really teaching reading if I do not make use of this guide? Anyway, I have brought in my own books and books from the library and although students have read many, I realize I've never asked them to comment on them. On Monday, I'm going to talk about reading with them. Share my evaluation of a book, then ask them to do the same. Hey, maybe they could even share their

comments with a friend, suggest a story to a friend.

Janice M. talked about giving students permission to abandon a book.

> I've always given kids choice in what they read, but I have always expected them to finish the book. Perhaps if I give them the choice not to finish a book they don't like, they won't be so uptight and won't take so long to decide. Maybe they'll be more relaxed.

The marginalizing of self—the disembodiment of reading and of knowledge—is so pervasive in schools (and in university courses) that to return to an examination of our local and particular selves becomes, as it did for these teachers, a welcome relief. It becomes, finally, a validation. But it comes with difficulty. Sharon decided to write about her childhood, to begin to tell her stories and participate with her students, not as the teacher, but a writer. She was nervous, both about facing the students and facing herself.

> The fact that memories that meant so much to me were languishing on the shelf begged the question: Why haven't you written this? Answers flooded back: I haven't the time. Who'd want to read it?... However, suppose that the writing helped me to deal with the past; to sort it and feel it and find the plot line. Maybe writing could help my life, as Ernest Becker says, "add up." I wondered if my experience with the memoir was shared by students. Are they sometimes afraid of what they will find when they give voice to their story? Perhaps in sharing my experience I could help them, I thought. Then I realized that the writer who needed help was me.

As they came closer to valuing again the embodied process of reading—that is, not denying their connections, their bodyreading—and as they began to believe more fully in their own power to make decisions in the classroom, the teachers also questioned other texts that tacitly wielded authority in their working lives.

Karen K. realized that she

> often felt that other educators knew all the answers and if I followed what they said I would be a good teacher. If it didn't work out, it was because of something I'd done....But I now think it is all right for me to question whether a new teaching strategy is as good as they say it is...we are all still searching for answers and we never really find them.

Carol R. was angry about an in-service offered by the school board which advocated practices inconsistent with the board's stated holistic philosophy about learning.

> There was once a time when I would have wanted to find out which of these views was the truth. I now realize there is no objective truth. People become a reflection of the way they are treated. The Industrial Revolution, with its specialization of labour, and especially the production line, have created a transmission of culture" model in education. We have to live with what that has produced while working to restructure institutions to work more holistically.

Although the workshop leader called Carol's comments divisive, Carol claimed that the school board's promotion of practices representing antithetical world views was "intellectual sloppiness." While there is no "truth," Carol argued, we can work toward coherence.

Janice M. re-assessed the assumption of the societal text that claims literacy is for all.

> These kids who don't do as well in school shouldn't be made to

feel that they have failed life because they have failed to meet our standards in reading and writing.... [L]iteracy is not a solution to all the world's ills and we are failing our students by ignoring the fact that we discriminate against those not considered literate. One of the most caring, loving, best parents I know is my cousin who reads and writes poorly and who has little formal education. She also has little self esteem and little confidence in her parenting abilities. How sad that school failed her so miserably. Her three children are articulate, intelligent, considerate people like their mother. We have to re-think what we value.

Peter S.'s staff had met with a local M'iqmaq Band Council recently and he later reflected on their day:

We listened to some amazing people talk about the effect the school system had on them, about the importance of their language and how the school system stripped them of it, and of the deep spiritual nature of the M'iqmaq culture. It was not hostile and it was incredibly instructive. They had very good reasons to fear white man's education.

He tied this experience with his reading of Iser's and Emig's work, and noted:

It is not the pretty pictures on the classroom wall or the plant by the window or the carefully constructed activities.... We need to be constantly looking for ways to understand how others perceive the world, to tolerate differences.

By tracking their understanding of their own reading process and by uncovering the ways in which they were were, as readers, shaped by the institutional narrative for teaching and learning reading, the teachers were able to rethink themselves as readers and teachers. Such revision, in many ways, enabled them to bridge the public and the private, the self and the social. Their

Exploring Reading

journals show that reading began for them as an experience associated with feeling, imagination, and a celebration of the senses. As a school activity, reading became ritualized and disembodied, became the text Out There. For women, who are still heavily socialized to please, having to choose the school text meant denial of the particularized and situated experience of their reading. While tracking their reading process, these teachers found others' maps helpful only to a point; what seemed more important was that they embark on the exploration themselves. Understanding reading requires both sense and reference, both what we know and how we live (Ricoeur, 1976). I hear the call for continued exploration in Maxine Greene's words:

> The idea of freedom, so long linked to self-direction and a separation of the subject from the objective world, may be revised and remade to the degree we understand situatedness and knowing in connection with action and speech, knowing as an aspect of vocation, taking place in the midst of life. (1988, p. 76)

References

Belenky et al. (1986). *Women's ways of knowing*. New York: Basic Books.

Greene, M. (1988). *The dialectic of freedom*. New York: Teacher's College Press.

Grumet, M. (1988). Bodyreading. In *Bitter milk*. Amherst, MA: University of Massachusetts Press.

Heilbrun, C. (1988). *Writing a woman's life*. New York: W.W. Norton.

Klinkenborg, V. (1990). Come and gone. *Harper's Magazine,* June: 34-36.

Kristeva, J. (1977) *About Chinese women*. Translated by Anita Burrows. London, UK: Marion Boyars.

Finding Her Place

Neilsen, A. (1989). *Critical thinking and reading: Empowering learners to think and act.* Urbana, IL: National Council of Teachers of English.

Neilsen, L. (1989). *Literacy and living.* Portsmouth, NH: Heinemann.

Neilsen, L. (1991). Is anyone listening? *The Reading Teacher,* 44, 494-496.

Ricoeur, P. (1976). *Interpretation theory: Discourse and the surplus of meaning.* Fort Worth, TX: Texas Christian University Press.

Rose, M. (1989). *Lives on the boundary.* New York: Penguin.

Smith, D. (1990). *The conceptual practices of power.* Toronto, Ontario: University of Toronto Press.

Among the books available to the teachers were the following:

Cazden, C.B. (1988). *Classroom discourse: The language of teaching and learning.* Portsmouth, NH: Heinemann Educational Books.

Emig, J. (1983). *The web of meaning.* Montclair, NJ: Boynton-Cook.

Fish, S. (1980) *Is there a text in this class?* Cambridge, MA: Harvard University Press.

Halliday, M.A.K. (1978). *Language as social semiotic.* Baltimore, MD: University Park Press.

Iser, W. (1978). *The act of reading. A theory of aesthetic response.* Baltimore, MD: The Johns Hopkins University Press.

Lefevre, K.B. (1987). *Invention as a social act.* Carbondale, IL: Southern Illinois University Press.

Piaget, J. (1926). *The language and thought of the child.* London, UK: Routledge & Kegan Paul.

Piaget, J. (1970). *Psychology and epistemology.* New York: The Viking Press.

Polanyi, M. (1958). *Personal knowledge.* Chicago, IL: University of Chicago Press.

Rosenblatt, L.M. (1938). *Literature as exploration.* New York: Noble & Noble. (1976 edition)

Rosenblatt, L.M. (1978). *The reader, the text, the poem: The transactional theory of the literary work.* Carbondale, IL: Southern Illinois University Press.

Suleiman, S.R. & Crosman, I. (Eds). (1980). *The reader in the text: Essays on audience and interpretation.* Princeton, NJ: Princeton

University Press.

Vygotsky, L.S. (1962). *Thought and language*. Cambridge, MA: MIT Press.

Vygotsky, L.S. (1978) *Mind in society: The development of higher psychological processes*. Cambridge, MA: Harvard University Press.

Wilkinson, A. (1975). *Language and education*. Oxford, UK: Oxford University Press.

Excerpts from a keynote address at the Second International Conference on Adult and Adolescent Reading, Banff.

—3—
Literacy and Gender:
A Patchwork Quilt

My talk today is a patchwork quilt in process, the sections still seeking patterns as I speak and as you participate. Here are anecdotes, remnants of theory, words, and ideas both smooth and rough in texture, shared and told in the voices of mothers, academic women, literacy workers, native women, and women in the workplace.

These fragments of our words and lives, however, share a common thread: What it means to teach and learn literacy—or anything else, for that matter—is related to what it means to be female or male, and to our experiences, our individual and collective histories of reproducing and nurturing, of our domestic life, our natures, our personal knowledge, and our politics. Language, as one of many technologies of identity, writes us into the design of this quilt.

Literacy has been primarily the work of women—as mothers in the home, as volunteers in the community, as elementary school teachers, and as secretaries at work. But women rarely have access to the political power and authority necessary in schools and society to effect widespread change in literacy learning. Our "just add women and stir" assumptions we use in research and in life are doing us harm: we have failed to conduct fair inquiry research and we have failed to make responsible educational decisions if we have failed to study the relationship between gender and literacy.

Women comprise two-thirds of all illiterates in the world and 90 percent of all refugee populations. In industrialized nations, women form over 40 percent of the paid labor force, but are paid only one-half to three-quarters of what men earn at the same jobs. Women head one-third of all families on earth (Morgan, 1989).

In her research on women in literacy programs, Jennifer Horsman notes:

> Many of the women did a lot of "work" helping children with school work. They gave children tests to help them learn and prepare for school tests, they explained problems the children were stuck on, and they helped children do research for special projects which required encyclopedias, visits to libraries and pictures to cut up. They also generally showed interest in their children's performance at school and encouraged them to do their homework. (1988, p. 176)

In fact, many of the women learners Horsman studied came to programs so they could eventually help their children with their schoolwork.

Dorothy Smith (1987) reminds us:

> What mothers do to support their children's school is done in this imaginary "mother" time which takes no time at all and not in real time where it competes with other work. Mothers are never off the hook. Lack of time or fatigue is never a reason for not reading with your child, listening to her spelling, going over

Literacy and Gender

her French dictation.... A few fathers contribute some time but not a lot, at least with children at the elementary level (33).

Jenny Horsman again:

> It is important to note what...the normal discourse serves to disguise: teachers are described as teaching, whereas parents are simply helping and the complex and skilled nature of the work expected of them becomes invisible. (177)

> But when things go wrong, teachers, experts and the media regularly explain working-class children's poor achievements in school with accounts that include the parents' failure to read to their children, their lack of interest in education, the poor example they set, and even their failure to raise their children correctly. (178)

A comment from a literacy tutor who declined to be named:

> One of the forces that drives working-class women to literacy programs is violence. It's a way to get out of the home. But it backfires. When women learn how to read and write it necessarily affects the balance of power and control in the family. Just as many women who enter literacy programs to escape violence leave them for the same reason.

Kathleen Rockhill notes:

> If we open the doors of our minds to the power of the fist, the power of the sexual, the power of the family, the church and other cultural forms, perhaps we can begin to find ways to address...the double bind (that women are in): to act upon their desire for change requires a choice that few feel they can make—a choice between love, family, home and violent upheaval. (1987, p. 166)

Eva Saulis, from *Enough is Enough: Aboriginal Women Speak Out*:

Finding Her Place

My mother did Indian medicine and we spoke only Indian until we went to school. That's when we lost our language because we weren't allowed to speak Indian on school grounds. My parents spoke Indian and French at home. We could hardly understand anything at school... Once I talked with one of the nuns about the old days and the nun said it wasn't their idea; it was the rules laid down, the policy that we weren't supposed to talk Indian. She said, "We had nothing to do with it ourselves. We were just doing what we were told."

Sandra Lovelace speaks:

At first we went to school on the reserve. The nuns taught us and we couldn't talk Indian—every time we talked Indian we'd get spanked and told we were dirty. We were made to feel ashamed. I quit school about grade eight. I figured if this is what the world is like, I don't want to be around white people.

Armstrong and Armstrong (*Looking Ahead: The Future of Women's Work* (p. 213) report that, although over half of Canadian women are now counted as active members of the labor force, about a third of them do clerical work.

We see the tragic humor in women's role in literacy here, in a poem by Helen Potrebenko:

Another Silly Typing Error

The nature of typing is such that
there are none but silly errors to make:
renowned only for pettiness
and an appearance of stupidity.
I don't want to make silly little errors;
I want to make big important errors.
I want to make at least one error
which fills my supervisor with such horror
she blanches and almost faints
and then runs to the manager's office.

Literacy and Gender

The manager turns pale and stares out the window
then resolutely picks up the phone
to page the big boss at his golf game.
Then the big boss comes running into the office
and the manager closes his door
and hours go by.
The other women don't talk
or talk only in whispers,
pale as ghosts but relieved it isn't them.
An emergency stockholders' meeting has to be called
about which we only hear rumors.
To make sure I don't accidentally get a job
with a subsidiary, allied company, or supplier,
I am offered a choice of either
fourteen years severance pay or early retirement.
A question is asked in Parliament
to which the Prime Minister replies by assuring the House
most typists only make silly typing errors
which only rarely affect the balance of trade.
The only time I get to talk about it
is when I am interviewed (anonymously) for an article
about the effect of typing errors on the economy.

—from Ursula Franklin,
The Real World of Technology, 1990, pp. 110-111

Written comments from support staff in a government organization in Nova Scotia, December, 1989:

Nancy: We are the typing and coffee dollies. I'm tired of not being listened to.

Maddie: I believe the only talents viewed as an asset when you are a secretary in government is the fact that you have eight fingers and one thumb that type and that you can answer a ringing phone. We know what goes on in the Branch and we're not stupid. I've seen the manager take offence when I've made a good suggestion - probably because he hadn't thought of it. (Field notes, March, 1990)

91

Finding Her Place

Excerpt from hallway conversation with male director in government organization after workshop with his support staff:

> So, Lorri, how are your meetings with the girls going? They figure they're going to take over the Branch, do they?

Cheris Kramarae (from "Proprietors of Language")

> When women take steps to change the language structure and their own uses of language, they are in fact acting to change their status in society; they are challenging the legitimacy of the dominant group. By calling the challengers and their proposals for language change silly, unnatural, irrational, and simplistic, the dominant group tries to reaffirm its threatened social identity.

Ursula Franklin, on technology:

> Attention to the language is important....whenever someone talks to you about the benefits and costs of (technology), don't ask "What benefits?" Ask "whose benefits and whose costs?" The discourse should seek out those on whom technology impacts. (There is) an implicit attempt to keep people from challenging technology by making their direct experience appear marginal and irrelevant..... We need to concentrate on redemptive technologies. (124-126)

This quilt is fashioned by secretaries who are doing literacy's housework with insufficient and often outdated equipment and even less decision-making power. It includes classroom teachers, community workers, graduate students, nursery school workers, among other women, caught in the complex social web that expects them to support, teach, and extend the literacy of people in their purview—all without the economic or institutional power that would ensure their success. In this quilt we see people whose ancestors have lived here for centuries being refused the literacy of their birth. We recognize too the many mothers, held responsible for literacy at home, but whose connected literacy they create with their children is denied and devalued at school, especially if they are not part of white mainstream culture.

We recognize ourselves, too, for this quilt is composed of us all. It is stitched with memory, designed by our decisions, colored by our values. The degree to which it provides comfort, safety, assurance, and shelter is the degree to which we recognize our own role in creating it.

My grandmother's quilt, which has been hanging on the west wall since her death, is a symbol to me of her dedication to family and community. It calls to mind circles of women in rural Western Canada working long evenings to create something necessary, something enduring. Surely we, too, can work together to stitch something necessary and enduring, large enough for us all.

References

Deem, R. (1978). *Women and schooling*. London, UK: Routledge & Kegan Paul.

Enough is enough: Aboriginal women speak out. (1987.) Toronto, Ontario: The Women's Press.

Franklin, U. (1990). *The real world of technology*. Toronto, Ontario: The Massey Lectures, CBC Enterprises.

Horsman, J. (1990). *Something in my mind besides the everyday*. Toronto, Ontario: The Women's Press.

Josselson, R. (1987) *Finding herself*. San Francisco, CA: Jossey-Bass.

Kanter, R.M. (1975). Women and the structure of organizations. In Millman, M. & Kanter, R. *Another voice: Feminist perspectives on social life and social science*. New York: Octagon Books, pp. 49-50.

Finding Her Place

Kanter, R.M. (1983). *The changemasters*. New York: Octagon Books.

Kramarae, C. (1980). Proprietors of Language. In McConnell-Ginet, S., Borker, R., & Furman, N. (eds) *Women and language in literature and society*. New York: Praeger Special Studies, p. 65.

Maroney, H., & Luxton, M. (eds). (1987) *Feminism and political economy*. Toronto, Ontario: Methuen.

Morgan, R. (1989). *The demon lover*. New York: W.W. Norton.

Rockhill, K. (1987). The chaos of subjectivity in the ordered halls of academe. *Canadian Woman Studies*, 8(4), Winter.

Smith, D. (1987). *The everyday world as problematic*. Toronto, Ontario: University of Toronto Press.

96

Work with the Pictou county teachers, support staff in the government, and with Bachelor of Education students shook my assumptions about researcher stance. This chapter describes my realization that the constructivism through which I thought I was working was, in significant ways, as nomothetic and researcher-driven as my earlier, positivist work.

—4—
Women, Literacy, and Agency:
Beyond the Master Narratives

As a researcher and a woman, I am becoming increasingly conflicted about my approach to inquiry, the role I can play in the academy studying and working with women, mostly teachers, and my beliefs about the emancipatory promise of literacy. Where once I saw forms, images, I now see kaleidoscopic montages of theoretical moments, shifting and slipping in elusive patterns. I have never felt more challenged, more un-constructed, more awake in my life. Each week it seems another given is taken away.

Rosemary Tong's (1989, p. 236) reminder that "as bad as it is for a woman to be bullied into submission by a patriarch's unitary truth, it is even worse for her to be judged not a real feminist by a matriarch's unitary truth" speaks not only to an anti-essentialist perspective I understand, but also to a larger, more pervasive pattern in educational research, especially research conducted by women with women: that of attempting to find a position from which to undertake research that isn't ethically and morally uncomfortable or repugnant, at the same time trying to resist the inevitable interpellation of current belief systems on who we are and what we think. In short, whether it's midlife resignation or the zeitgeist that is primarily responsible, I find I am less likely now to allow myself to be bullied into submission by anyone else's truth, regardless of the weight of the literature behind its claims.

And yet, whatever sense-making I do about my past or my present inquiry process, I recognize that the accounts themselves will continue to be "inscribed with dominant ideologies" (Manicom, p. 374). Our stories and the telling of them are always partial, always selective, always open to interrogation. The threads we use to weave the fabric of our stories will always saturated with ideological hues.

My work as a literacy researcher, which began years ago with the more simple task of manipulating syntactic variables, cannot be separated from my intellectual life as a woman. I have been variously swept away by positivist and post-positivist approaches, ethnography, case study research, collaborative inquiry, among others, each of which, for its time, seemed to provide the most promise for understanding what literacy is and what it does. I want to see the epistemological and methodological journey as an evolution; I want to write my own authority and agency into my memories of these affairs of the mind, but I am not so sure. An excerpt from Marge Piercy's poem "Stone, Paper, Knife" may capture best what actually happened:

> ....*How many men*
> *I have lain with who would only*
> *fit bodies together at one angle*
> *and who required exactly muttered*
> *obscene formulae, precise caresses*
>
> *until every woman they embraced*
> *was the same dolly of their will*
> *and all coupling mechanical, safe*
> *proceeding by strict taboos whose fabric*

98

Women, Literacy, and Agency

no wild emotion could pierce.
(p. 138, *Stone, Paper, Knife.* New York: Alfred A. Knopf, 1983)

Having allowed myself to be "a dolly of the will" of both feminist thought and prevailing research agenda over the years (but, being enough of a social constructionist not to feel particularly guilty about it), I take comfort, perhaps even joy, in now seeking, without apology, those inquiry approaches and rationale which wild emotion can pierce, learning to develop ways of doing and thinking about research in literacy that are closer to fusing mind and body, heart and head. At this point, I value theoretical pluralism, efforts to disrupt and expose the master narratives of the academy—those larger stories which write us even as we act out their plotlines—and the growing efforts of feminist researchers to make our work make a difference.

Over the last five years, I have been inquiring into the ways in which women in institutional settings use literacy to examine their life and their work. But as I learn from them how they use literacy to challenge the master narratives of the government workplace, the university classroom, the school, or society at large; as I describe their growing sense of agency in their work, I must also describe mine. For the master narratives, the many methodologies and ways of knowing I have lain with are inscribed in my practices as well. And it is my literacy which shapes my understanding of theirs, and represents it to you.

Dorothy Smith's (1990) work on the relations of ruling and objectified knowledge is a useful standpoint to understand literacy, especially women's literacy. For Smith, relations of ruling are not the usual structures we think about, such as the government or political organizations. They are, instead, the total complex of activities in all spheres "by which our kind of society is ruled, managed, and administered" (1990, p. 14). They

99

are those coded behaviours and expectations that mark our activities and that become embedded in language, particularly written language, as a form of objectified knowledge. The objectified knowledge carries authority in the conceptual plane; it governs how we think and talk in the multiple positionings of our daily lives. And whether a woman is working as a clerk or a secretary, as a graduate student, or as a untenured university teacher, "women mediate for men at work the relationship between (that) conceptual mode of action and the actual concrete forms in which it is and must be realized, and the actual material conditions upon which it depends" (1990, p.19). In other words, the relations of ruling as we know them confine the majority of literate women to the office housework of society. In so doing, we as women remain outside or subordinate to the ruling apparatus, and alienated from our own experiences. Our task, as Smith describes it, might be to "disclose to women involved in the educational process how matters come about as they do in their experience and to provide methods of making their work experience accountable to themselves and to other women rather than to the ruling apparatus of which institutions are part" (1987, p. 178). While I have worked with women to try to help them become accountable to themselves and other women, rather than to the ruling apparatus, it has only been recently that I have realized how essential it is that I engage in that process for myself as well.

An Ethnography Story from the Workplace

Three years ago, I completed an ethnographic study of writing in the workplace. Hired by a local government department to "fix up the writing problem with the professional staff," as the Deputy Minister described it, I set about to analyze the habits and processes of the production of reports, letters, and proposals among the largely male middle management staff. I was granted permission to do research on literacy in the organization as I helped to "retrain" the staff as writers (again, the Deputy Minister's words). It was a daunting prospect, but a financially attractive one, and one which gave me a ready-made research setting. It wasn't until we had completed several group workshops that I realized I was taking good money to be co-opted into marginalizing the support staff, all women, whose efforts, without exaggeration, had been keeping the organization afloat. It became clear that the inefficiency plaguing the organization was caused, in large part, by petty political arm-wrestling throughout the hierarchy of the management staff. The support staff with all the responsibility for document production but no decision-making authority were twice-victimized: Their workload typing, retyping, and photocopying multiple iterations of documents to feed the pecking order of approval wasted their energies and took away from more productive work; and their critiques of time-consuming, redundant, and counter-productive procedures were ignored and trivialized. (It goes without saying, of course, that their salary further victimized them: it was approximately one-third that of their supervisors).

Late into the contract, I urged for a workshop for the support staff alone. The workshop time was devoted to drafting a set of recommendations for change. The recommendations were followed a month later with statistics the women had collected to support the recommendations: they tallied time spent on various tasks, calculated cost-efficiency of the out-dated equipment, tracked documents to prove their claim that a typical letter took three-and-one-half weeks to leave the department, and translated into dollars the cost to Nova Scotia taxpayers of such inefficiency. Senior management read the report and while widespread changes were not made, certain procedures were adjusted, and the support staff gained a say in the production of documents they did not have previously.

As an ethnographer, I came to that setting looking for the meanings: how did people perceive the reading and writing they were doing? I was dutiful about the interviewing, about field notes, and about triangulating perspectives. A picture began to emerge of a hierarchy, the channels of which were hopelessly clogged with paper generated for purposes of jockeying for position rather than communicating. It became clear that the putative goal of my contract—to re-train writers and to make recommendations for greater efficiency—would not be realized because the relations of ruling saturated every piece of paper and every inefficient procedure. Everything I was doing was window-dressing. As a researcher, I began to focus instead on the work of the support staff, for two reasons: their commonsense claims spoke to a desire for order and efficiency not clouded by power politics; and their status as pink collar workers and their perceived lack of authority among the management staff appealed to my feminist sensibilities.

It was through my discussions with these women that my scripted stance as an ethnographer began to be revised, but only slightly. Although I had accounted for my own subject positioning in previous research (Neilsen, 1989), for the most part I was enacting the master narrative of Rosaldo's Lone Ethnographer: I was the literate recorder of utterances, the gatherer of artifacts. "In accordance with imperialist norms, (the) natives provided the raw material ('the data') for processing.... After returning to the metropolitan centre....the Lone Ethnographer wrote his (sic) work" (1989, p. 31). And in keeping with the loosening of the codes then apparent in the field (Geertz, 1989; Stoller, 1989), I even experimented with literary form by writing my account of the so-called fieldwork in the form of a play framed by quotes from Ibsen's *A Doll's House*.

What insinuated its way into my mind and my gut as I worked with the support staff and what began to change my inquiry process was my identification with them, and it was from that standpoint that we were able to engage in productive work. I was most useful not as a writing consultant, but as a researcher who was also a woman. Together we brainstormed strategies to make the case for improved procedures and I was able to bring to the table my experience in various forms of data gathering and statistical methods which they eagerly applied to the problems at hand. That was my most explicit, and obvious, contribution. What was left unstated until now was perhaps the most salient contribution, that of being a woman who has spent many years doing various forms of office housework, as a clerical worker, a receptionist, a keypunch operator in a bank, a graduate assistant, and most recently, but better paid, as a writing consultant to institutions. As a consultant, I work largely with male management and it is common to be teased about being the "hired English teacher." Ph.D. or not, my literacy and my work as a teacher help to further instantiate stereotypical perceptions of women who work with words.

This recognition of my partial identification with the support staff is key to my discussion here for it speaks to the dilemma that we all recognize in our work as feminist researchers. When I brought my written account of the work to a public audience, the work represented a researcher stance which Fine (1992) has described as "voices." One step beyond ventriloquy, in which "the author tells Truth, has no gender, race, class, or stance" (212), the "voices" stance allows us as researchers to "hide, unproblematic, just under the covers of those marginal, if now 'liberated' voices" (215) of the participants, or subjects of the research. This stance typically involves "a delicate tailoring of texts" (219), using just the words of the individuals we work with to make the point we intend to make, or intended to make all along. Writing about the support staff, their concerns about collaboration and voice, it was easy to cut and stitch fragments of field note conversations to stretch over pre-fabricated frames provided by Carol Gilligan, Nona Lyons, Rosabeth Moss Kanter, and the literary work of Henrik Ibsen. While I wasn't exactly ventriloquating the women, neither was I working from an explicitly activist stance, at least what I would today call activist.

The dilemma for the support staff was that they were perceived as Other, were alienated from the ruling apparatus even as their work supported it. My dilemma as a researcher was that I perceived myself as Other, believed my obligation as a scholar—indeed my very success—was dependent on my ability to maintain that separation, although the emancipatory work I was able to foster, in some small way, depended upon my being able to identify with them as women.

The Researcher as Teacher

A second strand of research that informs this discussion involved a graduate seminar in reading theory in which twelve women, all of whom are classroom teachers, chose to explore their own reading process as they read the works of theorists such as Polanyi, Vygotsky, Rosenblatt, Smith, Piaget, Iser, and Halliday, among others. They kept journals to track in detail their daily reading, wrote accounts of their school experiences, and delved deeply into their recollections of their reading experiences as children at home. As teacher-researchers, their goal was to understand better the roots and the growth of their own literacy in order to inform their classroom teaching. As they worked through an understanding of the theories espoused by others, they expressed the desire to develop their own theories of the reading process, or at least to articulate the degree to which these theories were reflected in their own experiences of working with children.

We agreed as a group that while they explored their reading as individuals, our discussions would provide a forum to discuss their discoveries, to make connections and comparisons, to allow common themes and obvious disparities to emerge. As the course instructor, I would pull together those themes and offer a meta-analysis of their individual analyses of themselves as readers. "This is what I think is going on here," I would say.

The teachers' journals and discussion indicated that reading began for them as an experience associated with feeling, imagination, and a celebration of the senses. Reading was an embodied experience; as early literacy learners, these women were "body-reading" (Grumet, 1988). As a school activity, however, reading became ritualized and disembodied; it became the Text Out There, the authoritative discourse inscribed in the master narrative of learning to read in school. Their accounts told the story of what reading was supposed to be: their fear in early years of "reading ahead"; their reluctance as adults to leave a book unfinished or to read in a non-linear fashion, skipping about the text; their private concern for unearthing the "right interpretation" in the course readings while they publicly espoused whole language approaches in the classroom. As these women re-visioned themselves as readers, they began to question their allegiance to the narratives that had written their lives as readers to date; it was only a short step for them to make the connection to what they do as teachers in the classroom. Their relationship to the readings in the course changed as well; Louise

105

Finding Her Place

Rosenblatt and Frank Smith (or at least their textual represen-
tations) became two of many participants in a conversation in
which these teachers and their classroom wisdom played a part.
The authority these teachers invested in the text was not
completely eroded, to be sure; and there is no telling the degree
to which the emancipatory notions offered by theorists such as
Rosenblatt or Smith were simply taken up and adopted to
support the teachers' emerging constructivist ideas. (Again, we
wander in the hall of mirrors that makes it almost impossible to
distinguish agency itself from the adoption of an emancipatory
stance that sanctions agency. As Britzman [1991, p. 63] notes,
"what must be addressed are the deep investments teachers and
students have in the available discourses, and the ways they are
borrowed, taken up, and reinflected with subjective meanings").

And where was I as this was going on? In the center, of course.
I was no longer the objective observer, the Lone Ethnographer
swooping into a field ripe with data for the picking. I was the
course instructor who set the overarching agenda, asked the
initiating question that launched their inquiry, coached from
behind as they established their goal and their approach. At the
time we all saw my stance as participatory, the research they did
as emancipatory, my pedagogy as student-centred, not teacher-
centred. Because this was the first graduate course for many in
the group, the stance I took as an instructor and co-researcher
represented a radical shift in pedagogy from what they had
experienced as undergraduates many years ago. My recording of
their process, the research I believed I was doing with them, was,
in fact, research about them. Our work together was bound by
the demands of the institution; my work as an instructor and a
researcher was guided by my sense of how I ought to conduct
myself and the course to promote student-centred inquiry and
pedagogy. The master narratives continued to hold sway; they

were simply more palatable ones.

(On reflection, I am loath to name our state of mind "false consciousness" because it assumes that someone out there, possibly me in this case, ought to have since woken up with the authentic version of what happened. The term is objectionable to me because it is rooted in the demands—and the arrogance—of yet another master narrative).

But something else, more important and more lasting, occurred during the course of the semester. We talked about our research, we compared notes, we told stories, we connected. As different as we were in background, age, teaching experience, or education, we were united in common experiences of the school as a patriarchal institution whose top-down text-centred approach to reading instruction alienated us all from our lives in the pages. When Janice talked about her shame at being caught reading ahead in her reader, I remembered. When Carol told about the moment she realized that the right answer was not the obvious one, especially on a reading test, we all remembered. We talked about our collective experiences as graduate students, and I recounted the many love affairs I had had with this theory or that, with my search for the One answer among many, the world view that made sense. Creating a space for the discussion of these common experiences wasn't necessary: it was what we did, and how we worked with one another. The experience of the course and the research we did together was not an event, and certainly not a field setting: It was a relationship.

Maria Mies (1991) talks about the dilemma of being at once separated and united as women work together on research that makes a difference in women's lives. She argues that there is a level at which women are bound by their experiences of patriarchy; that level, she claims, is deeper than class, skin color, language, and education:

107

Finding Her Place

Because this level exists women are in a position to communicate with one each other as people across the different barriers.
Labelling alone creates no communication. It arranges people
together as if they were things. Partial identification is hence
possible if we reject the total claim on our existence as a
commodity...if we do not sublimate to commodity relations
that part in us where we are afflicted and affected in our
human beingness...partial identification therefore makes possible the necessary closeness to the others as well as the
necessary distance from myself. (1991, p. 81)

Mies' comments might be labelled by some as essentialist,
and while most will say that the multiply-positioned nature of
our identities makes an essentialist position untenable, I cannot
ignore the experience I have in common with other women, the
"womanbeingness" we share by dint of our gender. (Besides, in
this radically re-assessment of who I am as a researcher and a
woman, I am increasingly impatient with our tendency in the
academy to fetishize concepts such as essentialism: my work as
a woman is not to contribute to the production of ideology as
commodity, but to work to end oppressive relations. But, who
knows, perhaps I too am fetishizing concepts even now).

Working with these teachers in the graduate seminar, I
became as much, or more, participant as observer. My history in
educational settings made my intellectual, experiential, and
emotional investment much greater with these women than
with the support staff in the government workplace. Because of
this investment, the research process became less a conscious
and applied methodology and more a state of mind. I kept notes,
certainly, noted patterns and followed them up, used my literacy
in an attempt to understand theirs, and found myself less likely
to want to attach their experiences to theoretical frames to
validate them, to enable the "findings" to insert themselves into

Women, Literacy, and Agency

academic discourse with a certain authority. Instead, theoretical frames, such as Grumet's (1988) informed, extended, and illuminated the discourse that emerged. Methodological purity and theoretical consonance seemed less important than conversation, connection, and talk of changed practice, of individual and collective action. The inquiry process was embedded in my relationship with these individuals as women and as a group.

For years, I have felt uncomfortable about the exploitative dark side of research and of teaching. Knowing colleagues whose publishing career has been built on teachers' voices packaged as empowerment vehicles—and being perplexed at the teachers' willingness to let themselves be so empowered and their reluctance to name or resist it for fear of repercussion—I wanted to resist that impulse. These teachers, these women, our learning, were not to be exploited. Britzman (1991) talks about the dualism created when we believe, as feminists educators, that our work can have an emancipatory effect simply by creating experiences for women as women to tell their stories:

> On the one hand, if teachers are persuasive, student may take on the desires of teachers as if they were their own. On the other hand, if teachers are successful, students will find their own voice. In this dualism, the only "true" voice is the teacher's voice and thus willingness can only be realized through coercion. (1991, p.74)

As a researcher, I was perpetuating the same practice, putting myself at the center of the work as I prepared to write about our experience. Fine's (1992) continuum of "ventriloquy," "voices," and "activism," speaks eloquently to the ethical dilemma many feminist researchers face. Fine argues that it is failure of our methodology, "and a flight from our own political responsibilities (not) to tell tough, critical, and confusing stories

109

about the ideological and discursive patterns of inequitable power arrangements" (1992, p. 219). There was no question, as course instructor and meta-researcher, the power arrangements were inequitable. But in feeling awkward about writing about the experience, in self-consciously watching my feet as I danced, was I not, submitting to the same dualism of which Britzman speaks? By concerning myself with my stance, was I not centering a concern for the power arrangement itself, centering methodology, placing on the margins the very substance of our work as literate women composing new understandings of ourselves as teachers? Which master narrative now was guiding my work? bell hooks' words, mimicking the colonizer's voice, haunt me:

> ...I will tell (your story) back to you in a new way. Tell it back to you in such a way that it has become mine, my own. Rewriting you, I write myself anew. I am still author, authority. I am still the colonizer, the speaking subject. (1990, p. 152)

If I am truly to be response-able, the most productive conversation ought to occur not only between me and other similarly-conflicted researchers, but among all of us collectively engaged in such research. If I am truly to be a response-able teacher, the conversation must engage us all equally in change, in interrogating our identities and our role in institutions: I must change too, not merely for the opportunity to flagellate myself publicly in print, to create another new academic commodity, but to "come out" as Fine (1992) says about the way I work. And if I am truly to be a response-able human being, I must begin to account for the many identities I live, the shifting power relations I participate in, and watch carefully the ways in which they dis-able others rather than enable them. Further, I must learn to celebrate, rather than repress or deny, those identities that allow me to be human, to be woman, in my work.

Institutional Disruptions and Habits of Mind

Jennifer and Rhonna stood out from the class of 58 Bachelor of Education students from the first day of class. A couple of years older than the average B.Ed. student, each has a strong sense of what is just, and what is not. They describe themselves as having different belief systems and different teaching styles; they are close friends.

Most of their classmates, facing a year of intense study and practicum experience, typically enter the program keyed up, on edge, ready to meet the demands of the institution, and prepared to succeed. Their academic and experiential preparation had won them a slot in the program over 750 applicants. They have little prospect of finding a teaching position when the year is finished; most will have to wait a couple of years before a position opens up. Their anxiety about achievement and employment runs high. They want to excel, want to know what's expected. Most are in their early to mid-twenties, some are married and have children.

As the newly-hired faculty member, charged with the responsibility of overseeing the B.Ed. program, the student teaching course, and school placements, along with my graduate teaching load, I was as green as these B.Ed. students were eager. Although my colleagues were very helpful, a combination of factors beyond anyone's control left me without a mentor in my new position. As a result, I was unfamiliar with institutional practices to date, institutional expectations for how the B.Ed program is run, faculty expectations for my duties, admission and registration procedures, the day-to-day relations of ruling that informed everyone's behaviour, and the details of daily practice

111

that one needs to acquire in order to do one's job. Further, my teaching experience to date had largely been with graduate students, most of whom were middle-aged women. Over a year, Rhonna, Jennifer, and I put into print to one another the concerns we have had to face being inducted into educational communities: they into the university program, schools, and the teaching profession at large; me, into full-time university life and institutional norms and practices. Our notes, journal entries, and letters arose from the challenges each of us were facing; no agreement was made at the beginning of the year to engage in a dialogue: it arose from the exigencies of our institutional lives. From the outset, I admired and respected both these women for their courage and idealism, for their insight into contradictory and paternalistic practices in educational institutions. As I re-read these exchanges now, and prepare to describe some of the issues surrounding them, I have no sense of presenting this as research per se, and yet, I submit that it might be. Perhaps it is just life. Further, although I search for its signs, I feel no sense of the moral hypochondria that I have felt up to this point about telling someone else's story, about re\presenting these women to you. The work we have done together in the course of living through a very difficult year has earned us, each of us to the other, the trust and solidarity to tell the stories that implicate us in one another's lives.

If this is research, and if there is a stance I ought to attempt to take in this quicksand, it approximates the Inappropriate Other that Trinh T. Minh-Ha (1991) describes:

> Like the outsider, she steps back and records what never occurs to her the insider as being worth or in need of recording. But unlike the outsider, she also resorts to non-explicative, non-totalizing strategies that suspend meaning and resist closure.... She refuses to reduce herself to an Other and her

112

> reflections to a mere outsider's objective reasoning or insider's
> objective feeling.... She is this Inappropriate Other/Same who
> moves about with always at least two/four gestures: that of
> affirming "I am like you" while persisting in her difference;
> and that of reminding "I am different" while unsettling every
> definition of otherness arrived at. (74)

Trinh Minh-ha argues there is no authentic inside or outside
anyway, and when we cease to be impressed and intimidated by
the "magic of essences", the need for an authorial referent from
which emanates judgement, we recognize our own constituted
nature, our role in the production of meaning. This is "not to say
that the historical "I" can be obscured or ignored, and that
differentiation cannot be made" but that "more or less is always
more or less in relation to a judging subject" (p. 76). I am, after
all, as you are, a fabric of many-textured threads highlighting
many different patterns according to the moment. I am middle-
aged, academic, first-born child, sister, mother, wife, researcher,
descendant of Irish, Scottish, French, and Cree; heterosexual,
friend, technology buff, menopausal woman, novice gardener,
and so on. My need to tell you this, as Trinh Minh-ha notes, is not
borne out of a need to be self-indulgent and/or self-critical. It is
borne out of a need to de-naturalize I, the researcher; I, the
woman. It is to lay bare the many points at which the relationships in which I engage will always be partial, will always move,
like shadows, part of who I am and yet beyond my reach.

The first incident that gave rise to writing about the institutional narratives we questioned arose from Rhonna's student
placement. She had been placed in a classroom in which the co-
operating teacher used teaching practices and disciplinary strategies that Rhonna found abusive. After three days, Rhonna
insisted she could not return to the woman's class. As she wrote
in her note to me:

Finding Her Place

*I still carry some feelings of guilt from when I was a child and
witnessed first hand episodes of physical abuse. I remember
sitting and begging my mother to call the authorities about the
goings-on within this family who were relatives. Of course, my
mother was in a position whereby in a small community she
would have appeared to be the villain if she were to say
anything. I was just a child but I remember feeling very
powerless. In that class, the bottom line was that I felt powerless
in a situation where I could feel pain.*

We talked about a new placement, and I encouraged Rhonna
to speak to the classroom teacher to let her know her reasons for
leaving. Professionally, it was the responsible thing to do, as a
courtesy to the teacher; but more importantly, Rhonna's comments would provide a necessary mirror to the woman's practice
that could result in the classroom teacher's reassessment of her
methods. It was difficult for Rhonna, but she met with the teacher.
Later, I visited the classroom informally to talk the issue through
with the teacher and, within a few short minutes, found myself
startled by the teacher's tone and manner with the children. I, too,
left the room with a knot in my stomach recalling, not coinciden-
tally, my own experiences with a verbally-abusive mother.

Rhonna's refusal to return to the classroom forced me to
confront our institutional practice. Students typically have no
say in their selection of schools and their criticism of co-operating
teachers is usually considered a result of their anxiety of entering a classroom in the first place. Rhonna's complaint, her
resistance, was different.

Placement issues continued to emerge that term. As the one
charged with organizing placements, I heard endless complaints,
some of which I perceived to be valid; others trivial. Our commitment as an institution to placing student teachers in culturally
diverse settings means that students often have to travel great

distance to the school to which they are assigned. I grew impatient with requests for transfers to more convenient locations not only because my political beliefs supported diversity, but also because I felt a pressure to follow institutional practices to date. This expectation was never explicitly presented to me, but I felt the imperative in my first year to do what had been done before, to play out the master narratives guiding institutional life until I understood them well enough to be in a position to change them. My impatience also arose from what I perceived to be whining on the part of the students. They seemed, at least from my conversations with them, to be more concerned with ease of transportation than with the opportunity to work in a classrooms radically different from their schooling experiences to date. During a class early in the term, their anger and my frustration came together in an unpleasant incident. After a barrage of complaints, I cut off conversation by stating: "This is the real world. The jobs you are offered may not be in a convenient location. You can't all be placed in white, middle-class schools." Later, in a letter to me, Jennifer noted: "In one line, you insulted the intelligence of everyone there, and totally disregarded a reasonable statement." The next term, I placed the decision for location with the students themselves and received a memo from a colleague who described my actions as "imprudent."

During the year, after many conversations, and many words in print, Jennifer, Rhonna and I developed shared understandings of our individual and collective attempts to live out the expectations of the institution, at the same time holding to our beliefs about just and equitable behaviour. I became the Inappropriate Other, Professor Insider/Outsider, believing with the faculty that some practices ought to stay "as is" and that many challenges the students made to those practices were borne out of their high anxiety, their learned dependence on evaluation, and their collective lack of so-called real world experience. At the same time, I came to recognize there were few spaces for students to develop independence and autonomy within the program: they had little power or authority, because of their so-called station in the institution, to challenge the sexism they saw in one class, the neurotic power-plays they experienced in another, the inefficient registration process they endured that year, the overcrowded time-table, the exploitative practices of certain school administrators who believe student teachers are extra pairs of hands, and the most insidious master narrative of them all, the evaluation practices.

During their entire academic lives, these people have been living by the grade. Evaluation holds great sway, to the extent most prefer silence over resistance: they aren't going to rock the boat until the grades are in. Jennifer and Rhonna were two exceptions, regularly questioning, offering alternatives, challenging, arguing, and to a few faculty including me, writing their thoughts. Their grades were important to them, but naming and challenging injustice was more important. Together, as each incident arises, we worked at change. Their work offering insights and critiques and representing the opinions of others to the faculty at large resulted in several changes for next year. Jennifer, for example, will head a group to provide counsel and assistance to incoming students in next year's program.

As I learn to understand myself in the institution and in the changes I hope to effect, I see myself as both student and teacher, resister and oppressor, friend and faculty member, insider/outsider. But I am not comfortable even with those dualities, because the work we have done this year, unless I am deluding myself again, more closely approximates an on-going dialogic relationship that accepts our conflicting identities. Yes, it would seem on the surface I hold the institutional power over Jennifer and Rhonna, for example, but I too am being evaluated, re-minded of my transgressions, neither fully inside the faculty or out of it. It is the very ambivalence about identity that I share with the women who are called students; and it is only from that ambivalence I believe that I can do the work that needs to be done. Like the idealistic politician who hopes to change the system only to be co-opted by it, I fear the more I become "institutionalized" the less I will be able to see what the students see, feel what they feel. Perhaps Jennifer's comment, in response to a faculty member who said "You should be glad you are here at all," is one I ought to place on the bulletin board, along with the dream-catcher from Rhonna:

> *I am an adult, I have done a lot of good things with my life. I will be a good teacher. I deserve to be treated respectfully. You should be glad that I am here.*

Beyond the Master Narratives

Michelle Fine talks of the emergence of a new generation of epistemological dilemmas and possibilities: "what makes this research? when does intervention stop and reflection begin? How do I/we 'know' what I/we 'know'? what are our grounds for disproof?" (1992, p. 230). Susan Lytle and I have explored not only what counts as research, but also where it begins and ends and what lives beyond it (Neilsen & Lytle, 1992). Madeleine Grumet's reminder that we live values first and describe them later (1992) makes me think that perhaps the same is true for our inquiry processes; and that perhaps even the naming of activity, particularly activist work in any setting, as "research" or as "inquiry" jeopardizes the very work we hope to do, for these terms are still so saturated with androcentric assumptions.

Finding Her Place

Suzanne Chandler wonders why "rather than tell about human lives, we speak of theories, methods, and designs" (1992, p. 130); she talks of the theory adoption practices that foreground research, and argues for a theory adaption practice that foregrounds "the lives, stories, and emotions of real students, real teachers, real schools, and real communities" (130): A practice, it would seem, that embraces "the wild emotion" of which Marge Piercey spoke, and which we know lives in our work.

At this dis/juncture in my work, I find myself wondering whether I am more comfortable living my research processes than thinking about them or describing them. Is the work that I do called inquiry, or is it simply called life? I know that as I reflect on the writing and talking with Rhonna and Jennifer, as I am challenged to change the institution as a result of our work, and as I sift through their notes to me again and jot down my own—I know there is a systematic examination of critical issues that in some circles could be called research. In other circles, it is simply called untenured university work. But are the important questions not what our inquiry is but what it does? Is it worthwhile to consider that, after years of attention to research methodology and issues, we can, in great measure, take on habits of mind—inquiring habits of mind—that become second nature, that are lived before they are described. Am I now, because I am more at home with dilemmas and more resistant to being swept away by mechanical demands of the paradigm-of-the-week, am I now more literate as a researcher, more free to reject the strict taboos that lurk in patriarchal hallways? Is my academic respectability more vulnerable the further I remove myself from fashionable and/or recognizable theories, and does that matter? I have no answers. And at this point, I am comfortable that I don't.

We write; we are written. If we are to have a sense of agency, to change the world as we know it, the writing must be done together. Each of us alone has difficulty, I believe, challenging the stories that presume to tell our lives, whether those stories are of the "how to do research" variety, or how to be a teacher, how to be a student, how to do school. As women, I believe our shared experiences do meet at some fundamental level in our common and visceral understandings of what Alice Walker calls "womanist" things. It is in the strength of those shared histories, however tenuously they may cross, that resistance to everyday, unexamined stories begins.

In an examination of modernism, hyperliteracy, and the colonization of the word, David Smith offers a compelling thought:

> Preparation for writing inevitably lies as much in the realm of existential preparedness as in the practice of "the writing process" or "word processing." Being prepared to write involves an attunement or attentiveness to reality most closely allied not to epistemology (knowing how to write) but to wisdom (knowing what should be said). Writing is a holy act, an articulation of limited understanding... (256)

And there, I believe, is where I am in this exploration about narrative and identity, about agency and theory. I am no further ahead in my work, but I am perhaps more fully attuned to its mystery. I hope through greater identity (yes, identity) with the women with whom I am challenged and privileged to work, that we can together use the wisdom we've earned to know what should be said and done to get on with re-making our worlds.

References

Britzman, D.P. (1991). Decentering discourses in teacher education: Or, the unleashing of unpopular things. *Journal of Education*, 173: 60-80.

Finding Her Place

Chandler, S. (1992). Displaying our lives: An argument against display-ing our theories. *Theory into Practice*. 31: 126-131.

Fine, M. (1992). *Disruptive voices: The possibilities of feminist research*. Ann Arbor, MI: University of Michigan Press.

Geertz, C. (1989). *Works and lives: The anthropologist as author*. Stanford, CA: Stanford University Press.

Grumet, M. (1992). The curriculum: What are the basics? In Kincheloe, J. & Steinberg, S. (Eds.), *Thirteen questions*. New York: Peter Lang, pp. 21-29.

Grumet, M. (1988). *Bitter milk: Women and teaching*. Amherst, MA: University of Massachusetts Press.

hooks, b. (1990). *Yearning: Race, gender, and cultural politics*. Boston, MA: South End Press.

Jessome, R. Personal communication.

Manicom, A. (1992). Feminist pedagogy: Transformations, standpoints, and politics. *Canadian Journal of Education*. 17:3, 365-389.

Mies, M. (1991). Women's research or feminist research? The debate surrounding feminist science and methodology. In Fonow, M. & Cook, J.A. (Eds), *Beyond methodology: Feminist scholarship as lived research*. Bloomington, IN: Indiana University Press.

Minh-Ha, T.T. (1991) *When the moon waxes red: Representation, gender, and cultural politics*. New York: Routledge.

Neilsen, L. (1993). Exploring reading: Mapping the personal text. In Straw, S., & Bogdan, D. (Eds), *Constructive reading: Teaching beyond communication*. Portsmouth, NH: Boynton-Cook.

Neilsen, L., & Lytle, S. (1992). Seeking ethical praxis: The politics of literacy research. Presentation at National Reading Conference, San Antonio, TX.

Neilsen, L. (1990). When writing goes to work: Voice, power, and the culture of the workplace. Unpublished paper, presented at the First National Writing Conference, Winnipeg, Manitoba.

Neilsen, L. (1989) *Literacy and living: The literate lives of three adults*. Portsmouth, NH: Heinemann Educational Books.

Piercy, M. (1983) *Stone, paper, knife*. New York; Alfred A. Knopf.

Rosaldo, R. (1989) *Culture and truth: The remaking of social analysis*. Boston, MA: Beacon Press.

Smith, D. (1992). Modernism, hyperliteracy, and the colonization of the word. *Alternatives*, 17: 246-260.

120

Women, Literacy, and Agency

Smith, D. (1990). *The conceptual practices of power: A feminist sociology of knowledge*. Toronto, Ontario: The University of Toronto Press.

Smith, D. (1987*). The everyday world as problematic: A feminist sociology*. Toronto, Ontario: The University of Toronto Press.

Stoller, P. (1989). *The taste of ethnographic things*. Philadelphia, PA: University of Pennsylvania Press.

Tong, R. (1989*) Feminist thought: A comprehensive introduction*. Boulder, CO & San Francisco, CA: Westview Press.

Walkerdine, V. (1989. *Schoolgirl fictions*. London, UK: Verso Books.

Wallace, J. Personal communication.

These notes were written after several educational gatherings over a period of five years: a national conference in education, teacher inservice days, and after a summer institute for teachers. Engaged full-time in working with teachers by this time, particularly women teachers, I continued to struggle with finding room and space against or beyond the "master narratives." It is at this point I realize I am attempting to reject an antagonistic (or agonistic) stance and to situate work in the everyday, work that invites both men and women to examine their literacies and their inquiry.

—5—
At the Edge of Words:
Learning with Teachers

And Then Came Maude

A few years ago, I was invited, as a literacy researcher, to attend the Council of Ministers of Education Conference in Montreal, a million-dollar meeting billed as the First National Consultation in Education. We were invited—all five hundred of us representing education, government, and private sector interests in Canada—"to help set the national education agenda." Accepting the invitation may have been my first mistake. Or perhaps believing in it was.

For two days, strangers in working groups met to talk about priorities. It was clear, however, from the first morning, whose priorities we were there to discuss. The conference was organized around conventional educational themes: accountability, the relationship of education to work, and national standards. The Council of Ministers had prepared the agenda beforehand, including questions for which they wanted answers and a set of proposed actions by Sunday noon.

Anyone who has attended such a meeting knows that the first day is spent figuring one another out, driving rhetorical bumper cars, either being evasive or carefully attacking. It wasn't until the morning of the second day we began to show our colors.

What colors we had, that is. Our group was largely white, middle class, male and middle aged. There was much talk of gender equity, marginalized groups, the need for technology, the class discrimination against community college education. Everyone said all the right things, said them often, said them eloquently. Not much of that talk ended up on the action list. The call for research was reduced to the call for numbers: all else was "anecdotal reporting." I felt alone in my frustration, like a frog trapped in an airless container.

Funny how these things happen. Lots of refreshments, a wine and cheese bar with smoked salmon and rare cheeses one evening, fresh orange juice in the morning and cold drinks in the afternoon. Interpreters for the unilingual, sweets and ice water for the throats of the invited participants charged with this very important task. And where are you from? And what do you think, and how is your province dealing with cutbacks? The Globe and Mail editorial that day announced that "everybody who was anybody in education" was at this conference. The Montreal night life gave Maritimers and Westerners a chance to gather, to feel church-lady special, to feel sanctimoniously and truly Canadian.

And then came Maude.

After almost two days of being saturated by the educational jargon du jour, the National Chair of the Council of Canadians, Maude Barlow, woke us up.

Speaking to the assembled group, Ms. Barlow reminded us

that the only borders now are economic. Philip Morris's annual sales exceed New Zealand's GDP. Transnational corporations conduct 85 percent of the world's trade, and own 80 percent of the world's cultivated land. Ford's economy is bigger than Saudi Arabia's and Norway's.

One third of the world's workforce is unemployed, and the number is growing by 50 million every year. The top 10 available jobs in North America are in contingency work: retail sales, cashiers, office clerks, waiters, and others where workers have no pension, no security, no benefits. Part-time contingency workers will represent 50 percent of the U.S. workforce by the next decade.

In Canada, the federal government's own studies show that public spending accounts for only 6 percent of the deficit, and yet universality in three major programs—unemployment insurance, old age security, and family allowance—has been killed.

Over 20 Crown Corporations have been privatized. A leaked Bank of Canada document supports a "natural" level of high unemployment in developed countries. It is necessary, the report says, to keep wage demands low and job competition high.

Canada is first in the G7 countries in graduates in engineering, science, and mathematics. We have a glut of highly-qualified graduates in a number of areas. A survey of 5000 Canadian manufacturers indicated 99.5 percent believed a shortage of skilled workers is not a problem in Canada.

And yet, big business and the governments who back them, adds Ms. Barlow, continue to claim that the schools have failed to produce the workforce that business wants. Business wants contingency workers, she says. And the new economy wants people who are adaptable, flexible, loyal, mindful, trainable, expendable, and non-confrontational.

A vice-president of MacMillan Bloedel says the schools' core subjects ought to be English, Math, Physics, Chemistry, The Importance of Showing Up for Work, and How To Get Along with Others. "We get all the geography, law, ethics, and more than enough biology from TV," he says. Literacies for a new world, I thought.

We are well on the road to privatizing education, health care, and other public services. NAFTA, which does not address the issues of social programs, human rights, labor laws, or the environment, will change how we work and what we value. Collective bargaining will be unnecessary with contingency workers.

We're the frog in the pot, warned Ms. Barlow. The water is being heated slowly and steadily. To be told by our governments there is nothing we can do as individuals about the new economy, she says, is intellectual terrorism. We have to move fast, or we're cooked.

The applause was deafening. Many in this staid group stood. Outside, the conversation buzzed with the impact of the only speech at this feel-good conference that had any grit or substance. It seemed the effect was electric.

But later at the small group session, people returned to their assigned seats and the conversation returned to the original topics the CMEC had set. Again, people spoke eloquently of the need for change, again the shibboleths were passed and shared. Once there was a frisson of tension when a gentleman of the old school trammeled over the words of a young female student, but this soon passed.

The only action items on the flipchart could well have been written in 1984 or 1974. Maude Barlow's talk slipped out of memory as easily as the last movie of the week. Nothing much seems to stir the well-educated, the credentialed, and the comfortably employed.

As people refilled their glasses of ice water and passed around the sweets one more time, I hopped out the back door. It was getting mighty warm in there.

• • • • •

Where Inquiry Begins

As Department Head, she has asked all the English teachers to sit around the table this morning and talk. I am a guest, grateful not to be the One Who Tells today. This professional day will be different. I will be in the audience, I will listen and use words under their words, gently lifting the dry leaves of habitual conversation to uncover the gritty substance below.

The expert from afar to whom they tell stories, take shots, hurl questions like barbs can become a conduit for telling each other how it is. This person will field the comments from teachers: How she can no longer grade essays objectively; the kids and their lives are too complex. How he understands the plea for just two more points on the exam so Paul can leave school to support his baby. How she phoned every one of the 150 homes in September to explain her goals for the English course, and how the parents were surprised she wasn't calling about a problem.

Everyone at the table talks, casting experience into new shapes for me, and surprising us all as they do. Other days are filled with buzzers and clutter and voices and assignments with sneaker marks on them, but today is a professional day. Everyone listens. Everyone talks. The Department Head listens too. She planned this chance for them to talk, to come together, try to stay together. The school board and the public, who would ride teachers on an endless track toward an endless goal, typically don't understand these days and don't want to understand these stories. To understand them is to bear witness to pride and to pain. To listen to stories is to accept complexity, the stubborn particulars, as the late poet Bronwen Wallace calls them. Teachers know that outside the school walls, people prefer numbers. Numbers are results. Teachers are scapegoats to ride.

And so this is our life. Schools and children are the noble green path we once took eagerly. As the months and years fall behind us, the path becomes worn and twisted, but we stay. And today, on a professional day, with more than a hundred years of teaching experience, connecting a hundred thousand lives through poems and stories and thoughts and red and blue ink, today is a day when teachers realize once again the power we know when we come together to talk. The Department Head isn't concerned about results today. She is not gathering numbers. She knows teaching is a long journey, one taken easier with others.

Means and end. Journey and destination. The yin and yang of education ought to complement one another and give us strength; but instead, in classrooms, in research, and in policy, they divide us.

The pressure is on several fronts. Teach to the moment, or to the test? Give credit for how she learned the process, or what she wrote as product? On the research front, someone always draws a line between the number crunchers and the story-tellers, between scientism and humanism, between the individual and the group. In the race for knowledge, we aren't sure if we want levels of significance or significant understandings. We seem to be running through airports, a few goal-determined people in the lead, a few behind them, and others somewhere in between, trying to keep the group together. Yin and yang, push and pull.

And September, the invitation we can't refuse, will come again.

• • • • •

Post Script:
Late Summer, Sawlor's Lake, Hubbards

The air is not quiet. For days the rough edge of a distant hurricane south of us has skirted the waterline along the coast and carried sand and rock up as far as the road. The sea has been loud, and from the inside of the house I can hear the rolling waves, especially after dark. One night, restless as the ocean itself, I wandered the house looking for silence and waiting for sleep. Now and then, I dozed. Once in a dream, I saw my body tossing in black water in the cove, alone and within easy distance of the shore, fighting to survive while others slept.

The next morning, the sun was hot too early and the sea continued to rush high on the beach. This was the day to cut trees, clear the woods behind the house of deadfall, and sit with friends on the deck, talking about teaching, life, and the end of the summer. By mid-day when the chain saws had begun, the heat was intense.

I was tired from a long summer of teaching and yet in the afternoon heat, I wanted exercise more than rest. Perhaps by running through the path in the woods and over to the lake, I could work out the strange unease, the unsettled feeling that the sea was churning inside me as well. Perhaps by running, I could more easily face the prospect of clearing the woods afterward. My friend set a pace I could follow with my slow stride. We made small talk over the sound of our footsteps on the path. In the heat, the summer grasshopper noise was shrill.

We talked of the intensity of the summer course, his role as student, mine as instructor. We talked of the profound changes we saw in colleagues and friends, and the need for community in teachers' lives. Each of us is so isolated in our overcrowded schools, so alone. It is a time to look for hope: money is scarce, the public outcry against educators is greatest, and the profession itself is in flux. And as the sea boils below, we cling desperately to whatever flotsam seems, on the surface at least, to be an answer, a pedagogical raft.

At Sawlor's Lake, we walked into the property once owned by the American educational philosopher John Dewey. The cottage on the waterfront is now for sale. This stop in our excursion is an apt one. Dewey's *Experience and Education*, after all, had been part of our discussion on research this summer. John Dewey, Carol Gilligan, Deborah Tannen, Maria Mies, Maxine Greene, and the poets Sharon Olds and Bronwen Wallace: strange and powerful mix of ideas, and inviting. It all comes down to the story we call life.

The lake was still and clear. The dock, where I often sat last spring during my excursions, was now sloping to one side, near collapse. I crouched down on the rocks and soaked my neck with cold water. The clarity of the water reminded me of prairie summer lakes in my childhood and for a moment I wanted to take off my shoes and swim out, swim back to then.

The cottages around the lake were still; ours were the only voices I heard. We peered through the cracks in the two boarded-up cabins. My friend speculated about their age and pointed out which logs had needed replacing over the years. In all my visits I had never looked at the cabins with a builder's eye. Instead, I had been imagining the summer residents as they were forty

At the Edge of Words

years ago, warming themselves in the morning at the stone fireplace, pushing the rowboat away from the dock at sunset. I had been thinking I wanted to be a child here and watch the adults build the fire at night, hearing their voices in the dark as I fought sleep. Stories, I realize, are living structures, houses for conversation.

My friend spied a squirrel carrying a large mushroom to a high branch and wondered aloud how an animal knows which mushrooms are safe to eat. He tried the foothold on the stone chimney, thinking it could be climbed. I thought about how we wonder differently—is it gender, sex, experience, schooling that makes us differ?—and smiled: the reflections never end. As he examined the logs, he speculated on the building process. As I peeked in the dark of the cottage, I wished that the cracks in the boards cottage revealed more than the outline of a lamp on a table and the hulk of an old wooden boat.

The woods were cool and peaceful and I wanted to stay, swim, build a fire, and start a conversation that went beyond the moment. But our time was short and the others needed help with the clearing. As we left the woods and ran on the gravel, my friend saw a pair of spectacles, intact but for the arms, and as he tucked them away, we joked about the Dewey memorabilia he has found. His seeing this summer is transformed, he comments, literally and figuratively. I wondered whose face had worn the spectacles, and whether violence or carelessness had caused them to lie scratched and broken on the road. Behind every object, every inquiry, is a story. Perhaps all inquiry is story.

The path home through the bog was drier than usual because of the heat. In the distance we heard the chain saws on our property. My friend spotted a rabbit—twice—and I realized then how much I must miss when I run alone.

We have not run hard, at my request, and so when we reached

my house at the top of the hill I was too warm to continue, but not tired enough to stop. The unease I felt earlier remained. The smell of cut pine caught me by surprise, although it shouldn't have. The group in the yard had been steadily pulling wood from the back of the house, preparing the ground for new growth. They were hot and they were ready for a drink.

That evening on the deck, we spied the Dog Star, the mythical harbinger of heat and pestilence. By the garden plot, the stack of deadfall sat ready for burning, and nearby, I saw the pile of compost that needed to be turned for next year's garden. Some- one on the other side of the cove shot fireworks from the shore into the night sky. I felt scattered by small talk, but comfortably among friends. The breakers were still crashing white at the other side of the cove, and beyond the moonlight on the water, I imagined a rowboat on a silent lake and summers that endured like the best of conversations.

Part Two:
Knowing Her Place

—6—
The Academy
of the Kitchen Table[1]

*It is in the knowledge of the genuine conditions of our lives that
we must draw our strength to live and our reasons for living.*
—Simone de Beauvoir

*If ethnography produces cultural interpretations through in-
tense research experience, how is such unruly experience transformed into an authoritative written account? How, precisely, is
a garrulous, overdetermined, cross-cultural encounter, shot
through with power relations and personal cross purposes
circumscribed as an adequate version of a more-or-less discrete
"otherworld" composed by an individual author?*
—James Clifford

*By now most of us know that culture, society, fieldwork are all
contingent, ever-changing, slippery concepts. By now most of us
admit that social theory has failed to predict human behavior
reliably and validly. What is left, then, in a world so filled with
uncertainties? For a few, these uncertainties are liberating: they
allow us the latitude to play with established disciplinary and
literary conventions.*
—Paul Stoller

Knowing Her Place

We tell ourselves stories in order to live.

—Joan Didion

Each of us comes from a different kitchen table. Each of us imagines one another's table differently. And yet the kitchen table is, ultimately, where life comes home every day. Whether our family unit is one or many, whether or not we even have a roof over our head, each of us has a need to find a place where we light a fire, share a form of nourishment, tell stories about our world, and make plans to change it. The kitchen table is where we take comfort, where we take stock, where we can shed tears, vent our anger, tell secrets, crack jokes, feel fear, commiserate, and connect; a place where our souls and our spirits can be destroyed or take wing. The kitchen table is not a neutral place, and not always a safe one—sometimes the reflections of ourselves or the lives we make are unsettling, unwelcome, and frightening. But the kitchen table, for all its many moods and manifestations, can be a touchstone among individuals—strangers and loved ones— a place of possibilities and of renewal, a momentary home.

My mom worked in the home until I was in high school. No wonder, hey, with eight of us, and as the neighbors put it, the floors were clean enough to eat from. Mom made our clothes, baked, did laundry and always had a meat and potatoes supper every night. I can remember her reading to us every so often. She also took great interest in our homework. Actually, when I think about it, she personifies the kitchen table. My father was an invisible figure. What I remember most about him was the expression, "be quiet, your father's been working hard and he's sleeping." The irony, of course, is that is was likely nine or ten at night when mom was saying that, and she was still in the kitchen ironing.

The Academy of the Kitchen Table

Life, in its raw form, sits at this table and works in this kitchen. But academic concerns, research in particular, have not always found their way to this part of the house. The kitchen represents the unpainted complexion, the mess, the daily hunger and the unkempt emotions we prefer to conceal as we prepare to make our way through the door and out into the world. Around and beside the kitchen table happens much that marks the pain and passion of our lives. This a space that is usually worn and typically dust-free, but always symbolic of the material inequities between the labor of women and men and the labor of women with privilege and women without. This space is located in our house, our workplace, at the women's shelter, the school staff room, the local diner, and the community hall.

The academy, on the other hand, the community of scholars which owes its name to Plato's garden and its practices to medieval guilds, is a site of intellectual work we associate not with our private lives, but with public work in the realm of ideas. Here, as apprentice or journeyman, we are inducted into the mastery crafts of writing, theory-making, reasoning, and research in the public domain. Women are relative newcomers to the academy, having only within the last century or two achieved the status of "people" under the law and so entitled to access to university education or scholarly activity. It would seem that some of us, largely white middle class, have been accepted into the guild, albeit provisionally.

The privilege to work in the academy comes with a certain cost. As women who have gained access to the male symbolic order learn to work within that order, they become "more deeply embedded in their subordinate position" (Davies, 1989, p.3). They learn more thoroughly how their lives have been construed in androcentric terms, and as a result, must work through contradictory impulses of learning the master narratives while

139

resisting induction into them. This process is nowhere more evident than in the research enterprise. Whether we are faculty members, graduate students, or in-service teachers doing coursework in educational research, women in particular find ourselves making daily compromises which serve to reinforce institutional practices even as we hope to disrupt them.

One of the prevailing narratives in the work of the academy underwrites a view of research as a scientific enterprise marked by scholarly detachment, or objectivity, informed and guided by theoretical positions on what constitutes method, analysis, and results. Whether the theoretical postures dominating the research enterprise are labeled "positivist," "post-positivist," or "constructivist," among other terms, is in some sense beside the point (Carr & Kemmis, 1986). What is important is that, to date, the language of theory has exerted a "conceptual imperialism over experience" (Stanley & Wise, 1993, p. 162) resulting in the alienation of women from both theory and their own experience. This effect holds for men as well—embodied knowing is not only a female experience; but, when we consider the patriarchal and Eurocentric nature of institutions such as schools and universities, the issue of who has authority and which voices are heard is an issue more pressing and obvious for persons in those decentered, "comma-tized" groups we have been referring to collectively as the Other.

> *My childhood memories revolve around the kitchen and, as an adult, my best times are usually spent there as well. My father was a very strict British naval officer who would not allow his daughters to chew gum or say the word "sweat." As a result of our stern upbringing we always had meals on time, sat straight at the table, and conducted ourselves in a proper way. My father left when I was in Grade Four and my mother became more open*

The Academy of the Kitchen Table

> *to "helter skelter" from her girls and we seemed to become more of a family unit. The kitchen became a place of stories, school reports, family discussions, and stern talks. This area was the nucleus of our home, not the kitchen of a house. I had the great opportunity to buy that house from my mother and the kitchen table is continuing with new stories and memories.*

Questions of authority and stance have pushed educational research into new dimensions in the last decade, most dramatically in the area of what we have come to call "teacher research." The effect has fostered a growing understanding that when teachers redefine their relationships to knowledge about teaching and learning, they often begin "to reconstruct their classrooms.... When they change their relationships to knowledge, they may also realign their relationships to the brokers of knowledge and power in schools and universities" (Cochran-Smith & Lytle, 1993, p. 52).

Classroom teachers do this, of course, by critical reflection on their practice using a variety of approaches such as narrative inquiry, critical incident analysis, journal writing, using a variety of media, in projects that range from individual career histories to collaborative research with other classroom teachers or university teachers (Cole & Knowles, 1993). In so doing, as Cochran-Smith and Lytle have noted, teachers begin to reassess traditional, academy-driven notions of what counts as knowledge about teaching and who has the authority to know.

Much of our work as educators in this area has centered teacher practice as the fulcrum by which change in understanding and hence practice can occur. Those of us in faculties of education who work inside research—and must adopt institutional practices to secure our place in the academy—have a fascination, quite rightly, with classroom practice. It may be, for

141

many, the center of gravity in our lives. But, in the many shifting identities we live, being a researcher is but one.

Deborah Britzman (1991) notes:

> Subjectivity is both our conceptual orderings of things and the deep investments summoned by such orderings. It organizes an individual's idea about what it means to recognize oneself as a person, a student, a teacher, and so forth, and arranges strategies for the realization of these multiple identities. (57)

We are more than our identities as educators. At the risk of sounding like a bumper sticker, we are people too. Goodson (1991) notes, referring to narrative inquiry in particular:

> [This] is a welcome move forward, hinting as it does at the importance of biographical perspectives. But again, the personal is being linked irrevocably to practice. It is as if the teacher is her or his practice.... I wish to argue that a broader perspective will achieve more. (1991, p. 141)

Most certainly I am not suggesting we separate the dancer from the dance; I am saying that the dancer does not only dance. She looks for birthday gifts, pays bills (or doesn't), rides the bus, works at a crisis center, is a literacy volunteer, or a mother, or a lover or a recovering gambler. She (or he) constructs herself, her gendered identity—indeed all her identities—in everyday practice. By bringing together the academy and the kitchen table, by moving whatever conceptual furniture is necessary to make room, to shift and shift again the center of our inquiry into multiple—and perhaps conflicting—contexts, we will begin to truly live our notions of shifting identities, of the value of embodied knowing, of the connection between the personal and the political. By separating and privileging theory over experience in educational research, and by limiting our discussion of

The Academy of the Kitchen Table

experience as educators to classroom experience, we are denying ourselves an opportunity to "display our lives" (Chandler, 1992) and, in so doing, we are closing off other perspectives or pathways to understanding not only ourselves, but practice as well.

> *I worked full days in the Sixties in these domestic jobs for three dollars a day plus bus fare. At lunch time the food given to me was leftovers. I would not eat it. It went straight into the garbage can. While I was left in the kitchen to eat lunch on a stool at the kitchen counter, members of the family ate a freshly prepared meal in the dining room. As a black Nova Scotian, I was good enough to clean their house, but not good enough to eat the same food at the same table. I guess my motivation was survival.*

A project I began at the Institute for Reflective Practice at the University of Alberta in 1992, which I entitled "The Academy of the Kitchen Table" afforded me the opportunity of working with graduate students—all of whom are teachers—as they explored issues in feminist inquiry. Since then, I have worked with several groups of researchers, in and out of classrooms. What I have come to call kitchen table inquiry aims to collapse the distinctions that compartmentalize the way we have learned to view our work and our lives. It aims to disrupt the formal and public processes and products of traditional research, and the systemic relations that rule them. It aims to create a space in the academy to make our inquiring selves as researchers the subject of our own inquiry: the daily micro-political acts, the many issues, circumstances, and challenges of the ordinary which reveal the politics of our behavior in all our conflicting identities. The work at this table, like the person who does it, is purposeful; it is centered on doing in order to learn to do. It is inquiry that aims to make visible in research what has not been made visible, and hence not valued: the material work in the parentheses of our lives, the stuff of daily living that makes it all hang together or fall apart. It is inquiry that serves as a wake-up call for a long day ahead.

Going Home in Public

A woman whose daughter suffered under "expert" advice from birth decides to chronicle the years of struggle to preserve her own instincts as a mother about her daughter's abilities. She outlines in detail, using medical and personal records, the experience of being invisible in the knowledge-gathering about her daughter's condition. She feels that "experts" see her daughter as a textbook case and not the able child she has come to be. She sees now, as a classroom teacher, how this impulse to label and to provide easy answers, can sometimes be part of her own behavior, part of institutional expectations for the role of a teacher.

A graduate student in a large university campus walks into the men's room in the education building, uses the urinal, washes his hands at the sink, and then nods a greeting to the two women cleaning the room. He leaves the room and stops suddenly, struck by the realization that he, like every other white male of privilege on campus, walks by such women with no curiosity about who they are, no interest at all in their humanity. As a second generation Canadian, he recalls the stories of his family and their learning to live in a new culture. He returns that day to start up a conversation with the women that lasts until summer school ends and continues afterward, by correspondence.

A university teacher is working in a high school one afternoon when an RCMP officer in charge of victim services in the community gives a talk on violence to two classes of students in the library. During his talk, which is peppered with sexual innuendo, he makes several statements including one to the young men in the audience about rape: "Boys, when I was your age, 'no' simply meant 'try harder.'" The librarian and several of the students approach the university teacher after the talk, and because of her interest in violence against women, they solicit her help in writing letters to RCMP Headquarters in Ottawa, the Status of Women Office, and the Minister of Justice. The process eventually leads to the reassignment of the officer.

The increasing number of invocations in recent years to bring our research closer to home certainly indicate the degree to which we have, previously, been alienated from it (Chandler, 1992). In each of the situations I have just described, what counts as a suitable topic for research is what Cook and Fonow (1990) call the "situation at hand" (86). Turning the virtue of objectivity inside out, these people locate their inquiry closer to home and do so because they have a greater personal investment in what they are exploring; it allows them to explore more systematically those issues that are currently salient or about which they feel they need more control or understanding as people.

> *Every topic imaginable was covered there: sex, drugs, rock n' roll, politics, abortion, religion, family history, gossip, education. problems and possibilities, economics, business ventures, dreaming, arguing, laughing — the kitchen table was a meeting place, but also a place for learning...The most valuable things I learn are from shooting the breeze around a table.*

Over the last couple of years, those issues have included various forms of sexual harassment, "the glass ceiling" in administration, violence in the schoolyard, sexual identity, the patriarchal practices of Catholicism, the working mother syndrome, issues of mothers and daughters, expectations for the behavior of male nurses, the absence of stories of black women in Nova Scotia culture, gender politics in recreational sports for children, and the emotional aftermath of a coal mining disaster that killed 26 men in a small Nova Scotia community.

In each of these cases, the people involved had already begun their inquiry informally: the question, whether they had articulated it to themselves or not, was a part of their life. Enrolling in a course in "kitchen table" inquiry gives them a space to explore the issue more systematically with the others' support. Alongside their inquiry we read extensively—shared and individual reading arising from the issues at hand—and hold regular discussions about the inquiry. We redefine "research product" in light of the nature of the inquiry and decide individually, with the assistance of the group, which is the most appropriate form to articulate their new understandings and who the audience for these understandings or this information might be. They might compile statistics and stories about violence against young women for the parent group they belong to. They might analyze the inequitable power relations in a university-directed "collaborative" research project, and write their analysis in the form of a letter sent to the directors of the research. They might, after having recently bought a car, survey other female car-buyers for their comments and report the findings to the head offices of major car companies. They might decide an appropriate product is a children's book, a video, a painting, a collection of poetry or drawings shared with our group or with others. It might be that they decide to work with a family of New Canadians, volunteer in a rape crisis center, or organize a discussion group for rural women.

The Academy of the Kitchen Table

> *A ritual in our family was my mom and my three sisters and I having tea together after supper. My mom would read the tea leaves at the bottom of the cups, but first we could have a wish if we turned the cup upside down and turned three times without looking at the leaves. I think I got a strong sense of women sharing stories then. It's funny, but I don't associate men with the kitchen table...*

All of the inquiry begs the question: what is going on here? And what can I, as an individual or with others, begin to do about it? All are issues that bleed into the twenty-four hour days of the teachers who explore them and which often involve a familial or community group from which they derive support. In each case, because the inquiry is embedded in their lives, the rewards, the fears, or the insights are as well. Unlike a research project that begins and ends with the course syllabus and the semester, this inquiry tends to have a face and a future beyond the institution.

Stanley and Wise (1993), who themselves focussed their inquiry on an on-going series of obscene phone calls about their lesbianism, argue eloquently for inquiry which is concerned with the researcher's everyday life, because it is everyday life that we spend our time doing. Conventional research tends to focus on other people's knowledge, assuming that the life of the re-searcher—her or his mechanisms, experiences, conversations, actions—are unproblematic and uninteresting. Further, conventional research, even of the qualitative kind, Stanley and Wise claim, is dishonest; it is "based upon an ideology which legitimates the pretence of being 'representative,'" (167) and reinforces a power relationship which they view as morally indefensible. As many have noted, bell hooks, Liz Stanley, Audre Lorde, and Valerie Walkerdine among them, traditional researchers have typically ignored or disqualified the experiences of lesbians, the working class, people of color and classroom teachers, among others, on the basis of lack of objectivity, dismissing their research as non-representative, too local, emotional, not rigorous, and therefore not reliable. It seems that having the wits to name one's struggles according to the position at which one experiences resistance, oppression or silencing is the mark not of a lucid authorial being, but of an hysterical member of a special interest group. (The notion recalls sociolinguistic observations about women's uses of language in the service of changing status in society: the dominant group invariably tries to reaffirm its threatened social identity by trivializing and dismissing the challengers and their proposals). Stanley and Wise (1993), echoing a sentiment other feminist researchers have expressed—that objectivity is just another name for male subjectivity—argue that it is objectivity itself, not subjectivity, which is an excuse for sloppy work: "How many other professions, we wonder, make such a fetish out of ignorance, elevate it into the only possible claim to professional competence?" (1993, p. 169).

> *While my two brothers went to school, I stayed at home with my mother to help with the household chores. My early life was in the kitchen. I did not think about the inequality. Instead, I looked up to my mom who had never gone to school but was praised by all our relatives and neighbors for her virtues of being gentle, nurturing, and hardworking. Our Chinese social and cultural traditions have deprived many women of the chance of learning to be literate.*

The public/private split, which is articulated and reified in the canon of objectivity, has been explained in philosophical terms, as an artifact of Western Cartesian thought, and in psychoanalytic terms, as a legacy of Freudian thought about object relations (Flax, 1990). Much feminist work has analyzed and descried the subject-object, public-private dualisms which continue to inform research activity, and which many feminists claim account for their sense of anomie in the academy, the sense of being neither here nor there, not fully part of the community, but not excluded from it. Dualistic rational systems of thought, however greatly they may marginalize many of us in academic institutions, ultimately impoverish the entire research enterprise itself by failing to recognize their own limitations as thought systems in a pluralistic society.

Whether we frame a re-conception and re-vision of research as a feminist issue, rewriting inquiry from a perspective that centers women's experience; or whether we frame the issue as an ontological one (and these are connected), an attempt to crumble a foundationalist center, the project is necessary. Feminists/womanists/Other challenging patriarchy and postmodernists challenging representation seem, of late, to be working together toward a mutually productive alliance, one from which we can all benefit (Suleiman, 1992).

Since we moved in, this is the only room we've done anything with. We laid a wooden floor, sanded the cupboards. Why is that? I think because while I was growing up, my kitchen table experiences were memorable. My mother was married three times, but for about three years the kitchen table consisted of my mother, myself, and another woman.

Renovations

As the graduate students take up inquiry at the academy of

149

the kitchen table, so must I. My current work is to explain to myself and others what I mean by a renovated inquiry process and to learn, through constant and critical analysis, how to create spaces for this inquiry for myself and others. The context in which I do my research is the part of my life that I bring to the table for inquiry.

Incidents over the last few years have taught me, among other things, that the androcentric values of the academy resist notions that "the personal is political": that the so-called demo-cratic and progressive work we talk about is often not what we live as colleagues; and that as member of the academic guild who is still wet behind the ears, I am expected, above all, to uphold fraternal values of solidarity, even in the face of stark evidence that the Emperor, no matter how bad my vision might be, is still naked. I am learning about the penalties for violating the master narratives, and learning, as Trinh Minh-Ha says, that we are coerced into playing a game we don't want and which, "when we win, we lose" (1993). But I am also startled and dismayed to find myself making the daily compromises to institutional practice I vowed I would never make. Institutional behavior and habits of mind are stubbornly resistant to the deconstructive processes that can create the spaces necessary for change.

> *Ours was always a practical place, covered with well-worn vinyl, to protect the surface. For special occasions, such as Sunday dinner, company, a visit by the priest, she would use one of the tea-cloths she had sewn and embroidered.*

Spaces, such as a graduate seminar, allow us the opportunity to use feminist process (Schneidewind, 1987), to make the research process move and shift according to the needs of the people we work with, subvert grading or program practices, and

The Academy of the Kitchen Table

generally make this experience create its own standards for learning and for praxis. But where I work—where many of us work—these practices tend to stay within the classroom; they do not spill out into the practices of the institution at large. Crystal Taylor comments:

> We can't deny the personal text. We take it wherever we go.... My decision to carry out this research has sparked from my personal commitment to encourage more Black women to actively participate and involve themselves in women's issues...although there are close to fifty Black communities in the province, there is no research about Black women in Nova Scotia. I am non-existent, I have made no contributions.... I have completed a number of women's studies courses where classroom discourse has failed to address, or even whisper a mention of Black women. To be perfectly honest, I feel as though I have been "ripped off" by women's studies curriculum. I don't hold any specific instructor or institution responsible: the root of the problem goes beyond the two. And although I was interested in learning about Black women in these classes, I did not challenge the course design. I totally internalized the feelings of exclusion and discontent.

Christine Webb adds:

> I want to conduct feminist research...but all I have is a feeling about what it should be and do...there is no formula to plug into and I like that, but it is hard to proceed when I must conform to the guidelines of the institution for funding. How do I describe my methodological approach? I need funding to carry out this project...to get it I must conform to the rules and guidelines they define.... For the most part I always seems to be caught in the middle with my research endeavors...between the old and the new.... It's like working for two masters. I have to satisfy one so I can do what I really want or else the choice is to do nothing.... I need do action-oriented research and I love a living breathing project.

151

Materials List

To create spaces in institutions for research practice that displays our lives, rather than conceals them, requires on-going work. But doing such work, as we know, creates new understandings. And new understandings prompt new questions, causing cracks in the foundations to appear where before they were invisible.

And so, the seemingly ordinary curiosities of research take on extraordinary significance: How do the expectations for a product constrain or distort the process? Why are the funding guidelines based on only certain notions of what research is? Why are certain perspectives on research preferred by women? Why do you have to have a Ph.D. to obtain funding around here? Why are female graduate students drawn to work with male advisors when their female colleagues are equally competent? Are pseudonyms necessary when people prefer to use their own names? Why don't the non-academic staff in the university have more say in how the institution is run? Why do female faculty take on more clerical work than their male counterparts?

And then: Why does a university dedicated to the higher education of women continue to grant degrees with the nomenclature "bachelor and masters"? Why are all the faculty members white? Why are the admissions requirements geared to traditional students? Why does no one mention sexuality around here?

What did you do at school today? Did you eat all of your lunch? Did Nicholas behave himself today? Did you get a new library book? There's a man in the unit from New Waterford, and you think he's not good? The lamp is in at Sears? Is there a game on

---

The Academy of the Kitchen Table

> *tonight, Dad? What's for dessert? You said you'd pay that power bill on the way home. Bernice got into it again today with Heather, right in the hall. You better take a shower tonight Shane. Wasn't the baby gassy last night at this time?*

We find the questions lead to larger and larger issues, ones tugging the fabric of local and larger institutional practices. The conversations become deeper and broader. We find that we cannot pull only one thread; we must carry with it the whole tangled and knotted mess of loose and contradictory threads. Everything connects, but not in the easy linear, cause-effect way we have come to expect in our education. And not without emotion, frustration, fear, discontent, and tortuous work. Following Jane Flax (1990), I argue that, in this inquiry process, "if we do our work well, 'reality' will appear even more unstable, complex, and disorderly than it does now" (p. 183). We will decenter the world further, push outward from the academy into more local and particular settings, turn knowledge into knowing, and inquiry into life.

> *As a child, I spent much of my time at my grandmother's. It was there I did my homework and listened with one curious ear to the conversations between my aunt and my uncle. They both taught school and had lively reviews of the day. My grandmother preferred her chair beside the coal stove. From this perch she would interject with her opinions, jokes, support, as she sipped her tea and smoked her cigarette. Her kitchen was the hub of the house and she was the reason we gathered there. The image of that kitchen with its faded red linoleum floor remains with me yet.*

Who Are the Carpenters?

December 6 is an important date for me as a woman for two reasons: the birth of my younger son, who came to me late in my reproductive life and who continues to offer me breath-taking joy; and the death of fourteen young women at the Ecole Polytechnique in Montreal in 1989, killed by an assassin who separated the men and women in the classrooms, shot the women, and then left a note condemning all such feminists who had gained admission to the engineering school. Immediately following this mass murder, Ursula Franklin, a leading Canadian physicist and feminist, called for a senate inquiry into violence against women. In her address, she asked all Canadians to consider not only the question of how this man, Marc Lepine, got in the building, but how he got out. How was it that no man resisted or made a move to stop this man, but stood by, paralyzed in fear, an audience to a horrifying crime against women. "What does it take to make solidarity real?" she asks (Franklin, 1991, p. 9). We talk easily of being brothers and sisters in one human family, but in our everyday acts, whether in extreme and tragic circumstances such as the Montreal massacre or in the often-invisible daily practice of our working lives, we belie that solidarity whenever something we value is called into question. We shrug our shoulders, invoke institutional practices, turn away.

We had a lot of fun at the kitchen table when my father wasn't there. Water fights, butter fights were part of our meal. When my father was home we had to be proper. Supper had to be on the table when he got home. God forbid we weren't all home when he was ready to eat! As we got older my mother finally said something. As a child I hated him. Two years ago I finally got

154

The Academy of the Kitchen Table

> *tired of feeling sick every time I went home. I talked to my father about everything I had resented. I had written it all down. I talked for thirty minutes uninterrupted. He never said one word. I want my children to grow up with a father they can talk to.*

If we believe that the larger, unspeakable acts of the human condition have discernible roots in the everyday: if we believe, as many women and men do, that a fourteen year old shoving his girlfriend against the locker is part of a more powerful and pervasive text of violence against women, then we must believe that the work we need to do in the academy to create a space which is inviting to all is also connected to larger issues of alienation and marginalization in society at large. No lives are at stake when a colleague blocks a woman's promotion on the grounds of her "soft" and "subjective" research. No lives are at stake when a teacher is denied the opportunity to write her inquiry as a story, or when a Black woman cannot locate a scholarly tradition she recognizes within the academy she chooses. No lives, no massacre, at least not of the corporeal body. But change results as much from the symbolic violence in a nod or a word as from the barrel of a gun. Everyday practice alone is enough to wear us down, to shrivel the spirit. And this is precisely my point. And precisely where we must start the work.

Craig Owens (1992) talks of the difficulty of finding this support or solidarity in academia:

> Although sympathetic male critics respect feminism (an old theme, respect for women) and wish it well, they have in general declined the dialogue in which their female colleagues are trying to engage them. Some feminists are accused of going too far; others, not far enough....the feminist voice is usually regarded as one among many...thus feminism is rapidly as-

similated to a whole string of liberation or self-determination movements.... Moreover, men appear unwilling to address the issues placed on the critical agenda by women unless those issues have first been neut(e)ralised. (Owens, p. 337)

Helene Cixous describes the challenge set for women and others who wish to speak for themselves:

> I think we're completely crushed, especially in places like universities by the highly repressive operations of meta-language, the operation that sees to it that the moment women open their mouths—women more often than men—they are immediately asked in whose name and from what theoretical standpoint they are speaking, who is their master and where they are coming from; they have, in short, to salute and show their identity papers. (in Trinh Minh-Ha, 1991, p. 20)

And Lorraine Code talks specifically about the issue of subjective knowing:

> ...opponents...have been so hostile, so thoroughly scornful in their dismissals, that it is no wonder that feminists, well aware of the folk-historical identification of women with the forces of unreason, should resist the very thought that the logic of feminist emancipatory analysis points in (this) direction. (1993, p. 40)

When Kathy Flynn enrolled in the feminist inquiry course, she heard candid comments:

> ...they ranged from "I Hope you don't become one of THOSE" to "So what will this get you anyway—I mean what does this have to do with being a Resource Teacher?" Friends and family hit the hardest: "Sounds like bullshit to me—just an excuse to get a bunch of women talking," and "do they also give a course on Barefoot and Pregnant?" It's interesting to me to consider these comments in light of the fact that I know these people.

The Academy of the Kitchen Table

These are the kinds of barriers that hinder women's learning in a subtle way—these insidious little comments that can creep into a woman's psyche if no guard is placed at the door!

As I listened to the tape of my interview last night, I was struck by the very personal kinds of responses that reflected back to some of the seemingly small bits and snippets in this woman's life that had some very longterm effects in terms of the choices she made or was forced to make as a result of them. I'm interested in searching among the day to day experiences of ordinary lives for threads of truths—their truths—as well as the connectedness among them. This is where having faith in the power of process comes in for me. I have always been able to work with that in the personal and am delighted to see it gingerly moving into the public arena as well. (1993, e-mail correspondence)

This project—making inquiry less alienating, more activist, and less constrained by the institutions that define it—is difficult for all of us in all our identities. The distance across a table, like the distance between male and female, can be vast.

Finally, Michael Corbett's comments have taught me about how much work remains to be done. Michael was one of few men in the feminist inquiry courses I held under the title of "the academy of the kitchen table." A sociologist himself, he was adept at theorizing and equally quick to engage in examination of the personal.

I now find myself in a position where I am expected to make explicit who I am and what happens when I read the social text, the personal text, and the challenging text that is feminist theory. I seem to be chipping away at a block, slowing and painfully only to reach the conclusion that it is me at the center of my labors. Maybe I should have begun by chipping outward. It's an awkward analogy because this is a very difficult idea. (As a sociologist), I had come to believe that I can construct the truth for others beside myself.... It is interesting that what seems to be an empowering and liberating experience for many of the students, particularly women, I expect, is scary to me, because I know what I will come up against: my white privilege.

In his analysis of a "highly charged" discussion in the kitchen with his wife about the leave-taking of her near-adult daughter, he is confronted with memories of the circumstances that led to his leaving home many years ago.

Ah, how focussed I was then on me. I saw my parents as quaint, silly people.... I was drinking a lot. I stayed out half the night driving around in my old car, a 1972 Maverick, equipped with an 8-track, fuzzy blue seat covers, with a suicide clutch and three-on-the-tree. I was the quintessential rural Nova Scotia asshole you'd all cringe to see show up in your high school chemistry class.

On the day of my graduation I came home from work and from a few drinks out at the camp to find my mother and my girlfriend waiting in the kitchen. Mom asked me if I knew it was graduation day. I replied that I wasn't going. My mother was standing in the middle of the kitchen crying and my girlfriend was comforting her. I was standing flatfooted, stinking of beer, wondering what possible difference this could make to a grown woman. Later, my father told me I had a month to find another place to live.

It is in the context of analyzing his own leave-taking that Michael is able to understand the current chasm he has created between himself and his family about his stepdaughter's leaving. Through this, he recognizes his incomplete commitment to feminism:

My feminism has meant that I do the kind of work that men in this little village never sully their hands with... but I have not significantly considered my own role in structuring domestic reality in my family.... Analyzing these incidents has helped me to see the context and the history out of which I make my judgments...no wonder I so often feel like that seventeen year old boy standing in the kitchen trying to figure out why his words have caused so much pain.

Academic knowing and academic constructions—whether they are called feminist or otherwise—theorize about social relations and material conditions. We call the places where this knowledge is created and transmitted "places of higher learning." It's a simple notion, really. The word "higher," with its assumptions of hierarchy, has not served to liberate knowledge or women. Sitting around a table, we are forced to consider the tensions and the power of working together at the same level, facing each other, eye to eye.

> *I guess what we bring away from the table depends a lot on how hungry we were, what we were craving, what we weren't expecting as much as what we were.... I've been thinking a lot of the incredible effects of invisible acts on our everyday world in an everyday way and how these are not the kinds of Important Issues on the agenda for the 21st Century in education or other fields..*

Note

1. My thanks go to the students and colleagues whose comments about the kitchen tables in their lives appear here, and whose permission to use their words was freely given.

References

Britzman, D.P. (1991). *Practice makes practice: A critical study of learning to teach.* Albany, NY: State University of New York Press.

Carr, W., & Kemmis, S. (1986). *Becoming critical: Education, knowledge and action research.* London, UK: Falmer Press.

Chandler, S. (1992). Displaying our lives: An argument against displaying our theories. *Theory into Practice,* XXXI (2), 126-31.

Cochran-Smith, M., & Lytle, S. (1993). *Inside outside: Teacher research and knowledge.* New York: Teachers College Press.

Code, L. (1993). Taking subjectivity into account. In Alcoff, L., & Potter, E. (Eds). *Feminist epistemologies.* London, UK: Routledge.

Cole, A.L., & Knowles, J.G. (1993). Teacher development partnership research: A focus on methods and issues. *American Educational Research Journal,* 32:3, 473-495.

Cook, J., & Fonow, M. (1990). Knowledge and women's interests: Issues of epistemology and methodology in feminist sociological research. In Nielsen, J.M. (Ed). *Feminist research methods: Exemplary readings in the social sciences.* Boulder, CO: Westview Press.

Davies, B. (1989). Education for sexism: A theoretical analysis of the sex/gender bias in education. *Educational Philosophy and Theory* (21), 1, pp. 1-19.

Flax, J. (1990). *Thinking fragments: Psychoanalysis, feminism, and postmodernism in the contemporary west.* Berkeley, CA: University of California Press.

Franklin, U. (1991). Commemoration for the Montreal massacre victims. *Canadian Woman Studies,* Summer, p. 9.

Goodson, I. (1991). Teachers' lives and educational research. In Goodson, I., & Walker, R. (Eds) *Biography, identity, and schooling: Episodes in educational research.* London, UK: Falmer Press.

Minh-Ha, T. (1991). *When the moon waxes red: Representation, gender, and cultural politics.* New York: Routledge.

Minh-Ha, T. Public lecture. Halifax, N.S. James Dunn Theatre, Dalhousie University, October 14, 1993.

Okely, J. (1992). Anthropology and autobiography: Participatory experience and embodied knowledge. In Okely, J., & Callaway, H. eds. (1992). *Anthropology and autobiography.* London, UK: Routledge.

The Academy of the Kitchen Table

Owens, C. (1992). The discourse of others. In Jencks, C. (Ed). *The postmodern reader*. London, UK: St. Martin's Press.

Schniedewind, N. (1987). Teaching feminist process. *Women's Studies Quarterly*, XV: 3 & 4 (Fall/Winter 1987), pp. 15-31.

Stanley, L. (Ed). (1990). *Feminist praxis: Research, theory and epistemology in feminist sociology*. London, UK: Routledge.

Stanley, L., & Wise, S. (1993). *Breaking out again: Feminist ontology and epistemology*. London, UK: Routledge.

Suleiman, S.R. (1992). Feminism and postmodernism: A question of politics. In Jencks, C. (Ed). *The postmodern reader*. London, UK: St. Martin's Press.

Walkerdine, V., & Lucey, H. (1984). *Democracy in the kitchen: Regulating mothers and socialising daughters*. London, UK: Virago Press.

Weedon, C. (1987). *Feminist practice and poststructuralist theory*. Oxford, UK: Basil Blackwell Ltd.

162

—7—
Feminist Inquiry
in Educative Settings

Poetry and prose responses at the heart of feminist inquiry.

●   ●   ●   ●   ●

GED 645.1 : Seminar in Feminist Inquiry

One of us stirs guts and bones to thicken paint, create
bright dyes, while compost heats up in her yard.
Art is living in this sprawling space
of generous, wanton searching. One
of us turns a page, the word, the holy Father,
Blessed Virgin Mary overturning in the light,
dismembering the night, the day, the seasons new,
now spinning strange. I am a recovering
catholic, she jokes,
and her eyes, her eyes do not smile.
Rising from the table now, one of us hip-holds a child
hears crying in the hall, tries to answer phones and
voices, voices everywhere.

Knowing Her Place

Her kitchen is so very small,
so very large. One of us reads words to children, old books
again in aging tongue, and writing reading, writes herself again.
And one of us is waiting, waiting
silent as a call around an empty table, yearning for
sounds of home she will not hear, the sight of words she can not
    read
again. Before the day arrives, one will watch a child,
her night-time cut in half,
her days the only thread not yet unwoven.
Another is a child again, her face the face of children
come to this land, the woman talking is her mother years ago.
D.P., she was, D.P., the words burn in
her daughter's soul. And one of us,
a mother too, talks of risks, but oh, how strong
she is to live them. One dares to look for more
than what she meant to find. And one, a man, sees how all
the maps he reads lead back to home, but not the home he knew.
    And
all of us,
all of us see the path we make,
the leaves we overturn, the seeds
we water, the roots we plant, the light that breaks when
we give ourselves the right to set out walking.

•   •   •   •   •

Proposal Writing in a Feminist Key

...Well, if we frame the proposal with, say three or four dimensions or continua or whatever about conventional ways of thinking
about research relationships, set it up to talk about the role of the
researcher in the work, about power and control, those things....

...yes, and then we use those as points of discussion for the participants...

...and if we've told some of our experiences in the beginning in the introductory part of the session, they can—Jesse, honey, don't play with that—uh, our stories, yes, then they'll have their own—Jesse! put that away, dear. That's dangerous. No, you cannot have a knife. Just a minute, Susan....sorry. Okay, I'm back....

...The stories are going to come out, you know. These sessions allow for that. Too much at that conference has been 'stand and deliver' and not enough time given to talk about the real world exigencies of doing research. But we have to hurry on this. It's due in three days...

...I know—Jesse!!—Sorry, hang on. Honey you cannot use that knife. I'm on the phone now, long distance, and as soon as I'm off I will be glad to help you. What do you want? apple? Okay—Susan, this is crazy...

...Not a good time, I know. Don't worry about it.... We've got something here, I think. I like these ideas. This is good. We can get some lively discussion going, using that framework, and give people a space to talk about their own re—Wait just one minute! Hold on, dearie. Is that my scarf? Whose scarf is that?—Sorry, Lorri, it's my daughter. She's off to her feminist reading group and that scarf looks familiar—Is that mine? Okay, kiddo. See you—Where were we? By the way, what do you hear about the job?

...Not much. I won't hear for awhile. The deadline is April 10, so I'm dealing with that old graduate student feeling of not being able to write a good enough letter, like writing a good enough thesis. Well, it's not even that. You want it to be the one that knocks everyone's socks off...

165

Knowing Her Place

...Tell me about it. My colloquium is April 9. It's making me crazy. It shouldn't though. This is my own department I'm talking to. I mean, standing up and giving a presentation to all the people I work with day in and day out. A lot of them, men in particular, don't even think that what I do counts as research...

...Are we going to have time to fit this in. This proposal has to be in by the fifteenth. Can we do this, and still do colloquia and letters and all those things we need to do? Will life always be this crazy?

...We have to do this because I have to leave for Stanford next week. We can do this. We can. Where were we? Which part of this will you write up? If you do the framework and fax it to me by tomorrow....

•　　•　　•　　•　　•

Deconstructing Jack
(for Ann and Dorothy)

You might in one sense
be Lesbian and I might
in one sense be Other/wise
but these are words
that build the structure
that make the windows
and frame the doors
for this is the house
that Jack builds.

Jack does not know, of course
that over the hill and
out of earshot

where wildflowers still grow and
the earth knows remembrance
Jill and her friends tumble in the meadow
laughter rising from our mouth as
we swing the pail brimming, singing
thunder drumming
knowing shelter needing
no hammers, and
no words.

• • • • •

Middle: Life

This heat is unbearable. Like an incantation, we have been muttering and moaning these words around the seminar table these last three weeks. Summer school, all day every day in the humid heat of July is beginning to feel like a mistake. Why would anyone in their right mind gather willingly each day around table in an airless, dimly lit building to talk about gender and genre in everyday life?

I look around the room. Among thirteen women, five of us grew up in alcoholic homes, collectively we have born thirteen children, two of us are grandmothers, one is pregnant, and ten of us are married. One of us is an "out" lesbian, at least four of us have dealt with with the death of a loved one in the last year, three of us care for elderly parents, four are Roman Catholic. In the last three weeks we have come to an acute awareness of how the world around us communicates, through subtle signals. our sense of ourselves as lover, wife, mother, daughter, teacher, sister, caregiver, and friend. We have read the words of Gloria Steinem, Nel Noddings Pam Gilbert, Camille Paglia, Germaine Greer, Betty Friedan, and the Pope. We have read and written

167

poetry, personal essays, scientific reports, plays, dialogues, transcripts, and fictions. We are the words, We are the fictions. We exist here. And not here.

We have talked about how we have impersonated ourselves over the years, about gender bias in math and science, women as researchers, about bulimia, wiccen spirituality, women in leadership, and embarrassing exam-time menstruation stories. We have told feminist jokes—yes, they do exist—and we have shed tears. Many. We began to reach out carefully in a room of strangers on the first day, and today, the hottest of the month to date, we are drawn to this table like chilled bodies to an open fire. It's hot outside, damned hot, but this heat we create here is different. We have each tossed ideas and stories into the center, shards of ourselves, broken glass seeking to be fired into new forms, chemicals looking for a new state.

It is a simple wish of women, I think: to hear our lives in the stories of others. I do not believe women fear being alone; we look for solitude, in fact. And we know we will run out of time. All things in time do. But what we fear in moving beyond time, are memories absent of grace. We fear not our bodies gone, but the stories suspended, erased from the memories of those left in time, stories like ghostfingers beyond the reach of those who might need them. As we have. And so we write. Auto Bio Graphy. Self. Life. Writing. And in the middle is life.

•   •   •   •   •

Literacy of the Invisible

Alanis Morissette is an angry woman,
he announces, lifting the bottle from
the ice bucket. It is not a comment,
but a proclamation. The others nod.

Feminist Inquiry in Educative Setttings

His goatee jerks as he drinks, he
leans back to receive his entrée,
allowing the waitress room. He does
not look at this woman. She is invisible.

I watch her watching him. I know
who she is. She is one of
the sixty million
missing women.

At the Dominion, I read the
face of the black-eyed woman
holding two cans of tomato soup, pausing.
Her baby reaches for
the shelves, and a ghostly boy
with eyes like caves waits for her
to choose. This will take time.
Other shoppers push by, carts filled with
frozen pizza, balsamic vinegar,
bottled water. No one looks
at this woman, no one feels
the fist closing in her gut:
not enough again this month.

That night, as the bars on George Street empty,
I listen in bed to car doors, the
pulsing of a rock beat over engines,
you stupid bitch, a bottle bouncing
off wet pavement. I pull back the curtain
when I hear a cry.
She is up against the door way on
Bond Street this damp summer night.
With one hand, he pushes at her breasts, with

169

Knowing Her Place

the other, he holds a bottle high.
The window above them is open, her children
sleep inside. His moans at her neck turn to
tom cat howls, the streetlight catches
his wild eye, her small empty face.
He writes his needs on her invisible body
without spilling his beer. It is three in the morning.
She reads the signs, she knows
she is the last call.

UNICEF tells me millions of woman are missing.
I don't need a newspaper to tell me that.
I know
the numbers
by heart.
Five thousand Indian women
died last year. Their dowries
were not good enough. Young girls bleed
to death, the secret of their joy sliced
away, turkey skin for sexual feasting.
Girl babies are flushed away from
the thighs of Chinese women. And by the time
I have written these words, a hundred
women will have walked into a bullet.
In Africa, young girls carry water
to feed their brothers who have gone to school.
Mothers who cannot read watch their
infant bodies wither. Women who cannot
write their name make Nike shoes and Liz Claiborne
clothes and a dollar a day.

Invisible women hide faces under veils,
scars under sweaters, voices in our throats.

Feminist Inquiry in Educative Setttings

You have no idea what we swallow.

Yes, professor, Alanis is angry.
I am angry. We memorize anger
like a nursery rhyme at the breast of
our mothers, and their mothers before them.
We can draw it, taste it,
smell it. Dance it.
Some of us are the lucky ones. We have money
to buy wine in a restaurant, fill our grocery
cart. We have the gum to tell you to fuck off.
We do not fear being seen.

In your world, you play with words:
hermeneutics, ontology, post-colonialism.
We work with words:
restraining order, minimum wage, grocery store coupons.
You talk of hegemony, the post-modern diaspora,
of cultural appropriation. At dinner, you speculate on
the semiotics of a singer
and a jagged little
pill.

Isn't it ironic?
Your waitress and I smile at
each other. We read you like a book.
Call it the semiotics of
resistance. Call it the literacy
of the invisible.

172

A version of this essay appeared in James Flood, Shirley Brice Heath, and Diane Lapp (Eds), *Handbook of research on teaching literacy through the communicative and visual arts* (New York: Macmillan, 1997).

—8—

Re-Making Sense, Re-Shaping Inquiry:
Feminist Metaphors and a Literacy of the Possible

The invisible woman in the asylum corridor sees others quite clearly, including the doctor who patiently tells her she isn't invisible.... The invisible woman has great compassion. So, after a while, she pulls on her body like a rumpled glove, and switches on her voice to comfort the elated doctor with words.
—Robin Morgan, *The Invisible Woman*, 1970

Unable to see her, I speak in a kind of blindness, not knowing what dance is being made of me, what puns of the thumb, tough similes of the fingers, how I translate into bone.
—Margaret Atwood, The Signer,
Morning in the Burned House, 1995

Our responsibility as literacy educators, we claim, is to bring literacy to life. We are midwives, we think, who watch reading and writing the word become the Freirean reading and writing the world, who see inquiry into literacy as a process of changing the abstract noun into the transformative verb. Becoming literate is a form of intellectual inquiry, in teaching and in life. So we stand behind or beside, offer skills, arrange perspectives, invite dialogue, nudge, nurture, critique. And wait.

Over the years, as a feminist teaching literacy and the inquiry process, I have come to realize that only when we come to an understanding of the cultures of the home, the school, and the academy as sites of struggle and hope, encoded and inscribed with politically-charged values, expectations, and assumptions, do we begin to see inquiry and research in literacy as partial, limited, shifting, and actively constructed. We also see literacy as not merely an intellectual activity, but a way we are in the world. Teachers who come to this understanding begin to see their own literacy as they see and know themselves: instrument, aspiration, connection, limitation. They begin to see themselves as integral, and hence responsible, to these cultures into which they inquire.

This process requires more than changing a noun to a verb. It is more than the cognitive transformations we often hope for, and it is much deeper. For the literacy we have been fostering in schools and in inquiry these many years has been a literacy devoid of our response-ability: of our ability, as passionate and breathing creatures, to respond to our world. To live in it, here: now, with all the ecological implications and baggage of a past and future together. Literacy, more than the head, is also of the heart, and of the body. Of many bodies, breathing together. To be attuned to the world in ways that make us clear-eyed conspirators in life we must pull literacy off the page and out of the individual intellect into our sense-making, body-resonant, and earthly-connected selves. It is this aim that shapes the work I do as a literacy researcher and teacher educator.

Claiming feminist as a descriptor for my work and my life (and I cannot separate these) poses challenges not only as an academic but as a researcher. I know I want, like Marge Piercy, to see the earth split open, to see notions of science/inquiry and literacy turned in our collective hands, held against the heat of the sun until their essences have evaporated, their core images bleached, their edges blurred and rendered invisible. Our modernist notions have reified science and literacy, so that definitions meant in their day to clarify have, instead, closed off possibilities. But an exploration of a postmodern stance, a stance which makes essences and foundations problematic, does not mean that nothing exists, that no positions are taken. It only means that we must be comfortable marking a path on shifting ground, easy with the notion of seeing meaning between the cracks, locating signifiers in spaces that were not there yesterday and may not be there tomorrow.

It is this project of creating a path by walking which I describe here. Revisioning research into literacy required me to revise the work that I do with teachers. My teaching in feminist inquiry and literacy research has changed dramatically over the last ten years as my senses of what counts as research and what counts as literacy continue to change. At this writing, I believe feminist inquiry to be a stance to the world which knows interpretation to be an ecological process, a project of integrating and furthering sustainable growth. We are connected, and we are response-able. And bringing history into our present, we are always just beginning.

Impossible Metaphors

Traditional notions of literacy and literacy research have been guided by impossible metaphors which constrain our notion of literacy. Like carefully-dressed, clipboard-carrying assistants trailing theory down its many well-defined hallways only to discover darkness, dead ends, or a painted movie set, these metaphors have succeeded in shaping methods of inquiry. But they have not achieved what we hoped they would achieve: robust and generative understandings of what literacy is and does and can be; ways of supporting and sustaining growth in literacy for children of all cultures, between and within our national and global communities; educational reform, including schooling practices which invite students and teachers into, rather than alienate them from, themselves, their communities, and a sense of all that is possible.

Even our pluralizing the concept of literacy—computer, media, visual, among others—has not mitigated the stifling effects of how we think about those literacies; how we tend to define, and hence confine; to describe, only to prescribe; and to teach, which, too quickly, turns to test. The results are more than disastrous. They are dehumanizing.

The guiding metaphors which have taken us away from ourselves, turning us away from the possible, are multiple. Three I have found to be pervasive—the industrial model, the medical model, and the training model—have roots in educational research, but the growth still creeps among the public and policymakers, covering more ground than we have any hope of reclaiming. Each of these models is informed by a verbocentric ideology; each separates reading and writing from other ways of knowing. Each is more limiting than enabling.

The industrial, or mechanistic model (A. Neilsen, 1989) characterizes literacy in terms of parts and components within a well-functioning machine. Learning literacy involves learning perfectible subskills; teaching literacy involves sequencing the instruction of these skills in such a manner as to result in a well-functioning machine. In society, this industrial metaphor plays itself out in functional notions of literacy as a competence which is definable and measurable. It is also autonomous, largely pan-contextual, and inert.

The medical metaphor characterizes our literacy in terms of wellness or pathology. Terms such as deficiency, diagnosis, and treatment mark this approach to teaching and learning how to read and write. This view of literacy is similar to the industrial metaphor in that diseased parts and aberrant behaviour can, with the correct treatment, be replaced or eradicated. "Healthy" literate behavior is normal, standardized behavior: school reading and writing become the primary indicators of literacy and the sites for evaluation and assessment. Compliance becomes a marker for health. Like the industrial, functional view, the medical metaphor has definable boundaries for literate and non-literate, and abnormal and normal.

The most popular metaphor for literacy education is the training center, a place where children, like caged animals, learn to press the right buttons to receive their reward. The rewards range from stickers to smiley faces to gold stars to scholarships. Those who do not perform as required receive frowns, F's, the threat of being held back, or continual reminders of their status in the academic basement. The legacy of behaviorism lingers: during his first year of school my younger son's teacher devised a sticker system to encourage his sitting still to do his worksheets. My refusal to allow this both shocked and puzzled her: she sincerely believed that he would work for stickers. In the same way, our classroom practices assume a stimulus/response path into literacy which have the effect of disembodying text, textual practices, and knowing itself. And like the medical and industrial models which are its companions, the training model assumes cause and effect, and a dangerous linearity, instrumental utility, and predicability. Each of these metaphors externalizes the learning and teaching of literacy, perpetuating the myth that literacy is something we think about and do, rather than something we live. Each of these metaphors spawns research activity that serves to encode further the power of the metaphor in practice. How many years, for example, will we continue to isolate strategies for reading comprehension, teach them to an isolated sample in an anywhere-but-here classroom, and turn the results into textbook activities and teacher materials for widespread application? How much longer will we entertain the naive notion, whether it is wrapped in the garb of skill kits, whole language or process writing pedagogy, that there is a One Right Way?

But, more germane to this discussion is that these metaphors for literacy learning and research are verbocentric and patriarchal: they reinforce the text's power to create us in its image, an image whose values include preservation of the hierarchy, of competition, and of accountability, and whose means of naming the world have limited imaginings of text and textuality. Outside the discursive and textual practices we call literacy and literacy research there remain silent presences awaiting ears to hear, hands to touch. By looking to the spaces, the presences between, and their many shifting forms, we can seek revisionist and feminist metaphors of the possible. Like Shakespeare's sister, these presences may have been there all along, if we would only imagine them.

Countless feminist researchers and educators have written about the tendency for institutions to appropriate text into their discursive practices in ways that alienate, silence, and violate the majority of the world's population striving for a literacy of the possible (Rockhill, 1987; D. Smith, 1990). As Magda Gere Lewis tells it:

...if we are not men, if we are not economically advantaged, if

we survive by the labour of our hands, if we are not heterosexual, and if we do not embody and display the valued assets
of the privilege of Euro-American culture, schools are not the
sites of possibility which the rhetoric of educational discourse
wishes to portray. (1993, p. 193)

As a researcher and teacher educator, I must work on my own
practice. I must seek an integrity between my pedagogy and my
inquiry so that these practices continually find each other out.
The questions, then, are not about course syllabi but about daily
work in the relations among people and ideas. What do I do in my
own classroom to perpetuate silence and disembodied knowing
about literacy? And, by promoting principles of feminist inquiry
which have evolved in my practices as a researcher, how do I
avoid creating another regime which silences and alienates
teachers from themselves and their inquiry? How do I engage in
my own inquiry to nudge myself toward a more response-able
way of living?

Living Inquiry

*The nights are cooler now that summer is passing; they seem
darker, full of unplayed drama. An early morning walk reveals
the goldenrods, now as tall as my child, and the velvet white
stalks of pearly everlasting along the path. The air is heavy, even
sweet, and the woods are so silent that, when I step on the spongy
moss, I cannot hear my steps. It is only the tensing, and then
breaking, of filament against my skin, a spider web spun across
trees in the night, which reminds me that I am both myself and
Other here. Here? Where is here? In these woods, in this part of the
country, this season of my life, of my mind, of my body; this world
of worlds.*

179

Knowing Her Place

Now what kind of blissed-out academic prose is this, you may wonder? Bear with me. August is a rich month for me and it demands my experience of it by mediation of all my senses and means of understanding: somatic and kinaesthetic, visual, verbal. And so I walk, smell, swim, watch the stars, draw, write poetry, eat the summer harvest from the garden, sleep near an open window. I come to embody August.

Similarly, I come to embody inquiry and writing. Words have shaped, guided, informed, constrained, and told my life across many texts and many years. I sometimes see my writing in that cinematic trick-cum-cliche of the 1940s, the black and white pages of a calendar flipping, scrolling into another time and place, another dimension. Trinh T. Minh-Ha, describing Helène Cixous' writing as a process of inscribing, notes that the forms of Cixous' texts "cancel themselves out as they appear, [and] challenge the work's status as object [temporal, finite]. Infinitely dividing and multiplying, they are engaged in a movement of otherness which never comes back to the same" (1991, p. 141).

My love affair with words, like any love affair, is fraught with tension and passion. To begin writing, I do a dance I have since found is common: I read, I tidy the house, I ponder, flirt with an approach and then, with a shrug, abandon it, pore over books and papers and leave them open on the floor, the desk, the bed. I embrace the rhythm of certain ideas (right now I'm waltzing with both Frederick Franck's notion of the reflex arc and Donna Haraway's revisionist take on objectivity). I will move across many floors of understanding, shadow dancing with many theories, until the gestures, the nuances of these ideas become part of me, part of how my mind moves into words and the life they carry. (Here, I am also tempted to play with an eating metaphor, describe how I chew on certain ideas, letting their juices drain down the back of my throat into some river of theoretical waters.

Re-Making Sense, Re-Shaping Inquiry

The comparisons are many).

I will create a working environment, for a week or a month, which looks to others as though the room has been tossed by the Mafia. My mind will buzz with words, with continuities and discontinuities, and I will argue with myself until I reach clarity, insouciance, arrogance, humility, or boredom; any of these states will be fine. It's the processing, the induction, after all; the reaching for a state "in medias res," hearing the hum in the center of silence. To write, I must wade into a textual ocean and disappear in order to appear. I come to embody words.

This state, I assure you, has nothing to do with finding the Muse, or being a prose prima donna. I believe insight (or perception, or creativity, whatever one wants to call the state) has more to do with how attuned we are to the world around us, how passionately we want to apprentice ourselves to its offerings, to cultivate awareness, than with divine intervention or cosmic chicanery.

Similarly, when I draw, an avocation of my youth which tapped me forcibly on the shoulder when I began teaching courses in feminist inquiry, I must become so saturated with my seeing that my fusion with the so-called object transcends conventional physical borders. Frederick Franck (1993) calls this a state of seeing/drawing, meditative activity which requires me not to "look at" (for that is what separates us from objects, creating Other), but seeing: fully perceiving, the body, the eye, the hand becoming acutely sensitive antennae. Words fail here: I can only describe the state as a high thin wire of concentration, immensely relaxing, a state, paradoxical as this sounds, so inside the activity and myself that I am open to the universe.

And that is where writing and inquiry begin, I believe. At a place, or is it space? as individuals where we are so attuned to the process we are connected to the world. This space is where

181

literacy lives and breathes, where struggles and connection shift and strain. It is not an easy place to be, but it is alive. Name a human experience that calls on us as fully human and multi-dimensional and we all can list examples of that state of being. Settling into the fourth mile in a long run, kneading bread in the quiet of the morning, sitting in the audience in the last act of Les Miz, breast-feeding a child, weeding a garden, holding the hand of a dying friend in the dank and acrid smell of a hospital room, playing a video game, tinkering at the piano late on a winter's night. Each of these experiences opens up our perceptual pores, awakens in us a dimension, a responsiveness to the world in all its pain and beauty which may have lain dormant for some time. Typically, though, we let the stirring giant go back to sleep again, promising ourselves to allow life in more often.

What I want for myself and hope for children is to be fully alive, to be a sensuous, sensual, somatically-aware being, one who feels and knows anguish and joy, sees the particulars of the world as well as its wholeness, celebrates and challenges what we mean by human in a diverse world.

Morris Berman (1989) agrees. He is not, I think, hyperbolic in his assertion that when we lose awareness of our bodies, our sense of ourselves as a tiny cell in a larger living planet, we look for isms, and "from there it is a short step to seeing other isms as life-threatening, and to seeing the Other as an enemy" (p. 343). The despair of mothers of sons across enemy lines is silent testimony to our failure as a species to cherish life more than the contest of ideologies. The alarming rate of extinction of species on this planet reminds us, on that rare occasion when we stop to think about it, how we have made an Other of the organism which feeds us. Creating an Other allows us to avoid response, and hence, response-ability. Our romance with Cartesian simplicities has been a costly one, and we must draw it to a close. (But we must be careful, too, not to recast our talk of our humanity in neo-romantic terms: we fool ourselves if we think a spine-tingling chorus of "We are the World" can make us feel sufficiently at one with the universe to drown out cries of terror or fill the tomb-like silence of famine).

When We Dead Awaken

My aim, as a researcher and an educator, is to hone my own response-ability, and to foster that ability in others. In part, this response-ability must start with a "coming to our senses" that affirms our humanity:

> There is, here, a stretching out to a Gaia-politik, the conviction that the flesh of my body is also the flesh of the earth, the flesh of experience. To know your own flesh, to know both the pain and joy it contains, is to come to know something much larger...
> (Berman, 1989, p. 344)

Once that awareness is re-awakened, once we begin to hear, see, know, feel, and touch again, our alienation from others—from colleagues, from ideas, from the many Others we create to simplify our thinking and to dull our feeling—seems to diminish. We come back to ourselves, back to who we are and where we live. As researchers, we are better equipped to communicate our experience when we see the inquiry process as a relationship, not only among people or participants, but with our unarticulated selves and the earth which bears us.

One of the great disjunctures of education is the fact that, as adults, we are alienated from the thinking and feeling of our body selves (John-Steiner, 1985); but children, the putative beneficiaries of the school structures and curricula we create on their behalf, are not: they passionately and with joy use all their senses and abilities to create knowledge and to embrace the world (John-Steiner, 1985; Gardner, 1982).

Maxine Greene (1988) claims the passivity and disinterest prevalent in classrooms, particularly in the areas of reading and writing, is a result of our failure to educate for freedom in schools. To do this, we must focus on "the range of human intelligences, the multiple languages and symbol systems available for ordering experience and making sense of the lived world" (1988, p. 125).

Literacy educators are only now recognizing the powerful effect on learning and development of what Charles Suhor has called transmediation (1984), moving across sign systems in a way that Marjorie Siegel (1994) claims "offers learners rich potentials for gaining new insights and perspectives on the texts and concepts being explored—understandings that might remain untapped if language were the sole sign system used" (p. 3).

But how can we focus on the range of human possibility in children, when we fail to nurture those same possibilities, the uses of a myriad of symbol systems and ways of knowing, in ourselves? Where do we demonstrate or nurture our transmediative potential as adults? We can decry education's neglect of the arts and know that it is a long-standing neglect, borne of a utilitarian, functional, and materialist approach to education. We know that our attempts to weave the arts into curricula are an uphill struggle. We know there remains a hierarchy of symbol systems and intelligences which define schooling and literacy: verbal and mathematical literacy continue to claim most of the nation's attention and the taxpayer's dollar. We watch, too, as the association of early literacy learning with nurturing and motherhood (Grumet, 1988; Neilsen, 1993) becomes a double-edged sword: the body and the role of the mother in early

184

education is at once idealized and trivialized. The embodied knowing associated with early learning, fully human sense-making, is tolerated until later school years, when induction into the Word of the Father becomes necessary. Reading and writing become objects of study and control, separate from the learner, and employed to meet the ends of various contests of merit and manipulability, including assessment.

Nevertheless, in spite of these overwhelming obstacles, we have not adequately addressed our own complicity: what are we, as educators, doing to awaken in ourselves the responsiveness necessary to hone, promote, and celebrate our own multiple ways of knowing the world, of making sense? What are we doing to resist institutional practices which stifle our growth as professionals?

The metaphors we have used for literacy shape the educators as well as the learners. If we seek other metaphors, we may find our perspective on literacy and learning changes, and so do we. In seminars on qualitative and feminist inquiry, I have attempted to promote new perspectives on our many human literacies in the hopes that educators will take these perspectives into their lives and their classrooms and, as a result, teach with more confidence, autonomy, humility, and joy. Some may prefer to call these approaches methods of inquiry; perhaps they are simply (and complexly) the many ways we are human. And perhaps, as researchers and educators, we can argue for their cultivation not as curricula, but as habits of mind.

Creating a Path by Walking

It will be hot in the city today but, here, on the rocks of Peggy's Cove, the early morning air is cold. The sun will burn off the fog by ten, but for now, we have sweaters and jackets as we walk among the whale-sized rocks whose lines dip toward the Atlantic. Teachers all, we are careful to wear our sensible shoes; the notice posted near the lighthouse reminds all visitors that the sea here is merciless, that waves can, and do, reach up over the rocks and pull us in. I choose to walk among the rocks and around the cove itself, stopping to admire the brightly-coloured homes of the residents. What must these people think when visitors arrive, as we have, at 7:00 a.m.? What must it be like having your community be the most well-known tourist attraction on the East coast of Canada?

Agnes is on the wharf, talking to the fishermen who are loading their lobster traps. John is behind the lighthouse, at the edge of the water, using a tape recorder to capture the sound of the waves crashing against the boulders. Linda is perched next to a pool, a microcosm of aqualife nestled in the boulders, observing the movements of insects and suckers. Patricia is sketching, using an HB pencil to show the play of shadow and line in the rocks as the sun begins to break through the fog. At the peak of the largest boulder, I can see Allison, prone on the grey expanse, a notebook in her hand. Near the shore, Carole aims her camera at a gull poised like a weathervane against the sky.

We are here before the busloads of tourists, and for a reason. The stunning beauty of Peggy's Cove is guaranteed to pull us out of words and print into the physical power of the so-called natural world. It is guaranteed to bring us to our senses, and it does. This day-long event for graduate students, one which I often include when I am teaching a summer course, serves to remind us, as teachers, how bound we are to rooms and desks and constructions of words in various formats and guises. Invariably, we renew our long-forgotten commitment to worlds beyond the page when we are free to roam, to explore using all our senses, to record and reflect. And when we return to print, it is with

186

revised, sense-charged notions. Typically, a day such as this produces poetry, which always surprises the writer: she or he will return to class the next day, poem in hand, full of wonder and renewed inspiration. I felt alive again on those rocks, and I wrote this: Is this real research, she will ask?

And it is here, then, that we can begin. What is research? Who does it? What counts as knowing, and whose knowing is valued? From the outset, I make my agenda explicit. As a researcher and as a teacher educator, my aims include the following:

1. To demystify and to reclaim research and the inquiry process;

2. To encourage the use of multiple sign systems, particularly as they reawaken body understanding and aesthetic sensibilities, in order to open up the inquiry process, and in so doing, to revitalize professional commitment;

3. To promote an understanding of our multiple selves in relation to the cultures of the home, the school, and the academy and in so doing, promote our response-ability in those cultures;

4. To encourage resistance of practices in the educational and institutional hierarchy which de-value situated inquiry and multiple ways of knowing; and to be open to understand how I am co-opted by those practices, and how I perpetuate them.

Knowing Her Place

1. To demystify and to reclaim research and the inquiry process.

> *As people mature, they cease to believe in sides or Headmasters or highly ornamental pots. At any rate...it is notoriously diffi-cult to fix labels of merit in such a way that they do not come off.* (Virginia Woolf, p. 101)

Coming to the point of being able to articulate these aims for teaching and research has been a long and difficult process. Woven in the story of who I am and what I do as a researcher are, of course, the stories that form my history as a student, a teacher, a graduate student, and an academic. My struggle, which was much less painful than most, has served to remind me of my responsibility to other students, particularly women, who have felt outside themselves, silenced, and trivialized in education as a whole, and in the research process in particular. After all, research has created "a place where none of us lives and works—an 'objective' place wherein we are contrasted, compared, de-signed, and interpreted" (Chandler, 1992, p. 130). The study of research perspectives is often characterized by curricula which present research as hygienic and "out there." This disjuncture between our intellectual work and our lives is crazy-making, creating invisible women (and men) walking the corridors of academe in search of something familiar to their lived worlds. Desperate for connection, we relent, and like Robin Morgan's invisible woman, don a body and voice not our own, but which render us, for the time being, visible and heard.

The language of theory creates a valuing of propositional knowledge (Eisner, 1988), which generalizes more than it par-ticularizes, and whose coin is the testable assertion. But, as

Re-Making Sense, Re-Shaping Inquiry

Eisner states, our reliance on propositional knowledge diverts our attention from what he calls direct experience because we "know more than we can tell" linguistically (p. 16). Propositional knowledge is not only often contradictory to experience, particularly the experience of women and underrepresented groups in education, but its lifeless disembodied nature can, in fact, distort experience, and close possibility: "Our awareness is always limited by the tools we use. When those tools do not invite further sensory exploration, our consciousness is diminished" (16). We cannot see ourselves in the research reports and theoretical treatises that shape the research enterprise, and in trying to see ourselves in those terms, we blunt and diminish our exploration. Coming to research, we are required to wear the body of knowledge like a glove, and speak words only to make others happy.

We learn posturing so well that we risk mistaking it for the "real thing." Teachers who are also students of educational inquiry are doubly obligated to be in drag; not only must they wear the dress of academic theory and jargon, but in their own work in classrooms, they have been expected for years to be "professionals": to silence or mask their preferences, their cultural practices, their ethnicity and their politics to uphold a discourse of neutrality and objectivity. They must play their role so well that they are capable of inspiring shock in the student who sees them in blue jeans at the market, buying oranges and wine with their partner.

The task of demystifying and reclaiming research and the inquiry process begs the question, "What counts as research?" Discussions around the seminar table with teachers invariably reveal how deeply encoded conventional notions of research have become. Men and women alike, even those who have conducted their own classroom research, continue to believe that "real" research searches for an objective truth, is synonymous

189

with "science," is conducted in institutions elsewhere by funded academics, and has little practical relevance to their home or their working lives. Research is logical, value-free, tidy, and replicable. Academic practices, which so often go unchallenged or deconstructed (and which I realize I perpetuate even in this article), reify text as the sole purveyor of research knowledge, elevate "scientists" and "science," and perpetuate verbocentric practices in inquiry at all levels. The practices of quoting research to settle issues of "proof" and of lifting arguments with a highly developed set of bibliographic muscles prevent everyone around the table—faculty and student alike—from recognizing the validity and authenticity of their own experience and from learning to open that experience to scrutiny.

As the seminar facilitator, my task becomes showing the many ways by which we can take apart existing research "products," to look behind them to see how they are constructed within political and personal exigencies and constraints, and to recognize their fleeting and mutable nature. Teachers who want to explore classroom talk, for example, and who see that other researchers have published studies in that area, must be first be convinced that classroom talk is not closed as a topic, "been done," or "covered already." They must then work to understand that their perspective on a subject will be unique. (Much of the work I do, I realize, is enmeshed in the problems created by our lack of professional esteem, how we are schooled to defer). I remind people that everybody comes from somewhere, including the researcher. Using my own studies works well: I can explain how the historical influences and relations of ruling within the field of literacy research and within my particular institution shape the way in which I do inquiry and write about it. The text they read, then, is connected to a face, a voice, and a history, none of which are "objective" or unflawed. The words I wrote, the published text, can then be seen as partial, provisional, explor-atory, tentative.

What works best to dismantle notions of "research" and "researcher," however, has been to invite teachers to engage in their own inquiry; in particular, inquiry that arises from their own experience, not as individuals, but as situated, relational beings. This "kitchen table" inquiry, as I have called it, aims to create a space in the academy to make our daily micro-political acts, the many issues, circumstances, and challenges of the ordinary, legitimate areas for study. Such inquiry both reveals experience and makes it problematic, and because it is dialecti-cal, it serves necessarily to change the circumstances in which we live and work by forcing new syntheses, different identity relations. Like tai chi, the movements are not static; the body moves fluidly from one position to another, poised momentarily, each movement leading to the next in order to maintain balance. At each position, our perspective changes. To do inquiry, as we do tai chi, we learn to recognize that we have been making those movements all along, albeit with less purposefulness and disci-pline. Stylized moving with awareness, in tune with the world, makes inquiry come alive.

2. To encourage the use of multiple sign systems, particularly as they reawaken body understanding and aesthetic sensibilities, in order to open up the inquiry process, and in so doing, to revitalize professional commitment.

> *The governing of our kind of society is done in concepts and symbols.* (Smith, 1987, p. 87)

Knowing Her Place

The work of C.S. Peirce provides a basis for an understanding of sense-making, or meaning-making as a semiotic activity. A sign, he claims, is "something that stands to somebody for something in some respect or capacity." We make sense through a process of semiosis, in which our responding to a sign creates a "thirdness," our meaning or apprehension of/for the sign. What we have ignored in literacy education research, with only a few notable exceptions (Siegel, 1994; Harste, 1989), is the potential for semiotics in extending our understanding of reading and writing and the transmediative power of alternative sign systems in learning. Even those attempts to see literacy as a semiotic activity have tended to focus more on alternative modes of cognition, rather than full-bodied perspectives on learning. Not only our classroom practice in supporting literacy learning has been affected; so too has our inquiry. What counts as research and inquiry continues to be what can be documented and written in conventional text.

Marjorie Siegel's (1994) discussion of transmediation, the process of boundary crossing/mixing among sign systems in order to explore one way of knowing in terms of another, draws on children's work in schools. But the potential for such transmediation holds for the research process in academic institutions as well:

> Transmediation thus stands as a critique of the status quo in schools, where the emphasis on rote learning and the display of ready-made knowledge has dulled the minds and senses of a generation of students and led them to believe that there is no ambiguity in learning, no risks to be taken, no new knowledge to be made. (4)

So too are teachers dulled in their means of recognizing and creating the conditions for meaningful inquiry. Research is often

Re-Making Sense, Re-Shaping Inquiry

presented as a product, a current truth, a template for teaching. Why watch this reading group, they may wonder, when the list of readings from my graduate course tell me children will do X,Y, and Z, anyway? Why not simply read what others have studied rather than watch, hear, draw, record, smell, or interact in the busyness of classroom life in front of me? Here again, the dominant metaphors for literacy learning, mediated through the printed word, shape teachers' practice. A simple shift in meta-phorical thinking, from "if it's broke, fix it" to "if it's alive, feed it," might make all the difference not only in the way she or he teaches, but in the means they use to begin their own inquiry.

The courses I have taught in inquiry (whether a general course in qualitative inquiry, or more specifically, feminist inquiry), have invited teachers to go beyond conventional texts and ways of knowing to exploring—or renewing—their multiple ways of making sense of the world. The courses require them to engage in learning using many sign systems (from music to the visual arts to performance art, among others), to communicate their learning using those systems, and to consider their class-room teaching in light of these multiple sense-making literacies. What are they doing about stretching themselves as fully sense-making humans, and what kind of environment are they creating for their students to do the same?

With the permission (or perhaps, requirement) to explore sign systems other than conventional written text, teachers exchange insights using video, pencil and charcoal drawings, watercolour and oil paintings, dramatic performances, scripted plays, musical compositions, photographic essays, computer graphics, children's books, fabric arts, dance, and comic routines. Typically, they relish the freedom that such expression affords, but they are also somewhat reticent to declare their enthusiasm to colleagues. As exciting and renewing as these media are, they

193

are nevertheless held in the same regard among professionals as they are in the school system: making a video for a university course, for example, is not considered as "rigorous" as reading three books and writing a term paper. Teachers begin to see that, regardless of the work in discourse these many years, one definition of "text" prevails.

Like emerging limbs of a sapling, our many ways of knowing the world can be cut off early in our lives. School becomes a site for learning compliance, and robust and fecund creativity—the sort we see in artists and highly productive people—is seldom nurtured. The stories often told about highly creative people, such as those studied by Ghiselin (1952) or John-Steiner (1985), indicate that they often endure or ignore schooling to keep their creativity alive. But, unfortunately, so do we all. As adults, we squirrel away our instinctive needs to work in differing sign systems by slotting them into home or extra-curricular activities such as organized art and music lessons; we trivialize these needs as childish or as play (and hence disruptive of our work ethic); or we meet the needs in socially approved and sanctioned ways, allowing glimpses of the possible only through the doodlings on the cover of a notebook, the dramatic hallway impersonations of a teacher or colleague, or the performative art of lying our way out of trouble or obligation.

But mature trees can often, given the proper conditions, support diverse growth, and I have found consistently in my inquiry courses that teachers who conduct their own inquiry into making meaning in diverse ways will renew their professional enthusiasm. Bridging various sign systems, playing with their inter-educative potential, reminds teacher researchers that they are "whole" beings, aesthetically and somatically "real" and alive. Their confidence in having risked and thrived, the inter-relationality of the learning that ensues, and the liberation from the word as the only signifier all

combine to shift ground, to propel them forward to a fertile awareness of themselves and their own students.

Piaget's student, Howard Gruber, describes the "whole thinking" person as working with a number of interacting subsystems.
Howard Gardner's description of Gruber's perspective touches
closely on the notion of transmediation, albeit in terms sounding
more structural than semiotic: "A creative individual typically
spawns a network of enterprises—a complex of searches that
engages his (sic) curiosity over long periods of time. These
activities usually sustain one another and give rise to an incredibly active creative life" (Gardner, 1982, p. 354.) Not surpris-
ingly, the creative individual, Gardner claims, also experiences
a "strong, almost primordial tie to the subjects of his [sic]
curiosity...a special intimacy with the natural world" (355), a
pleasurable tie with the work that he compares to sexual involve-
ment with a loved one. It may well be that opening our senses
opens awareness, and such awakenings kindle or rekindle desire
in all its forms.

Sign systems, however well we explore them, and however
well we integrate or encourage transmediation among them, are
not neutral, nor sapped of ideology. They are politically charged,
encoded in our social practices in ways that can build empires
and assign value. At a pragmatic level, disciplines and activities
in schools are marked, encoded with political, economic, and
social importance or irrelevance. When teachers realize their
response-ability in these cultures for assigning and assuming
value to certain sign systems, it can open understanding about
the everyday, and create opportunities to challenge the given,
the values which form an unproblematized backdrop to everything they do. Suddenly, they will see schools in a different light,
their work both as belonging to a culture of its own creation and
responsible for its critique and renewal. They begin to question

the verbocentric bias in the public education system which marks survivors and champions as those who learn to negotiate and perpetuate the relations of ruling (Smith, 1987).

3. To promote an understanding of our multiple selves in relation to the cultures of the home, the school and the academy and in so doing, promote our response-ability in those cultures.

> *So, I think ... "our" problem, is how to have simultaneously an account of radical historical contingency for all knowledge claims and knowing subjects, a critical practice for which recognizing our own "semiotic technologies" for making meanings, and a no-nonsense commitment to faithful accounts of a "real" world, one that can be partially shared and that is friendly to earthwide projects of finite freedom, adequate material abundance, modest meaning in suffering, and limited happiness.* (Haraway, 1991, p. 187)

While we engage in ongoing debates about the nature and existence of truth, looking askance at those claims that "no truth" exists as being equally problematic and equally modernist (if that matters), we still have to live and work, teach children, feed the dog, and pay for groceries. Some of us answer the phone to hear threats and abusive comments about our gender or our sexuality; others hide from a man who hits when he drinks; and still others watch as the administrative position available in the school, and toward which we have directed all energies, goes to a youthful member of the "old boys' club."

This is not mere information; these are experiences that matter, that bring us to our senses. These are the "stones in our shoe" (L. Neilsen, 1994). We are eldest in a large family from rural Canada, or we are the child of an alcoholic, a new citizen of the country, or the sister of a man who has just died of AIDS. Each of us comes from somewhere, but that "somewhere" casts a different shadow in each of our encounters with others. The recognition that each of us is a constellation of differing positions according to the culture or context in which we find ourselves - and that these "multiple selves" negotiate and monitor ever-changing positions in a complex web of relations in the world— need not be an awareness which strikes fear of chaos. It can, instead, be a liberating recognition that the "self" is provisional, growing, elusive, but nevertheless, for the time being, here. Such awareness also brings with it the obvious: that the self is as the self does. We are what we do.

This kaleidoscope of shifting selves that we carry into the world each changing day, creates a similarly complex set of relations for the teacher encountering a roomful of children, each of whom brings equally complex kaleidoscopes and webs of relations. The study of teachers' lives, whether described from narrative, postmodern, or critical perspectives, is beginning to inform our understanding about actual people doing messy work in classrooms. Researchers who make it a point to come clean about their own experiences will not only provide us with the kinds of exemplars we need to move the field forward, but will provide invitations for all of us to drop our masks. By divulging who we are and where we come from, we are less likely to dismiss others' understandings as deficient, wrong, or lost in false consciousness.

When I work with teachers in inquiry seminars, they work with the situations or issues in their own home, work, or community which trouble, chafe, or intrigue them in some way. Research closer to home is less likely to be turned into an object, an Other, and the participants in the inquiry are more likely to have a face and a voice. These are situations from which the researcher cannot stand outside, but in which she participates, and often, through the process, inspires or effects change. Thus, this "kitchen table" inquiry has a particularly striking effect on peoples' assumptions about researcher stance. Questions about research ethics rise to the forefront.

In a recent discussion, an art teacher described her colleague's recent practice of using a repetitive, cut-and-paste task with paper in her first grade classroom. Although the teacher had observed the class only one day, she judged her colleague as having "taught art badly," of having stifled the children's creativity. But, someone in the seminar group asked, could there other explanations? What are the assumptions here about inquiry and about teaching art? Another offered an alternative perspective on the activity: was this teacher, perhaps, aiming to provide young children with an opportunity to practice motor skills and task completion, and not seeing this activity as related at all to art? How do we frame what we do? How do we frame what we see? Ought we to judge? How does the observed see herself and her intentions? How does the researcher see the teacher? Whose perspective is closer to "true"? Are our observations different when we see ourselves as colleagues, not researchers? What is a research stance? Who benefits from it? Who decides?

It becomes more difficult, as we engage in inquiry closer to the communities in which we live, to put on the body of a researcher like the rumpled glove, and to speak words outside of ourselves. It becomes more difficult, as we sit in a circle around the kitchen table, the seminar table, or the staff room table, to point a finger at others in the circle who do not meet our standards, or see from our perspective. For this reason, I believe it is important that our inquiry be situated in places we know, and in which we participate. It is only then that we face our

Re-Making Sense, Re-Shaping Inquiry

response-ability, be less cavalier with our notions of what counts as ethical, and what constitute integrity and community. Flying into data plantations, in the colonialist version of "objective" research, has always allowed for the kind of symbolic violence that, around home or the kitchen table, would be resisted, might be considered intrusive, assumptive, arrogant, and exploitative.

4. To encourage resistance of practices in the educational and institutional hierarchy which de-value situated inquiry and multiple ways of knowing; and to be open to understand how I am co-opted by those practices, and how I perpetuate them.

> ...[academic scholarship] is in the mind, in logic, in a form of discourse which totally erases the body, the emotional, the symbolic, the multiplicities and confusions—and in all ways orders the chaos of our lived experiences so that we no longer feel their power, their immobilizing conflicts, as we live them.
> (Kathleen Rockhill, 1987, p. 7)

My doctoral studies were filled with what might be called transmediative experiences. I particularly recall one writing seminar held by Donald Murray in which we engaged in another creative process, such as playing the piano or drawing, and wrote about how the processes informed one another. In other seminars writing as an art form was valued, encouraged, and expected; discursive, highly bibliographic academic writing played a part, but not the major part, in my studies. The education department in which I now teach has long held a reputation for holistic teaching practices, albeit varying interpretations of those, and for response-able, flexible, constructivist pedagogy.

199

Knowing Her Place

Students in our graduate program typically must spend the first part of their studies unlearning the institutional expectations and assumptions about university teaching and academic work they brought with them. It takes several months waiting before I or my colleagues hear the incoming question "Is this what you want?" shift to "Let's talk about what I/we need to do, and how I/we can make that happen."

Still, as fortunate as I have been as a graduate student studying inquiry and a faculty member both teaching and engaging in it, tensions remain. The symbolic order of the educational research marks doctoral institutions such as the one I attended as being from a "soft" research perspective, not "rigorous" or a place where "real" research is funded or pursued. The narrative and reflexive research practices associated with institutions such as these are often labelled unscientific, merely anecdotal. Regardless of the educational site, from an elementary to a university classroom, ways of pursuing our knowing have become gender coded, inscribing a public/private separation, where stories and the "personal" are considered of the private sphere, usually associated with women, and which run counter to the goals of the school which is intended to prepare people, especially males, for induction into public life (Nicholson, 1994, p. 79).

Outside the places where I am able to live and work I realize, as Helene Cixous so accurately names it, I must salute and show my identity papers, or in Virgina Woolf's terms, to identify my Headmaster. While students in our program speak in passionate tones of the dramatic changes in their perspectives—indeed in their lives and their relationships with colleagues, family, and friends—as a result of studies in which they can explore alternative notions of literacy and inquiry, the universities which maintain the status quo, the patriarchal symbolic order, are nevertheless considered to be legitimate universities, the "schol-

200

arly" institutions. They are places where the student query "what do you want?" is answered by the prevailing master narrative or the accompanying bibliography.

In the meantime, I continue to celebrate and support, theoretically and empirically, work which, by redefining literacy and inquiry, seems to want to redefine scholarship as we know it. In a time of decaying institutions and irrelevant structures it is necessary that we engage in inquiry which calls on an understanding of our whole signifying beings and in so doing rewrites our institutional practices. We are at critical point; we must realign signifiers in new fusions of possibilities. How many years and how many millions of dollars will we continue to spend on dead and dangerous metaphors, grasping for new ways to revive them? How many years do we expect a love of literacy to survive with its heart cut out?

The inquiry I explore and which I propose here is not, nor should it be, the only form of inquiry offered or explored in feminist courses, or in any research program, for that matter. After all, theory-as-regime creates its own problems of oppression. What should these efforts be called? Feminist standpoint inquiry? situated, reflexive research? feminist ethnomethodology? interpretive inquiry? response-able research? Perhaps this work is a step toward the joining of partial views and voices into a collective subject position. Or perhaps the work is more interesting for the new spaces it creates, the positions it disrupts.

And so the circle turns, and this time the view is different. I consider it a step toward achieving Donna Haraway's "earthwide projects" and Morris Berman's "gaia politik" to resist the institutional practices which continue to define, and hence constrain research that grows out of a particular context by attempting to name it, and to compare it to others' in different classrooms, other inquiry collectives. Whose ends does it serve for us to agree on a definition of qualitative, or feminist, or science—to put fences around our isms and marshall our forces—if children and adults continue to wander the earth deadened to its promise and its pain? Virginia Woolf reminds me that we cease believing in sides as we mature, and the labels we use will come off anyway. Experience tells me, also, that even when I refuse a label, others will affix it on the work to quiet their own uncertainty. I cannot help that; but I can help myself and others teach and learn in more responsive ways.

Over the last five years my work with teachers has changed. Variously, I have encouraged a focus on observation, reflection, reflexivity, and resistance, sometimes, or usually, all at once. The ways of inquiring and "telling" have included most aesthetic and technological media available. The "sites" for inquiry have ranged from a girls' soccer season to an immigrants' social club to the local newspaper, an individual's experience of racism in school, the experience of motherhood, to the conversational dynamic of our graduate seminar. In all cases, the researcher—with her perspectives, dilemmas, insights, and activity—is the sphere from which the inquiry begins, the axis on which the related and relational worlds spin.

Throughout these explorations, I have encouraged the body awareness and attunement that brings alive teacher researchers too long buried under dry and bloodless words. I have argued for the validity of inquiry that arises out of uncertainty, and indeed, invites more troubling of experience. And I have worked to support as many strategies for seeing, hearing, documenting, and codifying—a triangulation of methods, if you will, especially of methods that invite the many forms of representing how we know.

A classroom is still a classroom, however, and my own practices with people are open to question and to critique. For some, I realize, the kind of situated inquiry I promote creates its own form of tyranny, opening issues a person would rather not address. My pedagogy can be a breath of fresh air for some, a terrifying open space with no guide posts for others. I must learn to adapt practices that recognize such differences. I must also recognize my own complicity in maintaining the symbolic order that excludes underrepresented and silenced groups, and places students at the bottom of a hierarchy. Grades and other such markers are still there, in spite of our work to take them out of institutional practice. We can support growth through critique and conversation, create all the communities of inquiry we wish, but the grade sheets continue to appear on our desks.

It is instructive to continue to ask the impossible: how can educational institutions, and the practices of pedagogy themselves (however "empowering") avoid becoming sites of oppression, silencing in their own way? We cannot aspire to other, more ideal classrooms, for I do not believe they exist. Classrooms are still situated within academic institutions which promote competition, and which, through policies and discourse find ways of excluding many combinations of identities, and the lived realities they hold, all in the name of standards and rigor.

Feminist Metaphors

Robin Morgan's Invisible Woman "sees others quite clearly, including the doctor who patiently tells her she isn't invisible." She "pulls on her body" and "switches on her voice" and, in so doing, calls attention to herself. Better to suffer this, she thinks, than for the young doctor to learn that "he himself is insane. Only the strong can know that" (326).

Historically, voice—and its companion notions of ventriloquism, silence, and mutedness—has been a productive meta-

203

phor for women's experience teaching and learning in the world (Gilligan, 1977; Belenky, Clinchy, Goldberger, and Tarule, 1986; Gere Lewis, 1993; Fine, 1992). But is voice the foundational sound of our "true" selves, or do we produce many tones in many ways over many years? And from where do voices emanate? Equally compelling and useful has been the metaphor of the body, the corporeal being, whether we articulate it in terms of invisibility, embodied knowing/disembodied knowing, skin as a cover, role-playing or masks (Belenky et al, 1986; Trinh T. Minh-Ha, 1991; Grumet, 1988). Too often, however, we use the metaphor of body as an entity distinct from the mind. Cartesian perspectives on our work in the world have helped to form a basis for the metaphors for literacy which we now find wanting. What might happen if we no longer separated mind, body, the world?

Shakespeare's sister, the 16th Century fictional young woman born with a gift of poetry, is the ghost in our collective conscious-ness, reminding us all of the blunted possibilities of women's imaginings. Virginia Woolf, describing how the downward spiral to the young woman's death might have occurred, imagines her facing the impossible: "all the conditions of her life, all her own instincts, were hostile" to the development of her talent. Be-tween her and the incandescence of mind needed to write poetry, were attitudes, social practices, and assumptions which were insurmountable, even in her own mind. "Her mind must have been strained by the need of opposing this, of disproving that" (p. 53), writes Woolf. In fact, Shakespeare's sister, shut in by the gates created in her world, would never have sought the horizon of her talents at all; from where she stood, it was impossible to even be aware of an horizon, let alone seek its possibilities.

Little has changed where issues of knowledge and inquiry for women and underrepresented groups are concerned. I continue to hear challenges about the "validity" or "reliability" of my argument for a living inquiry: how then can we compare, prove, sort, categorize, or place value such inquiry in the academy? A kitchen table metaphor for inquiry has a decidedly homespun, anti-intellectual flavour, challenging received notions of formal academic propriety. And yet I will continue to invite my colleagues to the conversation there. Such a conversation causes us all to examine again the split between the public and the private spheres: one, the political and social external world, and the other, the realm of privacy and subjectivity.

This, then, has been education. As Linda Nicholson (1994) writes: "As one moves from the elementary to graduate and particularly professional schools, one finds an institution less and less 'homelike' and increasingly dominated by characteristics associated with the public world and masculinity" (80). A living inquiry, as comfortable in the kitchen as the seminar room, attempts to bring research home, to be named and recognized in the same way we continue to lobby for recognition of unpaid labour, for the value of story beside statistic. It is work of the heart, the hands, our sensemaking body, our many-toned voices.

The issues are ones on which the world can tilt: learning about the world as though the body is inseparable from the mind; creating the discursive world from the axis of experiences of the silenced, the unnamed, and the disregarded; exposing and composing our lives as researchers by including and examining who we are and what we do in the name of inquiry. Such issues are issues of legitimacy, if we choose to use a morally-laden term, or perhaps, issues of value. What and who and how do we value, what means and why, when we set out on the inquiry path?

But like the histories of midwifery or herbal medicine—from necessary practice to a position outside the realm of "acceptable medical practice" to a growing, if qualified return to "legitimacy"—the history of inquiry, at least its history within the last 20 years, has been a battle of "regimes of truth" (Gore, 1993). But who is right is not nearly as interesting or productive as questions such as "Who benefits?" "What is the legacy of our work?" "Who and what are we not hearing, seeing, knowing?" Women who assisted at the birth of children are neither right nor wrong; they are variously witches, shamans, friends, lovers, pariahs, health care providers, and licensed midwives. The work is necessary, and will be done. The times assign place, and the politics ascribe value.

In fact, it is not my intention to force the adoption of my research and teaching practices on anyone, only to invite teachers to embrace them, take them in, like Shakespeare's sister, for a time, to reawaken aspects of themselves and their professional lives, to live the inquiry, and to be confident in its own particular truth. These practices of feminist inquiry, while they are satisfying and challenging, are part of the diversity and richness that marks the inquiry process as a whole, part of a mix of perspectives and methods we need to spark learning and force change. Such diversity, to the extent that the practices are not oppressive or irresponsible, is to be embraced in the same way our multimodal literacies ought to be embraced. My argument is that feminist inquiry of the sort I practice and support, ought not, like the talents of Shakespeare's sister, be blunted by the thick resistance of the status quo. Nor ought it to be skewered on a standard to which it does not aspire: to be the whole answer. Such feminist praxis ought to claim a space in the house we are constructing, not perceived as a faint shadow in an asylum hallway. After all, as Donna Haraway notes, "we could use some enforcible, reliable accounts of things not reducible to power moves and agonistic, high status games of rhetoric" (1991, p.188).

Metaphors become our lenses, our seat on the ferris wheel,

our foot on the rocky bottom of the ocean. They shape how we respond, and even who we are. Our metaphors for teaching and learning literacy with and for ourselves and our students have diminished our possibilities, closed us from the constellations of codes and living responses that life opens up to us. Thirsty children are given recipes for water; soul-diminished teachers are given keys to the textbook storeroom. Both ought to be out looking for the horizon, unravelling it, creating surprise.

No single metaphor can be selected here to speak for a feminist method of inquiry. But I am aware that metaphors that make sense—shape sense—for me in my teaching and inquiry practices are metaphors that call on the "body resonant." Living inquiry means that a relational being, living in overlapping worlds, touches and responds to those around her as she pursues the work she deems important. As she moves within/out of these worlds, she and they are changed. More than speaking a single voice, her presence re/sounds, re/verberates; her senses take in all that surrounds her, and she in turn, gives back. Her many-toned voice is part of her presence; sometimes a song, sometimes a cry, or a whisper. Her body lives in the world—mind, emotion, and sentience as a breathing whole—like a cell lives within a larger being, exchanging life-giving synapses of the heart, the mind, and all that she is. Our body resonant is less like a corporeal entity, and more like a permeable membrane balancing forces of air and water, fire and earth. Literacies of the body resonant are living literacies. They are the joy and pain of engaging ourselves in many ways our sensory systems offer, knowing all the while we are not aiming to reach an ideal holism, but rather to be awakened to the knowledge that links meanings with bodies, here and elsewhere. I am urging abandonment of metaphors for literacy that do not fit our world, that cut off our circulation, parch our possibilities and clutter our lives with miseducative and unsustainable activity. We need complex, situated, metaphors, opening a "view from a body, always a complex, contradictory, structuring and structured body, versus the view from above, from nowhere, from simplicity" (Haraway, 1991, p. 195).

No god's (or goddess') eye view is enough, and we have had too many in the inquiry business in education who aspire to that seat. Meanwhile, as academic arguments rage in the etherworld, the discursive system where "system/atic" inquiry is enforced, a Kurdish child new to Canada enters a school in Nova Scotia speaking no English. She feels the cold in the outside air and in the classroom climate. She aches with knowledge she cannot tell, and she sits near the window, her pencil poised at a paper with words to copy. Dis-embodied words, that do not touch any experience she knows. Elsewhere, the mother of two children enters a literacy program after thirty years of illiteracy and confesses she no longer feels like a nobody. Literacy will make her somebody, she believes.

No body. Some/body. Dis/embodied. Our metaphors for literacy have created a world of schooled people outside their bodies, outside themselves, unable to connect their life to their words. New ways of imagining our literacies and our possibilities might help us all read, write, sing, touch, hear, and in richer ways resonate with the lives and the struggles of travellers we have missed on the paths. We are passionate, resonant bodies seeking connection and survival; it is a compassionate literacy to which we must aspire.

References

Atwood, M. (1995). *Morning in the burned house*. Toronto, Ontario:

Re-Making Sense, Re-Shaping Inquiry

McClelland & Stewart, pp. 14-15.

Belenky, M., Clinchy, B., Goldberger, N., & Tarule, J. (1986). *Women's ways of knowing: The development of self, voice, and mind.* New York: Basic Books.

Berman, M. (1989). *Coming to our senses.* New York: Bantam Books.

Chandler, S. (1992). Displaying our lives: An argument against displaying our theories. *Theory into Practice*, 31, 126-131.

Eisner, E. (1988). The primacy of experience and the politics of method. *Educational Researcher*, June/July, 15-20.

Franck, F. (1993). *Zen seeing, zen drawing.* New York: Bantam Books.

Gardner, H. (1982). *Art, mind, and brain.* New York: Basic Books.

Gheselin, B. (1952). *The creative process.* New York: New American Library.

Gore, J. (1993). *The struggle for pedagogies: Critical and feminist discourses as regimes of truth.* New York: Routledge.

Greene, M. (1988). *The dialectic of freedom.* New York: Teachers College Press.

Grumet, M. (1988). *Bitter milk: Women and teaching.* Amherst, MA: University of Massachusetts Press.

Haraway, D. (1991). *Simians, cyborgs, and women: The reinvention of nature.* New York: Routledge.

Harste, J.C., Woodward, V.A., & Burke, C.L. (1984). *Language stories and literacy lessons.* Portsmouth, NH: Heinemann.

John-Steiner, V. (1985). *Notebooks of the mind: Explorations of thinking.* Albuqerque, NM: University of New Mexico Press.

Lewis, M.G. (1993). *Without a word: Teaching beyond women's silence.* New York: Routledge.

Minh-Ha, T. (1991). *When the moon waxes red: Representation, gender, and cultural politics.* New York: Routledge.

Morgan, R. (1970). The invisible woman. In Florence Howe (ed,. 1993, *No more masks: An anthology of twentieth century American poets.* New York: HarperCollins, 326.

Neilsen, A. (1989). *Critical thinking and reading: Empowering learners to think and act.* Urbana, IL: National Council of Teachers of English and ERIC.

Neilsen, L. (1994). *A stone in my shoe: Teaching literacy in times of change.* Winnipeg, Manitoba: Peguis Publishers.

Neilsen, L. (1994). The academy of the kitchen table. Unpublished

209

manuscript.

Neilsen, L. (1993). Exploring reading: Mapping the personal text. In Straw, S., & Bogdan, D., (eds), *Teaching beyond communication*. Portsmouth, NH: Boynton-Cook/Heinemann.

Neilsen, L. (1989*). Literacy and living: The literate lives of three adults*. Portsmouth, NH: Heinemann.

Nicholson, L.J. (1994). Women and schooling. In Stone, Lynda (ed), *The education feminism reader*. New York: Routledge.

Rockhill, K. (1987). The chaos of subjectivity in the ordered halls of academe. *Canadian Woman Studies*, 8 (4), Winter.

Siegel, M. (1994). Metaphor and the curricular possibilities of transmediation. Paper presented at the annual meeting of the American Educational Research Association. New Orleans, LA, April.

Smith, D. (1990). *The conceptual practices of power*. Toronto, Ontario: University of Toronto Press.

Suhor, C. (1984). Towards a semiotics-based curriculum. *Journal of Curriculum Studies*, 16 (3), 247-257.

Woolf, V. (1929). *A room of one's own*. London, UK: The Hogarth Press.

A version of this chapter appears in D. Alvermann, K. Hinchman, D. Moore, S. Phelps, and D. Waff (eds)., *Reconceptualizing the literacies in adolescents' lives* (Mahwah, NJ: Lawrence Erlbaum, 1998). Layering the textual conventions of script writing, dialogue, and academic discourse allowed for art/text/inquiry to merge in ways that foregrounded participants' voices and honored the art of writing/text-making.

—9—
Playing for Real:
Performative Texts
and Adolescent Identities

Olivia: Now, sir, what is your text?
Viola: Most sweet lady—
Olivia: A comfortable doctrine, and much may be said of it. Where lies your text?
Viola: In Orsino's bosom.
Olivia: In his bosom! In what chapter of his bosom?
Viola: To answer by the method, in the first of his heart.
Olivia: I have read it. It is heresy. Have you no more to say?
Viola: Good madam, let me see your face.
Olivia: Have you any commission from your lord to negotiate with my face? You are now out of your text, but we will draw the curtain and show you the picture. Look you, sire, such a one I was this present. Isn't not well done? (Unveiling)

—William Shakespeare, *Twelfth Night* (I:V)

Prologue

...Old paint on canvas as it ages sometimes becomes transparent. When that happens it is possible, in some pictures, to see the

Knowing Her Place

original lines: a tree will show through a woman's dress, a child
makes way for a dog, a large boat is no longer on an open sea....
This is called pentimento...the old conception, replaced by a
later choice, is a way of seeing and then seeing again...
—Lillian Hellman (1973, p. 1)

"Who am I?" is a question of central importance in adolescence. No longer children unselfconsciously acting out story in the school yard or playing dress-up in the basement, adolescents, with their feet firmly planted in the path toward adulthood, try on roles in their lives at school, at home, and in the community. Unlike the play of young children, however, adolescent play seems often marked by an awareness by the adolescent of its purpose: to explore identities through roles and to find a place in the world. While play at all ages is serious and important, adolescent performance-as-identity has a particular urgency and intensity. Eva Hoffman (1989), writing about her adolescent struggles to find the right persona as a Polish immigrant to North America, describes this intensity about life as being marked by "fire, flair, a holy spark of inspiration" (1989, p. 154). Adulthood looms, and passion intensifies: Who will I be today, tomorrow, next year?

This chapter explores the role of text in the lives of two adolescents in a Nova Scotia rural community. By text, I mean sets of potential meanings and signifying practices adhering for readers and writers in both local and larger discourse communities. A novel in English class, for example, is a text; so, too, is the conversation about such a novel in which the students and teachers engage (Fish, 1980), and so, too, are teen 'zines, mall cultures, and television sitcoms. The premise of this study is that our engagements with texts in everyday life help all readers and writers to shape their identities (and re-shape them, in an ongoing process); but that adolescents, in particular, engage in more fluid, intentional, and often more passionate identity-play in their encounters with texts. Whether their "text" is a school-sanctioned reading requirement, a beach novel, a style of dressing, a conversational pattern, or a popular film, texts hold potential as symbolic resources. In this study, these symbolic resources not only help the adolescent to make sense of her or his experience, but also offer opportunities for trying on or taking up often multiple and conflicting roles or identities. In this way, a text is both window and door. Text can serve to constitute us and determine us; and yet, as Judith Butler (1990) reminds us about discourse, to be constituted by discourse needn't mean we are determined by it. Adolescents, who typically demonstrate as much zeal in taking up roles as they do in resisting them, become performers in their own right simultaneously being both actor and theatre, performer and audience in their engagement with the world through texts. By reading and writing the texts of their lives, they are reading and writing themselves.

At some level, this study of two adolescents was undertaken over a period of twelve years. As researcher, mother, and community member, I have observed the participants, Eleanor and David, in a number of social, personal, and school settings since their first grade in school. The in-depth interviews about the role of key texts in the participants' lives, however, were taken over a two-month period in the latter part of the students' grade eleven (junior) year in high school. Emerging from transcripts of six hours of individual and paired interviews is a recurring theme: the fluidity of text in performance and role-playing as Eleanor and David make and shape meaning in their lives through literacy. Their understanding and "scripting" of principal, or what I refer to as "touchstone" texts in their lives is woven into their school and social behavior in a process of ongoing

215

revision. Here the touchstone texts are the novel, *The Catcher in the Rye*, and the film, *Pulp Fiction*; their motifs and influences shift, recede, and emerge, seeming at times like the phenomenon of pentimento in painting (Hellman, 1978) or layered scripts of a palimpsest, a manuscript whose erasures are written upon in successive layers. Because of the vitality of movement of these texts in their lives, however, perhaps a more contemporary, albeit mechanistic, comparison might be that of successive iterations in a word-processing document; what we see now on the screen represents changes, deletions, additions to the same text over a period of time: in process, the text resists stasis. In their taking up of texts to author their lives, adolescents also resist stasis and defy definition. The performative dynamism in the intertextual movement, however, is instructive.

Because of the centrality of performance and role-playing in the description of literacy in the lives of Eleanor and David, I am, as the researcher and one of the participants in the study, presenting the material here using the motifs of a play and the language and scene-setting of theatre. Some of this study is reported as stage-setting, some as conventional discursive analysis, and some as dialogue and monologue. The play, as it were, is in the reading of the juxtaposed texts you encounter here. As readers, you become both participants and audience as these texts weave through one another. As narrator and participant, I become, as does the reader, part of the inter-textual dynamics. The players, the texts, the readings, the contexts are presented in an attempt to create an interplay which is not linear, a text about text which does not adhere to Western rhetorical and narrative conventions. While I will offer implications for teaching at the end of this chapter, based on observations and comments reported here, these implications are neither conclusions

216

nor guidelines, but instead are questions to consider as we work with adolescents and literacy.

The Players

Eleanor

Eleanor and her older sister moved with her mother (a single parent) to this rural Nova Scotia community before Eleanor entered school. El (as she is called) now lives with her mother, owner of a local craft store, and her stepfather, fifth-generation Nova Scotian, in a recently-converted boathouse on the shore of St. Margaret's Bay.

Interviews with El took place during a family move from their former residence to the cabin (El's sister has moved out). El spent a good deal of her time alone in the old house, where she has her own room and her own telephone line. El was about to turn 17. Her older sister has worked as an *au paire* in France and will teach English in Japan next year. El has travelled alone to Ireland to visit relatives, travels every other weekend to see her birth father, works part-time at a local restaurant/coffee house and occasionally as a sign painter for a local artist. She catches rides frequently into the nearby city to see films, hang out in coffee houses, or to visit her current boyfriend, an art student and animation artist.

El is independent and unconventional by community standards. Her dress is distinctive, what some might call "nonconformist." She wears several earrings, including a nose ring and her dark hair has sported many hairstyles. She is short, quiet, but not shy, and often questions her parents' and her teachers' decisions. Art and music are important to her; art, drama, English and history are her favorite school subjects. She has attended school in the same school system since Grade Primary.

David

David, who is now seventeen, moved to the community from Western Canada thirteen years ago with his parents, both of whom are educators. He has a nine-year-old brother. David and Eleanor have been close friends since grade one, but never romantically paired. They socialize together, often without their respective boyfriends/girlfriends, and have, on occasion, disagreed strongly over issues.

David, like El, has been independent from an early age. He has travelled frequently out of Nova Scotia. He attended school in the same classes as Eleanor except in grades nine and ten when he chose to attend a school in the city system. Highly verbal, he has used performance where possible in school settings (as course work, and as class clown), has studied drama with the local theatre school since he was ten, and has served as a youth judge at the local film festival. David is on two baseball teams, has been an avid skateboarder and snowboarder, and when he is not spending time with his girlfriend, hangs out with El, Ross, Sophie, Simon, and others from school. Ross, David, Simon, and El have made several home videos based on material they have written or improvised.

David dresses in a style which he calls unique ("I am not preppie, not jock, and not punk"), but which resembles closely the dress of skateboarders (large shirts, long skirt-like shorts). Like El, David's heritage is European, largely Caucasian. His brown hair has been shoulder-length, worn in a ponytail, but is now short and dyed dark blond. David is tall, has the build of a linebacker, and has a loud voice. Like El, David has a strong sense of justice, and each uses this sense to challenge what they see as sexist or racist practices of their teachers or the community. Both El and David can be heard frequently "dissing" the rural community for what they believe to be its provincial attitudes.

Researcher / Narrator

As a thirteen-year resident of the rural community in which El and David live, I have researched and written about the literate behavior of selected adults in the area (Neilsen, 1989). As David's mother, I have seen both David and El in a variety of literacy and schooling contexts over the eleven-year period in which the two have known one another. Having moved intellectually from an atomistic, functional notion of literacy and literacy research in the 1970s, I am now engaged in on-going research into gender and literacy, research which might be characterized as poststructuralist/hermeneutic in approach. My beliefs in the social construction of gender and of literacy as well as my commitment to situated research practices make it necessary, I believe, to declare myself a participant in the study. I believe, too, that local research, driven by situated, integral understanding of the context, holds the opportunity for more finely-grained analysis and a more informed perspective. Not only have I had the opportunity to see El and David in a number of social and educational contexts, I have also worked as a teacher educator and volunteer in the elementary and junior high schools they attended.

The Texts

The Catcher in the Rye

J.D. Salinger's 1951 story of a prep-school runaway is per-haps one of North America's most controversial, popular, and enduring novels. Typically described as the only novel to success-fully "convey contemporary youth's dissatisfaction with adult society" (*Benet's*, 1987), it deals with the two days following Holden Caulfield's departure from school in which he drifts around New York, avoiding his return to his family, and spend-ing his money on "real world" adventures. Idealistic, sardonic, observant, and sophisticated, Holden Caulfield is considered by many adolescent and adult readers to represent the voice of disaffected youth. Indeed, although the generation that grew up in the fifties (the generation of this researcher) were avid readers of the novel (the language of the novel was frank and racy enough for the times to ensure a wide readership), the work continues to attract succeeding generations of young readers.

Critical acclaim for the novel would likely have been written from a New Critical perspective at the time of its publication (a perspective which holds that the text stands alone—indeed, from this perspective, literary works of art must be considered autonomous, without regard to social, cultural, or biographical influences). J.D. Salinger followed *The Catcher in the Rye* with other works about sensitive and troubled adolescents; but, as a novelist, Salinger has been absent from the literacy scene for thirty years. He has lived as a recluse since the mid-1960s. At a time when the zeitgeist demands that we, as creators and consumers of text, understand the embeddedness of text in context—and changes in meanings over time—Salinger's work is left to speak for itself. Or, perhaps it is more accurate here to say that the protagonist narrator, Holden Caulfield, alone can speak for the text. (Salinger's text has never been made into a film and, recently, a World Wide Web site on Holden, developed by a university student, was shut down as a result of pressure from Salinger's lawyers).

Pulp Fiction

The acclaimed movie about low-rent hit men won the Cannes Film Festival's highest prize, the *Palme d'Or*, and an Academy Award for Best Original screenplay for the writer/director, Quentin Tarantino. Celebrated as the coming-of-age of Tarantino, cinema's *"enfant terrible,"* the movie was also notable for its showcasing of actor John Travolta's long-awaited return to the screen.

Like Salinger, Tarantino has been praised for his authentic and engaging dialogue. Salinger's novel, its central character, and his voice, were considered highly original for their time. Tarantino's film is flagrantly derivative of other films and of pop culture narratives: ironically, it is this derivative quality, in part, which make critics consider his work original. The term "pulp fiction" refers to the five-cent novels popular a generation ago; and the movie is replete with pop culture images and references and allusions to well-known movies. The film includes a soundtrack which taps into the nostalgia of today's forty-something generation. The film continues to receive praise for its postmodern disruption of the conventional narrative and linear plot line. The story is not chronological; viewers must piece together "what happened" through a series of flashbacks (and jumps forward). Martin and Porter describe it as "trash masterpiece" in which the writer/director "spares the viewer little in this tale of the under-

Knowing Her Place

belly of Los Angeles where philosophizing hit men and techno-crazed druggies live on the thrill-packed edge" (1995, p. 103). Vincent Vega (Travolta) and Jules (Samuel Jackson) are the hapless gangsters whose antics we follow on the trail of a suitcase (whose contents remain a mystery).

The movie, like its director/writer, is not without its critics. Some have called the film "blaxploitation," claiming that actor Samuel Jackson's Afro and exaggerated sideburns (part of the movie's 70s motif) make him just another in a long line of black stereotypes, and that Travolta's "white negro" attitude, as well as frequent use by all characters of the word "nigger," makes the movie both dangerous and racist. Feminists, in particular, have attacked the film for its graphic violence: heroin addiction, execution-style murder, male rape and bondage, among other scenes, figure highly in the text.

Tarantino, unlike Salinger, is available as a "text" through which to understand the text of his film. The son of a sixteen-year-old single mother, he dropped out of school because he claims he couldn't do math, couldn't spell, and couldn't keep up with the class ("I fucking hated school. I was left back, so I was, like sixteen in ninth grade.... my mom didn't want me to quit because education was the bootstraps by which she pulled herself up out of a bad situation to a new life" [All Tarantino quotations are from Biskind, 1994/online. Page numbers not available electronically]). He became a film buff, got a job in a video store, and began to write, incorporating (or perhaps appropriating) storylines, motifs, and characters from a lifetime of film-watching. As a result, Tarantino's films have been described by filmmakers such as Oliver Stone as "movies about movies" rather than "movies about real life." He responds to these charges by noting that, as a post-Watergate and post-Vietnam child, he grew up believing that "everything is lies, everything is fiction." In fact, one commentator claims that the so-called "real" and gratuitous violence in Tarantino's movies merely shows (whether the director intended it or not) that audiences are easily outraged and shocked by such "little picture" events, and choose to ignore the "big picture" where insidious and more damaging violence, symbolic and otherwise, grinds away, within power structures removed from our limited sphere of influence (Fausset, 1996). Showing the gritty "realities" in the underbelly of "real life," Tarantino thus makes us question whether the "real life" we think we know is as fictional as the movies.

Theoretical Backdrop

This study was undertaken with the assumption that becoming literate is a lifelong process, and this process is not limited to the reading and writing of print material. Literacy learning and literate behaviors are semiotic activities (Neilsen, 1989) in which we learn to read and write within value-laden code systems; they are also pedagogical and political in nature. Becoming literate is a process not only of acquiring functional skills of decoding and encoding printed material, but also of developing critical awareness and agency in one's own life through the reading and writing of available signs both in and out of school: visual, auditory, sensory signs are available to "read" and to "write" as much as conventional print.

Adolescents in particular draw from popular culture to "actively create and define their own social identities...'reading' and 'writing' popular culture are thus inherently social processes" (Buckingham & Sefton-Green, 1994, p. 108). As young people learn to see themselves in social terms, they have the opportunity to see themselves as political beings, actively choosing to select or to resist the discourses and roles available to them. While it is true that choice itself is never free, but is instead framed or shaped by myriad personal and social influences, it is also true that the more diverse and discrepant the choices provided for young people, the greater their opportunity to make choices which move them beyond the insular and the local, and which foster their ability to approach their reading and writing with a greater understanding that literacy is saturated with social and political purposes and effects. David Buckingham and Julian Sefton-Green (1994) offer this observation:

> .. becoming critical could be seen simply as a matter of learning to reproduce the terminology and discourse structures of particular kinds of conventional critical (literacy)...in Bourdieu's terms, of acquiring a kind of cultural capital...on the other hand, the growth of critical understanding could be seen from a Vygotskyan perspective: as matter of cognitive or conceptual development...[emphasizing] the way in which critical understanding offers the individual a degree of power and control over his or her own thought processes. (1994, p. 182)

Adolescents supported in multiple opportunities to work with a range of texts, both school-sanctioned and popular, would seem, then, to be well-positioned for growth in their critical literacy development.

As they engage with texts, readers "constitute [fictional] realities...out of the sets of relevancies they have available to them at that time" (Davies, 1994, p. 101). Readers/viewers interweave their lives and the lives in the text, and as observers or teachers we thus have available to us a means of seeing how "power works through discursive practices, for example, in the maintenance of gender" (1994, p. 101).

Work by Pam Gilbert (1994), Bronwyn Davies (1993) and

Playing for Real

Meredith Cherland and Carole Edelsky (1993) has shown how young girls take up gender identities through reading as a social practice. Annie Rogers' study of pre-adolescent girls makes apparent that entry into adolescence creates for young girls a "crisis of courage" (1993, p. 290) in which they struggle to maintain their outspokenness and strength in the face of pressures to assume societal roles and expectations for feminine behaviour. Peg Finders' (1996a, 1996b) work on the "underlife" of junior high school girls' literacy practices illustrates how social roles are shaped and maintained through girls' reading of "teen 'zines" and how such reading (and the note-writing they do, for example) comprises an "underlife" beneath the school-sanctioned literacy practices. Quoting Goffman, Finders explains how "when worlds are laid on, underlives develop"; that humans, regardless of age, tend to resist an official view of who they must be and what they must do (1996, p. 97).

Boys, as much as girls, can be constrained by limited constructions of their gender identities in school and society. Masculinity in society is a construction which creates in boys implicit expectations for certain kinds of behavior, typically strength, physical power and the potential for violence, as well as sexual domination (Frank, 1993). Anne Haas Dyson (1994), however, reports on boys' and girls' encounters with gender relations and power through text and offers classroom possibilities which allow both boys and girls to challenge these social constructions of masculinity and femininity and thus "transform images of power and gender in the local culture of a classroom, images that are themselves interwoven in complex ways with race, social class, physical appearance, and personality" (Haas Dyson, 1994, p. 224).

Most work in gender over the last decade has affirmed that cultural values about males and females are inscribed in literacy practices and reinforce strongly the stereotypical male/female polarities of activity/passivity, dominance/submission, and public/private. Yet work such as Anne Haas Dyson's with young children, or Bronwyn Davies' and Barbara Kamler's work with mature women offers hope for the possibility of change through intervention using literate activities which create less simplistic notions of gendered constructions in schools and society. Indeed, Peg Finders (1996) calls for such work:

> ...examining the social, historical, and cultural motivations of particular roles available—in texts, classrooms, and the larger culture—will lead students to more critical awareness and thus, it is hoped, to the ability to revise those roles.... Students, both male and female, all keenly aware of disparate positions of power, need opportunities to practice dealing with intellectual uncertainties and political tension. (1996a, p. 126)

Faced, however, with school literacy practices as they currently exist, students find that their options are limited, that both the literary and the literacy canon privilege white middle class values, Eurocentric, male-centred reading material, hierarchically-organized and assessment-driven curricula, and, in high school, cultural values which reinforce achievement over learning, and control over educational possibilities (MacNeil, 1988). The high school itself is considered a masculine environment, in contrast with the feminine, nurturing environment of early schooling (Neilsen, 1993; Grumet, 1988); "content" acquisition, especially in the sciences and mathematics, is given primacy in the high school over "feminine" disciplines and pursuits such as English, arts, and drama. In the high school context, "hard" knowledge is often contrasted with "soft" knowledge, and hard knowledge is typically the domain of male teachers. Thus, it is typical for male ways of knowing to be privileged in the high school, and for males, either as active participants in school activities or as active resisters to school expectations, to dominate classroom discourse and public conversation, and for issues of power and control to dominate high school classrooms and culture (Robinson, 1992).

The "silence" of girls in schools is often characterized either as a result of oppression or as an act of resistance, and their literate activities as developing "underground" in private or underlife spheres. Valerie Walkerdine is right, I believe, when she claims that femininity and masculinity are "fictions linked to fantasies deeply embedded in the social world which can take on the status of fact in...practices like schooling through which we are regulated" (1990, p. xiii). But understanding silence as a result or a consequence of regulation need not lead us to assume that males do not have "private" literacies, or that females do not have "public" literacy practices. Indeed, it may be more useful to make the terms "public" and "private" literacy problematic for a number of reasons.

While we learn to take and create meaning through semiotic activity, reading the "signs" of our culture, our literate behavior, enacted in kitchens or board rooms, is always social in its nature (Vygotsky, 1962), even when we are alone. Speaking, writing, and reading all forms of text are literacy activities which are fundamentally dialogical and relational, regardless of the stage on which they are performed. In this way, so-called "private literacy" could not exist without the social creation of language, nor can "private literacy"—even when directed to oneself alone— be removed from its role in the rehearsal, consolidation, or extension of publicly-shared literacy.

Further, it is interesting to observe, as teachers and parents, how the texts of students' lives, regardless of the context in which they are introduced, often undergo a process which Henry

Jenkins (1992) refers to as "becoming real," even if they started in the private domain. First the text—particularly if it meets the interest of the reader/viewer—is incorporated into lived experience; then it is both re-read and re-written so that it is more productive and more meaningfully able to sustain its original appeal; and finally, it is shared within social practices as assumed and tacit knowledge, particularly among friends. As this study will show, the touchstone texts which inform Eleanor's and David's life undergo the process of becoming real in such a process, a process which culminates, finally, in the insertion of these texts into their social world. In this way, whether it is a *Saturday Night Live* sketch seen alone at home and then re-enacted in the school hallway as a piece of shared text (and then subsequently used as a "shorthand" reference for a social phenomenon), or whether it is a touchstone novel or film which plays an important role in their lives, these young people live the private in concert with the public. If we are to assume that the word "privacy" is equivalent to undisclosed text or ideas, we can also assume that each of these participants holds certain texts and understandings close to their chest, as we all do. For the purposes of this study, however, it is important to recognize the dialogical relationship between the individual and the social. Each script, or text, has the potential for re-enactment in public in some form, whether the enactment is explicit (incorporated into speech or writing, for example) or tacit (changed behavior, changed perspective on the world, for example).

Much research and commentary, especially in the area of cultural studies, is available to show the many ways in which societal texts, such as 'zines, films, television, and pop culture become "real" as appropriated exemplars of cultural capital and as recurring motifs in adolescents' everyday lives. Less is available to show the ways in which adolescents engage with written texts, such as novels, to incorporate the ideas or characteristics of the protagonists into their lives. Rachel Brownstein's (1982) work explores adult women's sense of themselves as heroine in romantic fictions both in and out of their lived worlds: "real women, like realistic novels, are haunted by the shaping shadow of romance" (1982, p. 32). Suzanne Juhasz (1994) writes of her lifelong love of escaping into fiction, and of its resonance with her shifting identities through the years as she grew away from heterosexual romantic fantasies to lesbian romance novels. It is generally accepted that for both reading and writing, women tend more toward personal engagements with the text, entering its world emotionally and passionately while males tend to keep their distance, objectifying the text as "other" (Bleich, 1986; Aisenberg & Harrington, 1988); yet this stereotypical rendering of male and female responses to literature has yet to be questioned in literacy research.

Finally, it is important to comment on the research process itself. Because I cannot separate myself from the process, I believe it is methodologically appropriate here that my perspectives be named and included as one of the multiple perspectives, including the readers' and the primary participants', on the observations, artifacts, and interview transcripts. I asked two questions of David and El: "Tell me about your reading and writing in school" (I asked this question of them individually, and as a twosome); and "tell me about your favorite 'text' (book, movie)." (I explained my perspective on "text," and that my meaning included other media). Each talked extensively with only my occasional "what do you mean?" or "can you say more about that?" to encourage elaboration.

Because we know each other so well, the conversations were, at first, awkward, as though we each recognized the performative nature of such talk. Our conversations over the years on academic matters have rarely been sustained, and never recorded, and so it took a session or two to be comfortable in our new conversational mode. For David, especially, knowing me as "mom," interested in his learning and his academic progress, he seemed at times caught between what he wanted to say and what he thought I might want to hear, both as a parent, and as a researcher. As a researcher, however, I did not consider this wrinkle problematic: issues of stance and disclosure, identity and performance adhere in most research interviewing, regardless of the relationship between interviewer and interviewed. El and David may have been performing, as all of us do, but this does not mean that their comments were inauthentic. Rather, their comments seemed remarkably candid and willingly offered; (in fact, they appeared pleased to be given the chance to talk). Later, they read transcriptions of our recorded conversations, made changes, read a draft copy of this chapter, and revised areas where they wanted to be represented differently.

Finally, these interviews and observations are offered to the reader in a format different from conventional research reporting. With a growing number of researchers, I argue for expanding our limited notions of rational, linear discourse, and for transcending restrictive options for particular genres, tones, and styles of reporting (Denzin, 1996). Therefore, the choice to write this chapter in this format is as much a theoretical decision as it is rhetorical. Similarly, the invitation to you, the reader, to become audience, to engage with the texts as presented, is meant to make an important theoretical point about literacy and text. It is an attempt, like breaking down the fourth wall in theatre, to collapse the distinctions between text and audience (or text and reader)—to make this a reading event, not an object—and to move away from viewing our own interactions with text as an activity separate from who we are (Rosenblatt, 1978). Here then are the voices of El and David. In our collective interactions with their words, as readers and educators, we create the textual play.

Eleanor

> Then I'd throw my automatic down the elevator shaft—after I'd wiped off all the finger prints and all. Then I'd crawl back to my room and call up Jane and have her come over and bandage up my guts. I pictured her holding a cigarette for me to smoke while I was bleeding and all. The goddam movies. They can ruin you. I'm not kidding.
> —Holden Caulfield, *The Catcher in the Rye*, p. 104

Why El Likes *Catcher in the Rye*

I think it's just the way he goes on these spiels, this complete train of thought...there's this one chapter—I actually did bits of it for a monologue once in drama—and Holden's in this crap hotel, and he's in the lobby, in this —as he calls it—"vomity- looking chair," and all of a sudden he starts thinking about Jane, the girl he's still in love with, and it just goes off for the whole chapter about Jane, and he comes back, and says, "and so that's what I thought when I was sitting in the lobby in this vomity-looking chair"—just the way he goes all over the place and he goes so deep into the way he's thinking, and you just relate to that, I mean that's how it happens in life...chapter eleven...here it is (she reads):

> ...all of a sudden, on my way out to the lobby, I got old Jane Gallagher on the brain again. I got her on, and I couldn't get her off. I sat down in this vomity-looking chair in the lobby and thought about her and Stradlater sitting in that goddam Ed

231

Knowing Her Place

> Banky's car, and though I was pretty damn sure old Stradlater hadn't given her the time—I know old Jane like a book—I still couldn't get her off my brain. (Salinger, p. 76)

and then he just goes on and on and on...

...And this is probably my favorite part in the whole book...when they're out on the screened-in porch and it was the first time they had even got close to necking, and they didn't really, and it was raining, "raining like a bastard out" and

> ...all of a sudden this booze hound her mother was married to came out on the porch and asked Jane if there were any cigarettes in the house. I didn't know him too well or anything, but he looked like the kind of guy who wouldn't talk to you much unless he wanted something off you. He had a lousy personality. Anyway, Jane wouldn't answer him...she didn't even look up from the game. (Salinger, p. 78)

Jane just started crying. And he [Holden] talks about how this teardrop fell on a red square on the checkerboard, and how she just rubbed it in. And you can just see it so well, the way he describes it. So well. It makes me really feel the respect that he had for Jane, and how he cared for her, I dunno. You almost think he doesn't have any respect for anything else but her. Everything else, he just blows off. But she's the only thing he really cares about...well, except Phoebe [El pronounces this "foe-bee"], his sister. I love to hear him talking about his kid sister, and how she dances, and the little things about her that make him happy.

...Another scene that really gets to me is when he was in his sister's school, when he went to get Phoebe to tell her he was leaving, and he saw "fuck off" written on the wall, and he was so angry, he wanted to go and smash the guy who did it, that it was

Playing for Real

so horrible that little kids would see this...he was really protective of his little sister. I mean, she'd be seeing this, and all the innocence she had would be lost...

On Seeing Catcher in the Rye as a Film

Never. No way. Because I have got it so clearly in my head if it was on film it would ruin it, unless I was the one who made the film...I mean the only thing anyone ever says about him is Sally, and she talks about his crewcut, so I don't know what he looks like. He's probably not big, cause he was worrying about old Stradlater stretching his jacket, and he's tall, I think, and he has a little bit of grey hair, it says that somewhere. I see him, like now, how he would dress now, because I don't know what the fashion was then. Because you can see him now, it does relate now, it's timeless, really. Completely.

I mean I can't even think who I would have play him as an actor...I wouldn't. I couldn't. Because then it just turns all Holly-wood. I don't want to see it like that. Yuk! Tom Cruise as Holden Caulfield? If it was going to be a movie it would have to be someone young, not big, who had never played anything before. Everyone else has a reputation and that takes over their character in a lot of movies. Like the guy who plays Kramer on Seinfeld could never, ever, ever be anybody else. If you saw him in anything else you couldn't take him seriously. I mean, the character is too important here. I could see people I know playing Holden Caulfield, but not anybody well-known....I know he's tall, skinny, with short hair, not a crew cut, short at the back, kind of long at the front. With casual pants, button-up shirts. I can hear his voice in my head, but I could never describe it exactly. Kinda low, but not real deep.

Knowing Her Place

Reading and Re-Reading

When I first read the book, I was in seventh grade, and I finished the book and I was, like, so sad. Just because I want this person to be alive, to really exist, so that I could know them....when I finished the book, I thought, what do I do now? Because I just felt like I knew this person....I wanted him to be around to talk to. I think I was a little in love with him.

But the more I read it—like the last time I read it through was a while back—and I was more distanced from it, I think. I just felt he was too pissed off at everything, and that bothered me. Nothing pleased him....I've heard people say it's a really depressing sort of book, I don't find it that way, but I think the more I read it, the more I get out of it. Maybe the first time I read it I didn't really understand what he was going through. It was just a story, he was just a cool guy who did whatever he felt like doing....

He couldn't relate to society because he thought it was all bullshit. When you think about lonely and sad he must have been, he couldn't really enjoy life, and that's why he wanted to get away, that would be the only way he could deal with the stuff he was feeling. I think he probably went home and his parents probably did that, sent him to an institution, I mean...you become so close to Holden you wonder how he could end up there. Why is this guy, who is really a normal kid, who sees the world for the way it is, why should he end up put away? A lot of people would like to have the guts that Holden did, just to say screw it and leave school, and get away, but they don't. I dunno, he just sounds like an adolescent sounds, even now. He says "goddam" all the time. I just love that. He just says what he wants. And all these people he knows; they all represent different people in the teenage social structure. I know people like Stradlater. I'm friends with people like Holden.

Playing for Real

And I know people like Ackley—the guy with the mossy teeth—
people who have disgusting fingernails and stuff. I know these
people. Well, now I do. Maybe I didn't when I first read it when
I was younger.

...Sometimes I see all the negative stuff in Holden, and I just
want to tell him to smarten up...other times it seems as though
it's the complete truth. I'll probably go and read it again now
that we've talked about it. I think I re-read it because it sounds
realistic, and I would re-read it just for the section on Jane and
the tear on the checkerboard. That really struck me. It was just
so obvious that he cared about her so passionately. That really
gives him another dimension. And I re-read that and wondered
about the step-father and Jane, whether we were supposed to
take from that that there was some kind of abuse going on. It's
subtle, but it's there. And Holden's feelings of protectiveness
toward Jane. If you didn't re-read and see those things then he
wouldn't be a good character, he'd just be a joke. He'd just whip
around New York doing what he does and talking about what
happens to him, but he has another dimension. There's so many
people like that. They'd never tell their little sister what they're
thinking, like how much they really cared about her. I remember
the time at the end when he was so exhausted, and sick, I think,
and he was watching Phoebe going around and around the
carousel, he was so full of happiness he wanted to cry. He loved
her but didn't say. He didn't talk to Jane the whole time even
though he had the opportunity...he's deeper than you'd
expect...But last time I read it, I wondered actually if Holden
was homophobic. Remember at the end when he leaves his
drunk teacher's house so quickly? Who knows if the guy was
making a pass at him, but I think Holden thought so.... And
something else I noticed the last reading. Remember how he
went to see his teacher, Spencer, and old Spencer showed him

his terrible essay on the Egyptians? Well, at the end of the book, he's in the museum, and he starts telling these little kids all about the Egyptians, like he actually knows something about them. It's as though he finally found a use for all that information in real life. He becomes the teacher. You know what I mean? It's like he's in-between being a child and an adult, and when I re-read that, I could really see it.

On Playing

Every single person Holden meets is interesting. Like his professor, and the woman on the train. I just laughed at him telling her all those lies about her son.... Me and Nic have this routine that we do sometimes. It's sort of like Holden's. We act like I'm from Ireland and he's from Germany and we're just travelling around Nova Scotia, and we put on accents and have this great big story we tell people downtown. Even when I'm sitting next to people I imagine things I could be saying to them, but I don't. Remember when Holden was dancing with that girl and he told her she just missed seeing a movie star? That was so funny. I'd love to do that.

On Connecting with Male and Female Characters

A lot of my friends are male, I spend a lot of time with guys. I have friends who are girls, too, but I connect with guys more I think.... For music I choose mostly women artists. Sinead O'Connor...But I like older music and they're mostly male artists. Like Donovan, The Doors, Cream, The Beatles, Neil Young, America—I heard A Horse with No Name so much when I was young, about two years old. My dad would play it all the time, and *so I remember hearing it in my head for about a year.... It was my sister, though, who suggested I read Catcher. And my science teacher just freaked out when she saw I was reading it—she didn't read it until she was in university. I think she was just shocked because most people my age were reading the Babysitter's Club and Sweet Valley High books. I read those in grade five: they were, like, chewing-gum reading. Something to occupy your mind for a couple of hours. It's amazing the crap that girls are reading; those Sweet Valley High chicks are just so ridiculous, so horrible. I wish there was stuff for girls to read that wasn't so empty. Things you'd want to read, that would be interesting, but that would also make you think a little bit, maybe learn something. Instead of living in Sweet Valley and wishing for a convertible. I would never even think of re-reading those Sweet Valley High books, I mean, I'd throw up. They're so cliched. I like novels, and poetry, and stories where there is more interpretation and where your own experience comes into it.*

On Pulp Fiction

I liked the way the story was told —the storyline all jumbled. I liked the cinematography and the dialogue. It was both vulgar and smart. I liked the way the dialogue got into detail about little things. Like Vincent and Jules get into this big thing about Mia and foot massage outside the door of where they're supposed to pick up the briefcase. It had nothing to do with what they were there for, they just went on a rant. Like the kind of rant that Holden would go on. Into detail about little, everyday stuff.

I went not because of Travolta, but because everyone was raving about it. It scared me, actually, because of my reaction to the violence. Some of the violent scenes just were nothing, which made me wonder if I was overexposed to violence, they were brutal, but what got to me—when I really freaked out—was when Vincent was putting the needle into Mia's heart. You know, the adrenalin to revive her. I mean he was saving her life, not killing her like all the rest of the violence in the movie, but saving her, and that's the part that really affected me.

David

In the middle of the restaurant is a dance floor. A big sign on the wall states, "No shoes allowed." So wannabe beboppers (actually Melrose-types) do the twist in their socks or bare feet.

The picture windows don't look out on the street, but instead, B and W movies of 50's street scenes play behind them. The waitresses and waiters are made up as replicas of 50's icons: Marilyn Monroe, Zorro, James Dean, Donna Reed, Martin and Lewis, and the Philip Morris Midget wait on tables wearing appropriate costumes.

Vincent and Mia study the menu in a booth made out of a red '59 Edsel. Buddy Holly (their waiter) comes over, sporting big button on his chest that says: "Hi, I'm buddy, pleasing you pleases me."

Buddy: Hi I'm Buddy, what can I get 'cha?
Vincent: I'll have the Douglas Sirk steak.
Buddy: How do you want it, burnt to a crisp, or bloody as hell?
Vincent: Bloody as hell. And to drink, a vanilla coke.
Buddy: How about you, Peggy Sue?
Mia: I'll have the Durwood Kirby burger—bloody—and a five-dollar shake.
Buddy: How d'ya want that shake, Martin and Lewis or Amos and Andy?
Mia: Martin and Lewis

Vincent takes a look around the place. The Yuppies are dancing,

---

the diners are biting into big, juicy hamburgers, and the icons are playing their parts. Marilyn is squealing, the Midget is paging Philip Morris, Donna Reed is making her customers drink their milk, and Dean and Jerry are acting like fools.

Mia: Whaddya think?
Vincent: It's like a wax museum with a pulse rate.

—Quentin Tarantino, *Pulp Fiction*
(http://colargol.idb.hi.a/tarantino/pulpscript)

Why David Likes Pulp Fiction

I thought it was hilarious. And I really liked the way Tarantino messed with linear structure and chopped up the film...that was just not done in any movies I have ever seen. Plus I fell in love with John Travolta—he was just wicked; it was his comeback movie. Plus the writing was really good. You know, the dialogue about nothing.

Often in movies, every word that someone says is critically important, you know, very, very significant. This was just casual conversation between guys...what they said was important, because it added to their characters or added to the scene, but it didn't have life or death consequences. Like John Travolta describing his trip to Amsterdam, talking with his partner:

...you'd really like it cause you can get a glass of beer at McDonald's. And you know what they call a quarter pounder with cheese at McDonald's?

You mean they don't call it a quarter pounder with cheese?

No man, they got the metric system. They wouldn't know what the fuck a quarter pounder is. What do they call it? Royale with cheese.

239

Knowing Her Place

> Royale with cheese?
>
> Yeah, Royale with cheese.

Later on, they go:

> You want some bacon?
>
> No man, I don't eat pork.
>
> What, you Jewish or something?
>
> No man, I just don't dig on swine.
>
> Yeah, but bacon tastes good, pork chops taste good.
>
> Yeah, it might taste like pumpkin pie, but I'd never know 'cause I wouldn't eat the filthy motherfucker. Pigs eat and root and shit; pigs are filthy animals.

..and they go on like that. This is right after Jules has found redemption because of some divine intervention where this guy hauled off and fired six shots from a hand cannon and missed them. But he's not talking about how he's found god, or how he's going to leave and find his true path, or nothing like that, he's talkin about bacon...you know what I mean? It's really well done. It's really laid back. It's hilarious.

On Having a Point

...There's Forrest Gump. *Where every word brought you closer to feeling compassion for Forrest Gump. Where you're really manipulated. But then there's TV, like* Seinfeld, *and all these new Generation X TV shows like* Friends *or the* Single Guy, Caroline in the City, *talking about nothing. Larry David and Jerry*

240

Playing for Real

Seinfeld came up with the idea of a show about nothing, and it's made millions. And that's what it is. Just casual encounters and funny situations. It doesn't have to follow a direct plot line. It doesn't have to be boy meets girl, stuff like that. It's just everyday life. That's what it showed in Pulp Fiction. *Just the everyday, underground life of two second rate gangsters. They might be a little more philosophical than most, but...*

I'm not part of Generation X, but I think these guys (Generation Xers) are sick of always having a plot line, or sick of things always having an inner meaning. I think every show has a point. But I don't think that it has to be a big one. I think life is like that. It doesn't always have a big point. Just lots of little ones.

On the Writer / Director

People just write what they know...all Quentin Tarantino knows is a whole bunch of movies, so I dunno, if you lived in Iceland you wouldn't write about the desert. Obviously Tarantino had a vast knowledge about certain kinds of movies. That's why he hasn't done a romance film, cause he really liked gangster films.

He's like a geek. It's not the same old, same old, let's cast Arnold Schwarzennegger where we can make a million dollars cause it's a film where we blow up everything. And it's not a Disney cartoon borrowed from a book. He's coming up with original stuff. Pulp Fiction *was never a book.*

...Pulp Fiction...ten cents. Book format...cheap entertainment, you know? Maybe the movie has some similarities with those old novels, not that he's borrowed from them, but it's not like Harlequin Romances. The entertainment value. They're second rate gangsters.

241

Knowing Her Place

On Fiction and Reality

I think it's a portrayal of that kind of life, but it's not real life, cause real life isn't like that. People want to see real life, but they want to see it done more cleverly and more exciting. They don't want to see it done over the top—at least I don't—I want to see it as close to reality, but still far away. That's a paradox, isn't it. It's an impossible reality, I guess.

On Cultural Texts

I mean, I understood all those things in the restaurant scene. Mamie Van Doren, cherry cokes, all that. I mean, I didn't live in the 50's, so I don't really know it, but I think the media has taught me to know what all that is, even though I didn't live it. So I could place it right away.

On Viewing and Re-Viewing: The Text Becomes Real

It certainly boosted my interest in movie-making and being in films. About that time I was in a lull, I didn't know if I was going to continue in theatre, I didn't know if I was going to study film, and then seeing that movie...it was like, ohmygod, this is something entirely new.... I liked it more when I got to see it more, when I was able to talk about it more, when I was able to share it more with my friends. I probably wouldn't have liked the movie as much if I was the only person I knew who saw it. My close friends and I got the sound track which was a kick-ass soundtrack which also added to my love for the film because there were excerpts from the movie on the soundtrack, which I memorized. Gave me a

242

greater appreciation for music at that time. One of Jules' lines, for example, is "That's all right...that's Cool 'n' the Gang."

We even went so far as to do our own Pulp Fiction *movie, Simon and I. We went downtown to an apartment building and did the scene about the foot massage. We took the video camera from Simon's house, decided to look for an old building that looked kind of 70's, carpeted and all that, we found a place on Queen, went up to one of the floors and asked Simon's sister to film us. We walked around, we were dressed up, and then we went downstairs and did the scene about Royale with cheese. It's just something we wanted to do, we weren't interested in making this whole movie or anything.*

Then we did the play at school which I directed. It intrigued me. I loved that script. The dialogue made the characters and the characters were wicked. I found the script on the Internet, printed off sections that I wanted. I would have printed off other sections but I couldn't because it was for the school, couldn't contain "motherfucker" and all that. I had to be selective. It was too bad, because I had to leave out some of the best scenes, like the foot massage one because it was talking about, like, oral sex.

Ross and I still want to put Pulp Fiction *in its linear order and see what kind of movie it turns out to be. It could totally suck.*

On Identities and the Future

There's always fantasy, like it would be cool to be Vincent Vega, to be like those guys. There's nothing more I want right now than to live in the big city. I want to live in a city, to know the goings-on, to be able to walk out my front door, and be there. But do it outside Canada. There's times when I would like to be Quentin Tarantino. To have made it.

Knowing Her Place

...*I hate Canadian movies. I know they are deeper, have more meaning, win all these awards, but that's not the attraction for me...I mean if I were in Canadian music, I would stay here. Canadian music rules. Our music business is the best. Canadian music—that's where it's at nowadays. But not our movie industry. It's too boring.*

I'm attracted to the fame, I guess, and you won't get that in Canada. It's not exciting enough here. I'm not just talking about Pulp Fiction *now. I'm talking about my life. I want my life to be exciting. To mean something.*

On Performing

Quentin Tarantino seems like us. Hanging around making films. Hanging out with friends. Our conversations are like that kind of dialogue. Or like Seinfeld. *I mean, maybe we're mocking them, but...we joke around with each other. A lot of our dialogue we borrow from* Pulp Fiction, *from shows, and stuff—that's the way we live our interactive life with each other. I mean I might live differently with my parents, or with Cheryl, but when I'm with all my friends together I'm being myself but I'm also performing, and everyone is. Cause we're all putting on our cool show for each other. We borrow from PF and are funny. We argue about nothing and are funny. Like Ross will go, hey, I like your shoes, let's just say. And I go, yeah, man, they ARE the shoes. And Ross will say, Oh, they ARE the shoes. And then we just go off talking about shoes. Just think of a situation and we'd try to one-up each other, playing, not like competition, but to try to come up with better lines. One-up each other.*

I think teenagers do this. Adults are adults and they have lived a lot of their life, and they've had time to mature, develop

244

Playing for Real

into a person, and I know they keep learning, but teenagers are so impressionable. And we're like borrowing from everything we see that we think is cool. I mean, like maybe this will fit on me. This will look cool on me; this kind of conversation, this kind of attitude. According to what we think is cool at that time. Your favorite song might be from the 60's but mine is still changing. You've lived your life, and although it's not close to over, your adolescence and your young life has, and you might have lots of great songs, and you hear new songs, but you always have your favorites. Right now, I'm picking my favorites. I'm trying out new personalities from different sources, whether it be Pulp Fiction, *or some other movie, or a television show, and if I think it's cool, maybe I'll try it out and maybe it will be me. Then again, maybe it won't be me, but it will stay with me, and so that adds to my personality, and so I also have that little facet of me, because I use it as knowledge. So by doing this my whole life I kinda gain a personality or a way of being.*

...I think certain attributes of mine are going to remain the same. I think I'm a funny person, and I know I'm not very good at listening. I've always talked a lot and I don't think that will change. I think you just change according to your surroundings, your age, your experiences, but that core personality that you start out with is still there.

...I don't think you ever lose anything as a person. It all helps to make up who you are. Maybe, like with Travolta, you gain his coolness, but then by gaining the coolness you've added his arrogance, which means you've lost your kindness which you used to have. But maybe it's not lost, maybe it's buried underneath there, underneath this John Travolta mask you're wearing...

...For a lot of time I even had my hair like Travolta. I don't think that twenty years from now I could look back on Vincent Vega, and say, how could I ever have liked him? I think he's super

cool. If you can look back and it still intrigues you, still draws you in, still makes it happen for you then it's part of you. For me, though, it's both Vincent and John Travolta. I couldn't think this way if it had been Tom Hanks.

On *Catcher in the Rye*

When I read that I walked around for a week annoyed at people because all they were doing was bullshitting. Everyone seemed to be so phony. Holden was a character I really liked but he didn't touch me personally, not like Vincent. Holden gave me an insight into how some teenagers live and think, but that's about it. That's the only book that ever touched me in a way. I'm not a book kinda guy anyway. I don't like to read. I like movies and films. And music.

El and David On Teachers and Teaching

David: *I read...not very much, to be honest. I read the newspaper.*

El: *...I will read the global news I know about. The other day I read something that concerns what I've been learning about in history this year with Mr. M.*

David: *Bosnia, and all that.*

El: *Yeah. I read something about Communism, too, which interested me. I never would have read before.*

David: *Uh, and lately, I have been reading a lot of stuff off the Internet.*

El: *I don't do that because I don't have a computer.*

David: *I'll find something I'm interested in, like a Beastie Boy interview, or* Rolling Stone *kind of stuff,* Spin, Skateboarding *magazine. The* Pulp Fiction *script...*

246

Playing for Real

El: *But..school comes first for me. So that if I have two options, like a book for English or* Spin *magazine, I will read the book...*

David: Spin *will always be there, but the English paper's due tomorrow.... But, you know, even though we have no more history seminars, cause it's exam time now, I still think I'd read something on Bosnia.*

El: *...the interest is sparked...It's our history class. I learned so much I didn't know...I mean, Mr. M....*

David: *He rocks!*

El: *Mr. M, we love you!*

David: *I learned a lot last year in history—about Roman times and that—but this year is so much more useful knowing how political and social things got to be the way they are because of events fifty years ago....*

El: *Like I never knew what a Fascist pig was...*

David: *I knew the name Mussolini, but until we had Mr. M, I used to think he was like this Italian mobster, from Sicily who killed guys...*

El: *Amazing the conclusions you come up with yourself.*

David: *I find out he was the first Fascist leader. And here I thought he was Jimmy Hoffa, or the Godfather.... Mr. M gives us amazing detail...*

El: *Yeah, he's still so passionate about it. He's been teaching the same course for sixteen years....and he still LOVES it....*

David: *And he's so powerful...he stands up there and he's so into it...*

El: *And he knows all the good gossip behind stuff.*

David: *Exactly. Details that just make it more interesting. Cause he makes it so personal....*

El: *He just talks all the time. He gets so excited. We can watch*

a film strip. We get two sentences into a woman
talking about something and....he goes "AND—" and
then he'll start into talking.

David: And he stops the film sometimes. "I forgot to tell you
something," he'll say...

El: We watched one filmstrip for five days! We never got
through it!

David: When a teacher is passionate like that it's a lot easier to
learn because, for instance, my English teacher—
who is actually the band teacher—she doesn't seem
like she gives two shits about anything....I asked her
something once, remember El?—

El: Yeah, I remember...she said...I dunno, and I don't care....

David: Yeah, I dunno, and I don't care. I'm like, ooo-kay...I love
English, I've always loved English, but this year I
don't care so much about it because she is so bored
herself...

El: In grade nine, I had a fifty in English, and then in grade
ten a ninety-eight. I mean, c'mon, there has to be
something in the way that you're taught....When you
have a teacher who cares, then you want to work for
them, you want to perform well for them because
they're such good teachers..

David: I had Mr. H. last year in English and I thought was such
a cool teacher I spent, like, 100 percent of the time
trying to impress the guy. I ended up with a ninety in
English...this year, I know I'm going to end up with
a low mark in English, when I shouldn't....

El: Well, you can't blame all on the teacher. But it does affect
your motivation.

David: ...I'm not motivated so I don't bother passing it in on
time, and so I get late marks...another is our drama

teacher, Mr. R.

El: *He didn't even know our names.... I remember he would do roll call and he'd go...this blank look, uh, Eleanor? and look around squinting, trying to find out...who I was. Well, it's obvious he doesn't care...so we don't care. Nobody memorized any lines for their plays, except for yours, David....this is what I mean. Today, in my history exam, I wrote eleven foolscap pages—*

David: *—I could have easily written for four hours in that history exam. I could have written twenty pages if I had time.... You don't even keep track cause you're into it so much..*

El: *I didn't even notice the time—*

David: *—My writing hand is sore...*

El: *Me, too...*

David: *In history this year, in Mr. M's class, we'd have about a seven page paper due bi-weekly, on what we are doing at that time. Also, and this is actually not so fun, we had to do the seminar paper before we got taught about the subject...*

El: *But I think that's cool. It teaches us how to do research. It's hard as hell, but you learn.*

David: *And when you go to class you already know something. And so when Mr. M starts to talk you already have the background information....and then we also have tests, and checklists, and stuff. I find all the work in history easy, we do, El and I, because we like it....*

El: *Yeah, he challenges us, but not in a way that, you know, is like trying to stump the students, play guessing games.*

David: *He doesn't do that cause he doesn't need to. You need teachers who are specialized, like him....*

El: *Who can answer questions that aren't on their little sheet.*

David: *Teachers shouldn't be the kind of person who has the book with all the answers at the back. You know what I mean? The teachers' edition. You got to have Mr. M. who knows everything there is to know about modern history...and you need Ms. M who is an actual artist...*

El: *...who went to art school...*

David: *And you need an English teacher like Ms. A. or Mr. H. and who have experienced life.... Mr. H. has been in Vietnam...he's been a hippie...he's seen world change...he was there when the Berlin wall came down, for example...*

El: *Interesting experiences at least....a teacher's life shouldn't affect how we learn, but it does. When you know somebody has a flair for life, they obviously have a flair for other things.... I know personally that I want to live, and I want to do stuff, and that I want to tell people about what I've learned and what I know, and that I'm excited about life...*

The Narrator on Implications for Teachers and Teaching

1. How do we as educators continue to reinforce the dualities in our thinking about literacy and learning, and how can we soften or erase those boundaries to make literacy learning more consistent with daily lifelong learning? Such dualities include teacher/student, private/public, society/individual, reality /fiction, curriculum/common knowledge, school/home, among others. El and David remind me, for example, that their on-going

curriculum is the lives they lead; that they make texts real for themselves, that they teach one another and can teach their teachers, that they will explore learning, grow in their literacy, and dream their dreams in settings often much more influential than school settings. What important paths to learning are we blocking off at the school door? How can we learn to listen to that learning and bring it into school settings and curricula?

2. How do we as educators write our role as arbiters and gate-keepers of texts inside the school walls? How can we make multiple (and possibly contentious—even questionable) texts from all media, including all relevant cultural texts, available to students? Can we bring in such texts without rendering such texts unappealing to students simply because we've appropriated them for the classroom? Where can we draw the line between responsible stewardship and censorship?

3. As a listener, I made little attempt to challenge, question, or approve/disapprove of the commentary provided by El and David. My goal was to listen to their perspectives on literacy in their lives, and later, when they revealed the primacy of certain texts, to have them elaborate on the ways they thought about and used these texts, and to represent those elaborations accurately in their eyes. In this way, I chose a conventionally constructivist stance as a researcher to hear the adolescents' perspectives. As an educator, however, I can extend such a study to support the development of students' critical literacy by engaging in conversations which invite El and David to examine these texts more closely. I can initiate conversations which invite critical reading and support their examination and critique of cultural assumptions. In fact, I have already taken up the opportunity with David and El to begin such critical readings. (Had the study been explicitly educative, I would also have encouraged mutual agenda-

setting throughout).

Nudging students into critical reading of texts invites such questions as the following: What cultural myths do these texts reproduce? What gender stereotypes do they reinforce or disrupt? Whose value systems do these texts represent and which are their intended audiences? What alternative readings are possible here? Whose perspectives are unvoiced or silenced, left unrepresented? Which assumptions are tacit, presented as a given, without thought to their effects on certain individuals, groups, or populations? What counts as racist, sexist, classist and who decides? How are each of these texts political? What power does each have and how is that power enacted or enforced?

4. How can we support play, role-playing, and the process of taking up identities in school in ways that honor the complexity of adolescents' lives? In what ways are we perpetuating the very logocentrism of schools (reading and writing print) and ignoring the many ways of knowing which tap into adolescents' learning and lives? In other words, how can we re-think curricula and school structure in ways that mirror the spirit of play and performance in adolescent life? In our own lives?

5. What role do we play as educators in living literate, enriching lives, and how can we make visible our passion for our work? How can we guard against just "doing our job" (relying on routine tasks and invoking institutional requirements merely to survive) and yet not fall victim to burn-out? How can we find ways to grow professionally and personally in order to maintain that "flair for life" (El) and learning which brought us into teaching in the first place? Further, how can we make visible the contextualized nature of our work so that students see us as individuals in context, not solo performers?

Epilogue

This study was undertaken to hear the voices of adolescents talk about texts, literacy, and learning. The monologues and dialogue tell us much about these adolescents, and perhaps, as teachers and educators, we hear the voices of other adolescents resonating in the words of El and David. While these students are not representative of all adolescents, to be sure, nor is this study meant to generalize based upon these observations, we do see similar themes recurring which define adolescent identity-building and literate activity.

Texts are symbolic resources for these two; they are imaginative possibilities, sometimes a costume, and sometimes a mask. Texts house dreams, too, and El and David dream through *Catcher* and *Pulp Fiction*. If I "read" them one way, I can read El's dreams as including the romance story; her reaction to the teardrop scene—through which Holden reveals his love for Jane—seems to indicate her wish to be loved the same way. (It is significant that Nic, her current boyfriend, is known for his anti-establishment beliefs). The admiration she has for Holden's love for his sister, Phoebe, also seem to show the centrality in her life of human values such as caring, preservation of the innocent, and the male's role as protector. Watching *Pulp Fiction*, El is struck most, for example, by the moment where Vincent's violent act (a needle plunged in the heart) revives Mia, the only female of significance in the movie, and one playing a supporting role.

If I "read" El's dreams another way, I can imagine her wish to have the freedom and flexibility that Holden has—and perhaps which many males share—to live his life the way he wishes, if only for a couple of days. El's stated wish to live an exciting life is consistent with her enjoyment of a character who has created his own excitement. Yet we are left to wonder whether she sees herself playing the lead role in her life, as Holden seems to do, or to play a supporting role on stage with a man. Does her text, like that of Viola in Shakespeare's *Twelfth Night*, rest "in the bosom" of another? Further, is El forced, because of lack of options in school, to see life through the curtain of male protagonists and male leads?

El dislikes anything that has "gone Hollywood," a phrase she seems to associate with inauthenticity and phoneyness. Her love for reading and writing propel her to use literacy to pursue what she believes to be authentic, particularly through journal writing and reading of poetry and novels. But, left without adult support in this goal, she typically finds male-centered texts to fuel her interest; what would happen if she found similarly strong and vivid female characters? (She once mentioned her youthful admiration of the Roald Dahl character Mathilda, which suggests to me her iconoclastic tendencies, and makes me, as an educator, want to seek out similar characters for her). As of this writing, I have begun to offer reading material to El— work by Eudora Welty, Alice Walker, Maya Angelou, Karen Connelly, among other well-known Canadian and American writers—material whose characters and lives show the range of women's experiences, including strong and compassionate roles for women. El has eagerly accepted these, and when she called today she mentioned how much she is enjoying Connelly's *A Thai Journal*. The English curriculum for her senior year does not look, at this point, to represent perspectives other than male Eurocentric perspectives, and so I will keep in touch with El, offering to pass along books or to assist her in any of her assignments.

David's dreams are made explicit: for this year, at least, he wants to be famous. He is unabashedly frank in his admiration of Travolta, Tarantino, and the character Vincent Vega, seeing them perhaps as role models to emulate, as symbolic resources to try on identities. Consistent with the social construction of masculinities, David dreams of having the power and control that his role models enjoy. David's observations seem to write the story of the hero, the master of his fate.

Just as I was struck by El's unassisted analysis of Holden's character, I am struck by David's candor and insight about his identity-building. He seems remarkably open about himself, at least for the purposes of this study. (As a parent and educator, I admit a certain alarm that cultural values such as the male posturing and Generation X dialogue are the stuff of his identity-building). David's role-playing is conscious and intentional, and very public. More so than El, he seems "never out of (his) text" (*Twelfth Night*). Further, as he re-reads he seems not to see more deeply into the text, as does El with her analysis of *Catcher*, but rather he uses the re-readings to memorize the roles, to master the nuances toward better performance. (This might also be explained by the obvious: that because Holden is a male living male cultural constructions, El cannot take up his behavior as easily as David can take up Vincent's behavior). Although David espouses anti-sexist and anti-racist practices in school and society, his re-reading of the film does not include a condemnation of what others see as its racist or sexist elements. When David and I had a follow-up conversation, he claimed that teachers, because of their role as sources of knowledge for students, must guard against racist and sexist practices. Filmmakers, however, are merely "showing real life, and real life is sexist and racist."

When pressed further about the ways in which inequities are perpetuated in this way, David denies that interpretation, claiming instead that an observant viewer will see beyond the racist and sexist elements. He does not want to engage in alternative readings.

Both El and David recognize the critical role that teachers play in their learning. But while both rave about their history teacher, a man whose passion for his subject is obviously infectious and educative, neither seems to question the man's reliance on performance as his principal teaching style. Neither seems to see teachers in a broader context, as members of a system which may constrain them as individuals; as a result, to them, the teacher's performance and personality become front and center in their estimation.

Clearly, then, we can open possibilities for students' engagements with texts, and for re-writing and re-reading their lives, if we use our roles as educators and mentors to help them develop alternative readings: of culture, of schools and teachers, of curricula, of print and visual media, of all texts in their lives. Playing for real is a process that creates roles for the future, and, since the roles of the past have been limiting and constraining for many, we must all—students and teachers—begin preparing now to write them anew.

References

Aisenberg, N., & Harrington, M. (1988). *Women in academe: Outsiders in the sacred grove.* Amherst, MA: University of Massachusetts Press.

Baker, C.D. & Luke, A. (eds). (1991). *Towards a critical sociology of reading pedagogy.* Philadelphia, PA: John Benjamins Publishing Company

Benet's Reader's Encyclopedia. (1987). 3rd edition. New York: Harper & Row.

Biskin, P. (1994). An auteur is born. *Premiere Magazine.* Online at http://colargol.idb.hi.a/tarantino/pulpscript

Bleich, D. (1986). Gender interests in reading and language. In Flynn, E.A., & Schweickart, P.P. (Eds). *Gender and reading: Essays on readers, texts, and contexts*. Baltimore, MD: Johns Hopkins University Press, pp. 234-266.

Brownstein, R. (1982). *Becoming a heroine: Reading about women in novels*. New York: The Viking Press.

Buckingham, D., & Sefton-Green, J. (1994). *Cultural studies goes to school*. London, UK: Taylor & Francis.

Butler, J. (1990). *Gender trouble: Feminism and the subversion of identity*. New York: Routledge.

Cherland, M.R., & Edelsky, C. (1993). Girls and reading: The desire for agency and she horror of helplessness in fictional encounters. In, Christian-Smith, L. (Ed) *Texts of desire: Essays on fiction, femininity and schooling*. London, UK: Falmer Press.

Connell, R.W. (1987). *Gender and power*. Sydney, Australia: Allen & Unwin.

Cook, J.A., & Fonow, M.M. (1990). Knowledge and women's interests: Issues of epistemology and methodology in feminist sociological research. In Nielsen, J. (Ed). *Feminist research methods*. Denver, CO: Westview Press.

Davies, B. (1994). *Poststructuralist theory and classroom practice*. Geelong, Australia: Deakin University Press.

Davies, B. (1993). *Shards of glass: Children reading and writing beyond gendered identities*. Sydney, Australia: Allen & Unwin.

Denzin, N. (1996). *Interpretive ethnography: Ethnographic practices for the 21st century*. Thousand Oaks, CA: Sage.

Fausset, R. (Undated). Trying to be the shepherd: Commentary on Pulp Fiction. Http://www.altx.com/io/pulpfiction.html

Finders, M. (1996a). "Just girls": literacy and allegiance in junior high school. *Written Communication*, 13 (1): 93- 129.

Finders, M. (1996b). Queens and teen zines: Early adolescent females reading their way toward adulthood. *Anthropology and Education Quarterly*, 27 (1): 71-89.

Fish, S. (1980). *Is there a text in this class?* Cambridge, MA: Harvard University Press.

Fiske, J. (1989). *Reading the popular*. London, UK: Routledge.

Frank, B. (1993). Straight/strait jackets for masculinity: Educating for "real" men. *Atlantis*, (18), Nos. 1 & 2, 47-59.

Gilbert, P. (1994). And they lived happily ever after: Cultural storylines and the construction of gender. In Haas Dyson, A., & Genishi, D. (eds). *The need for story: Cultural diversity in classroom and community*. Urbana, IL: National Council of Teachers of English.

Grumet, M. (1988). *Bitter milk: Women and teaching*. Amherst, MA: University of Massachusetts Press.

Haas Dyson, A. (1994). The ninjas, the X-men, and the ladies: Playing with power and identity in an urban primary school. *Teachers College Record*, 96 (2), Winter, 1994, 219-240.

Hellman, L. (1973). *Pentimento*. New York: Signet.

Hirsch, E.D. (1967). *Validity in interpretation*. New Haven, CT: Yale University Press.

Hoffman, E. (1989). *Lost in translation*. New York: Penguin.

Jenkins, H. (1992). *Textual poachers*. New York: Routledge.

Juhasz, S. (1994). *Reading from the heart*. New York: Penguin Books.

Kamler, B. (1993). Constructing gender in the writing process classroom. *Language Arts*, 70, 95-103.

MacNeil, L. (1988). *Contradictions of control*. New York: Routledge.

Martin, M., & Porter, M. (1995). *Video Movie Guide 1996*. New York: Ballantine Books.

Moss, G. (1995). Rewriting reading. In Holland, J., & Blair, M. (Eds). *Debates and issues in feminist research and pedagogy*. Clevedon, UK: The Open University.

Neilsen, L. (1993). Exploring reading: Mapping the personal text. In Straw, S., & Bogdan, D. (Eds). *Constructing reading*. Portsmouth, NH: Boynton/Cook.

Neilsen, L. (1989). *Literacy and living*. Portsmouth, NH: Heinemann Educational Books.

Robinson, K. (1992). Classroom discipline: Power, resistance and gender. A look at teacher perspectives. *Gender and Education*, 4 (3), 273-287.

Rogers, A.G. (1993). Voice, play and a practice of ordinary courage in girls' and women's lives. *Harvard Educational Review*, 63 (3), Fall, 1993: 265-295.

Rosenblatt, L. (1978). *The reader, the text, the poem: A transactional theory of the reading process*. Carbondale, IL: Southern Illinois University Press.

Playing for Real

Salinger, J.D. (1951). *The catcher in the rye*. New York: Bantam.

Tarantino, Q. (1994). *Pulp fiction*. Miramax films.

Vygotsky, L.S. (1962). *Thought and language*. Cambridge, MA: MIT Press.

Walkerdine, V. (1990). *Schoolgirl fictions*. London, UK: Verso.

—10—
Notes on Painting Ghosts and Writing the Poetry Report:
Some Things I Know But Not for Certain

Knowledge, however mundane and utilitarian, plays about in linguistic images and forms cultural practice.
—Toni Morrison, 1992, p. 49

The body is in the text of everyday life; by enacting that text it becomes not a product, but the processor of everyday life.
—Cranny-Francis, 1995, p. 113

Somewhere Out There, which was my youthful awareness of the world of knowledge and my outsider relationship to that world, no longer exists for me as merely an external space, a separate unknown. Everything we know is at once out there and in here, as is everything we will come to know. My place is to apprentice myself to the world, to paraphrase Merleau-Ponty, not in subservience and compliance, as the androcentric practices we have followed would keep me, but in reciprocity, curiosity, and response-ability. What we must seek are the transgressive experiences and the fresh words which reveal us, in Annie Dillard's words, "startlingly to ourselves as creatures set down here bewildered" (Dillard, 1989, p. 73).

Knowing Her Place

My perspectives on inquiry, just like my perspectives on feminism, have been variously monolithic, binary, constructivist, foundational/essentialist, and fractured, depending on whose terminology we use. However, like many researchers, my changes have resulted in my gaining research "literacies," complex and emergent understandings of inquiry in a post-everything world. Time and inculturation have combined to make inquiry a terrain where I live, rather than a place I visit on occasion. Inquiry is less a stance and more an intentional gesture, a re-bodied approach to working with people, particularly women, on projects which matter to them locally and globally. Inquiry is a conspiracy, a breathing together, for which we need the conditions of being "together" and sharing a climate, or air, for breathing. Inquiry values, rather than fears difference, sees contiguity or complementarity as necessary for working together without suppressing our diversity.

Working in the field of literacy research, we see changes in the field as we see changes in ourselves and our practice. The study and the applications of research methods has taken me from experimental work using statistical analyses into various approaches to qualitative research toward feminist inquiry practices (Campbell & Stanley, 1963; Carr & Kemmis, 1986; Denzin & Lincoln, 1994; Goetz & LeCompte, 1984; Guba & Lincoln, 1981; Holland, Blair, & Sheldon, 1995; McCarl Nielsen, 1990; Neilsen, 1997, 1993a, 1993b, 1993c, 1990, 1989, 1981; Schatzman & Strauss, 1973; Spradley, 1980; Stanley & Wise, 1993), each of which have refined and honed my understanding of my relationship to people, phenomena, and the work of the world. Discussions, observations, and theoretical commentary on methodologies (Fine, 1992; Gitlin, 1994, 1990; Guba & Lincoln, 1981; Mies, 1993; Mishler, 1990) continue to make the research enterprise problematic, and pose the challenge of knowing and articulating my ideas in relation to the ideas of others.

Both the practice of following method and the practice of taking stances on methodological theorizing can create a Bakhtinian tension: ideas and methods invite focus, centering, normalizing, cohering, reifying and replicating practices, often dangerously. Yet inquiry itself, its products and its processes, "spin outward, multiply, refuse to mesh with a hegemonic center" (Yaeger, 1991, p. 242). It is this centrifugal force, a destabilizing force which researchers have feared and which we now invite. The destabilizing turn might be named feminist perhaps, or post-modern. The name matters less than the intention, the inclination to openness and growth, to take risks, to create critical spaces. When we make the assumptions and the norms of research problematic, we make the assumptions and the norms of life together on this planet problematic as well. We begin to dismantle the Western knowledge project, and we begin to learn a fundamental humility. Expanding our research literacies keeps us full of wonder, in spite of the shaky ground and the shadows. We can learn more when our pen is a tool of discovery, not domination.

The research literacies I have gained are, by dint of my unique experiences, idiosyncratic; yet the ontological and epistemological waters in which these literacies continue to develop are social, political, ecological. Growing into and away from systems of ideas and thought collectives gives me both the freedom and the responsibility to articulate the dilemmas and the serendipitous discoveries along the inquiry journey. To do this is to take stock; it is also to reach out to others whose lives are devoted to inquiry. Re-imagining inquiry is re-imagining ways to work with people and ideas which keep us, like the painter, the dancer, and the performance artist, watchfully poised, momentarily still, and yet fluidly in motion.

Knowing Her Place

The words inquiry and research are almost inter-changeable for me. "Research" typically connotes boundaries of location, of time, and perhaps of method, as in "a research project"; "inquiry" has always suggested an inquisitive, integrative and responsive approach to learning and to life. Both words refer to systematic investigation; both processes, to me, are educative. As one who loves language, I might want to define carefully the differences, but instead, I resist that precision, preferring instead to leave their meanings fluid. Mishler (1990) makes a distinction between "the dominant model of hypothesis-testing experimentation," which he calls research, and his preferred term, "inquiry-guided" research, which sees variants of qualitative and interpretive approaches explicitly acknowledging and relying "on the dialectic interplay of theory, methods, and findings over the course of a study" (416). The assumption that inquiry is recursive and reflexive, an interplay of shifting semiotic processes, is an assumption I share with many, regardless of the terms we use. Re-search. Search, search again. Inquire, enquire. Ask. Watch. Learn. Research is the attuned mind/body working purposefully to explore, to listen, to support, to transgress, to gather with care, to create, to disrupt, and to offer back, to contribute, sometimes all at once.

Some things I know are these: inquiry is autobiographical, ecological, artistic. The degree to which inquiry opens us to connection and transcendence may also be its spiritual promise. Remaining open to the dimensions of inquiry, we continue to cultivate wisdom and transcend our biases through an ongoing de/reconstructive process. Our research literacies create more critical spaces, and what we think we know for certain must remain open.

Notes on Painting Ghosts

1. Autobiographical

Just as literate behavior has its own fingerprint, formed in the all-round growth of the individual in particular social, political and cultural climates, the way we approach inquiry and the agendas and issues in which we become engaged are unique. Others may or may not share the goals, depending on the degree of overlap of our particular interrelational contexts; but the questions which concern us arise from the experiences and issues in which we have been immersed. As individuals, we work from many locations, but the qualities of those locations may recede or gain primacy depending on the purposes and the sites of inquiry; and further, these may not be the identities which bring us to certain research agenda. My "good girl/good student" upbringing at home and at school, for example, must be considered when I recall the fierce attention to compliance and to "doing it right" for my first research project (Neilsen & Piche, 1981). I chose controllable ground.

The fear of emotion, passion, and intimacy characteristic of my largely Euro-centric heritage, but also of my birth family, has undoubtedly played a role in my decision to jump headlong into searching and recognizing traditionally "messy" and "female" issues in inquiry, and my ongoing struggle with integrating head and heart, mind and body. A need to understand myself, given my own family pathologies, has combined with my prairie upbringing to push me, finally, away from sheltered ground toward the wilderness of inquiry approaches I can not map, nor control (yet I am bound, in many ways still, to the demands of the "sacred grove" of the academy (Aisenberg & Harrington, 1988)). A project involving the politicizing of secretaries in a government workplace (Neilsen, 1993b) pushed me to praxis. At the time of the study, I was moving away from the need to identify with male authority, a need common for women academics, toward a position where I could name myself as feminist publicly.

"Autobiography, the structuring and voicing of experience, offers a route to the examination of the particularity and the partiality of knowing and telling, characteristics of both the living and the relaying of experiences" (Kelly, 1993, p. 84). Whether we write our stories, make explicit the autobiographic impulse or not, our actions in the world must certainly be marked by our unique particularity and partiality, our process of being who we are by doing what we do. Inquiry is such a process. For most of us, our inquiry efforts have been adopted as a result of our academic inculturation and our personal passions. For women, in particular, the desires to contribute, to be heard, and to become a member of an exciting and purposeful community are common themes. Each one of us takes these desires to a unique, individual place, and yet our work remains gendered, and in community. As Miller (1991) notes: feminism has "made it possible to see that the personal is also the theoretical; the personal is theory's material" (21).

Most important, too, is the recognition Joy James, an African American theorist, makes about the autobiographical impulse in our theory-making. When our work is grounded in our stories and our lives, we are "pulled off the sidelines as spectators and consumers" toward our role as actors. Autobiographical theorizing tends to discourage the objectifying and appropriating that marks the world of knowledge-making and research; as James notes, this appropriation is particularly insidious and dangerous for women of color and under-represented groups in the academy. (1996, p. 39).

Countless researchers (Frank, 1995; Kelly, 1993; Pinar, 1994; Stanley & Wise, 1993) write explicitly about the material conditions of their lives—their sense of place, their sexuality, their backgrounds—as being key to their stance and the process by which they engage in their work. What is remarkable in research and education is not that our work springs from the autobiographical (Graham, 1991); it is the degree to which we deny or suppress this understanding. We refuse to make this autobiographical impulse explicit, preferring instead to hide behind masks and false distinctions, such as public/private, subjective/objective, reason/passion, life/work.

If my work will be of value, I will aim to teach, learn and write according to the same principles I use to guide my relations with people and the world about me. To be sure, coherence is what we can only strive for, not what we can achieve. Our struggles, for example, to live the principles of diversity we espouse, causes us to re-examine the ideas we foster in our teaching. Our resistance to institutional discourse and our politic about non-hierarchical decision-making might, for example, invite us to look at who has a say in our classroom. Our aim to do what we say and say what we do pushes us into wakeful, more humane activity. The work pushes us, writes us. In Richardson's words, our work is the "continual cocreation" of the shifting self and social science (Richardson, 1994, p. 518). We cannot remain the scientistic ghost behind the words. The person we are writes others' worlds from particular positions at particular times. No textual staging is ever innocent (Richardson, 1994, p. 518), nor is it ghost-written. We must try to make visible what we have tried to keep invisible. We must drop the masks, own up to our responsibilities.

Our inquiry is autobiographical not only for the reasons or impulses which draw us to certain questions and contexts, but also for the manner in which we choose to inquire, the genres we are compelled to use, the methods which challenge and invite us.

Knowing Her Place

My preference for richly textured experience and phenomena and my passion for simplicity and attempts at artful expression bring me to qualitative work where writing plays a predominant role in making meaning. The growing wish of researchers who wish to negotiate meaning in relationships, both collegial and intimate, and to give primacy to relationships in the inquiry enterprise, makes the family of ethnographic approaches particularly compatible with their purposes. For me, the tension between knowing and not knowing, between comfortable and troubled, exists for me most directly in feminist inquiry where actively working alongside women to change the conditions of their lives can be a lifelong project (Mies, 1993).

And what of those researchers who choose autobiography itself as a form of inquiry? It is limiting enough that we resist the notion that whatever we choose to study, and the means we choose to study it, reveals much about who we are. But when we, as a research community, resist writing our own research auto-biographies or encouraging the teachers and students with whom we work to do the same, we lose the rich perspective that this "protean, multifaceted, and slippery" genre (Graham, 1991, p. 156) can offer literacy research and education.

From Aristotle onward, the genre of autobiography has remained within the realm of the popular but debased genres. Autobiography is considered a female genre (coded female more as a private act, however, than as a public one, for the literary autobiographies written by white men have become part of the literary canon). Lore Metzger (1994, in Higonnet) reminds us that genre and gender are etymologically linked. They engender "a semantic repertory...much larger and more expansive in French than in English, genre always including gender within its scope. Thus gender is genre's double." In literary as in other social texts, gender "interacts performatively with genre, gender

Notes on Painting Ghosts

identity is performatively constituted by the very expressions which are said to be its results" (1994, p. 83).

Narrative inquiry in literacy research, for example, is considered "soft" inquiry, feminine, not "hard science" like the studies of experimental researchers employing statistical tools and controlled settings. Reflexivity, telling the stories about our researcher roles, is often considered to be self-serving, arrogant, even irresponsible. And yet, it is worth asking whether the charge of narcissistic self-absorption against such inquiry is, in large part, a function of an academic culture which is fearful of passion, emotion, gritty details, unpleasant smells, pillow-biting mistakes, sensuality and sexuality, sharp noises, and messy processes. The typical researcher in literacy education, and I include myself here, has been given to rationalizing feelings, prone to posturing, and over-controlling people and circumstances. To many, telling the stories that account for why we research and what really happens in the process of research is beyond the boundaries of good taste: it is tantamount to flashing in a faculty meeting, or having to explain away one's tipsy aunt in the hallway.

Yet Susan Griffin claims that it is only when "one writes about the most intimate and seemingly idiosyncratic details that one touches others" (1992, p. 316). Bill Pinar argues that the "stories one tells must not be the ones we save for fellow airplane travelers or colleagues we meet annually at AERA. They are not stories to embellish and disguise the past and present...(they are stories which require) the dismantling of self-defenses" (1994, p. 217). Remembering Sidonie Smith's (1987, p. 50) comment that the "ideal woman is self-effacing rather than self-promoting," I take up Jane Tompkins' call to action: "The private-public dichotomy or hierarchy is a founding condition of female oppression. I say to hell with it. The reason I feel embarrassed at my own

269

attempts to speak personally in a professional context is that I
have been conditioned to feel that way. That's all there is to it"
(123, in Miller, *Getting Personal*, 1991, p. 5).

2. Ecological

Our social relationships are rooted in discourse and sustained by them. We live and work in the texts of the world, but
in educational research, just as in education itself, such living
inside the texts we create allows us to ignore the ways in which
these texts weave themselves into the larger ecology of interde-
pendencies and relations among people, ideas, and the particular tasks of living on the planet. But as Jardine (1994) reminds
us, ignoring the consequences of our ecological assumptions
about our work in education may, in fact, threaten the very
sustainability we claim to be working towards. An ecological
awareness reminds us of the tensions inherent in our unstable
interdependence: there is no "securable ground to the living
practices of human life, only ongoing shifting, ambiguous nests
or communities of interrelations which are constantly in need of
renewal, regeneration, rethinking" (Jardine, 1994, p. 510).

The first research study I completed was done in the ener-
getic positivist spirit of isolating factors which might inform an
understanding of writing quality (Neilsen & Piche, 1981). The
fact that I developed "student" passages for teachers to rate, that
these passages had no ecological validity at all, was of no
consequence. I had created what we would now call "textoids";
they served my research purposes, kept the study "clean," and
enabled me to avoid the messy lives and the ragged edges of
student-written passages. I do not repudiate this researcher, as
she was participating in the larger, "scientific" project to which

writing research was then devoted: to understand writing by understanding syntax as a function of cognition and production.

This researcher was a part of her research culture at the time. But as my research repertoire expanded, as my assumptions about knowing and learning shifted from positivist to post-positivist, and then toward constructivist, "meaning in context" (Mishler, 1979) became paramount. Like others experiencing similar shifts in assumptions, I researched the nests of influences in people's lives, the interrelationships of the histories and the experiences. Textured complexity was difficult to manipulate, to name and to write. The lines blurred: a research "project" seemed to have no edges. Meaning in context also meant the challenge of understanding the infusion of the political in the personal, the ways in which data and "facts" can never be bleached of ideology. As Opie (1992) notes, the task is to come with "an overt consciousness of ideology and an awareness that all ideology can obscure and enlighten" (1992, p. 66). Like life in the marsh at the edge of our village, the ecological relations of connection and limitation—the tenuous cycle of birth and death of ideas and other living things—play themselves out in our work as they play themselves out in a larger world. It is our ability to respond in appropriate, flexible, holistic, economical and substantive ways, that we must hone, not only for the sustainability of useful inquiry, but for the sake of generativity as an earthly project in itself.

An ecological understanding of inquiry recognizes that we participate in sets of relationships, and that the quality of our attention to the relationships can be the difference between emancipatory work and exploitative work, between doing to and doing with, between clumsy and wasteful and effective and generative. Inquiry is, at its most basic level, human, dialogic and intersubjective. It is a relationship we must talk about:

271

Knowing Her Place

"Dia"—togetherness, and "legesthai," meaning to tell, or to talk with one another, to argue, to negotiate, to exchange. The work of inquiry is to continually make explicit all the silences, the voices, the differences, and the shared assumptions. It is to use conversation not only to connect, but to disrupt, and to create upheaval, to dismantle old patterns, to reweave new ones. If the relationship is built on mutuality, an understanding that one can never truly know the other, that our points of connection are partial and tap into differing universes, we might then be aware that our respective relationships with the larger universe might give us common ground from which to work. Ethics statements are simply laws for ensuring that people within unequal, or differently valued power relationships are treated fairly, humanely, and with dignity. Ethics statements, however, in their formalizing of what should be common sense, merely serve to reinforce the chasms between the typically elitist, arrogant and isolated academic enterprise of scholarly inquiry and the "subjects" or "objects" of their inquiry. They also remind us how dismissive or unaware we have been about the ecological nature of inquiry. Perhaps if concern for the quality and the limits of our interrelationships were paramount, perhaps if this concern was not considered merely part of the formal requirements, protocols, or hoops to jump in inquiry, but was instead considered integral to the work itself, our inquiry might shift into more collaborative, and response-able dimensions. For this researcher, the quality of my relationship with individuals, with groups, in contexts and systems of contexts, has replaced the quality of my relationship with method as the critical feature and the greatest challenge in my development of research literacies.

The difficulties are stubborn. A feminist ecological perspective on research can not afford a distant manipulative stance as characterized by much traditional scientistic "objective" research practices, nor can it ignore the problems of so-called "full" identification. Feminist inquiry, while it enables me to work alongside women, often taking on their issues with them, is nevertheless a perspective which makes me more accountable for what I do than I have ever been. Living in the most ethical way we know how requires perpetual attention to inequities, particularities, tensions, emotions, desires, and aims. This requires a mutuality of purpose, a compassionate connection that neither elevates inquiry, nor allows retreat.

3. Artistic

To live and work in inquiry is, as Rasberry (1995) has written, "to honor the ambiguity and messiness of our pedagogical and methodological pursuits...to bring great value to the task of researching lived experience." Drawing on work by Leggo (1993) and Jardine (1994), Rasberry aims as a researcher/writer to embrace the poetics of educational research. Borrowing from Al Purdy (1994), he invites us to begin to hear the freezing music, "the mysterious everyday stuff" that takes place in classrooms and other imagined educational settings as "lake water sings into ice." It is an invitations to begin to live poetically in the work, to embrace the suspended moments inside which words dangle us—elusive, mysterious, fecund states which our controlling selves have traditionally been schooled to master, define, name, or categorize.

Artists seem more comfortable in this space than educational researchers, especially those of us trained in empiricist methods and taught to value logic and reason more than unbridled emotion and passion. It is a space that invites anomaly, and relishes ambiguity. For this reason, artists are an endangered species in all areas of education, from curriculum theory to inquiry (Greene, 1995). Artists are outside what Greene calls the "main text" (1995, p. 135); they invite the untried and the unexpected. Artists perceive patterns in new ways, find sensuous openings into new understandings, fresh concepts, wild possibilities. Artists help us subvert the ordinary, and see the extraordinary.

But what has been called scientific thinking can be creative as well; it draws on bisociation (Koestler, 1964), metaphor, and analogy (John-Steiner, 1985), among other processes, to invite anomaly. Unfortunately, the creative practices of science seem to be reserved primarily for the conceptual imaginings around scientific thought, and are rarely found in our methods, in the practice itself of doing educational research. It seems that educational inquiry, in its push to be scientific—typically through the methodological routes of psychology, cognitive science, and most recently anthropology—follows the impulse to name, to define, to use language to sort and to categorize. Only recently do we see educational researchers willing to use language to imagine, to explore, to let go, to explode forms, and create fantastic transgressions for alternate understandings (Neilsen & Clifford, 1996). Only recently do we witness an emergent resistance to fundamentalism, recognizing this need to fix ideas, grinding them into conformity, as an anti-poetic, anti-imaginative force, a force with more concern for control than for connection or transformation.

Language is fundamentally reflexive, and "only in poetic language can one deal with meaning in a revolutionary way" (Trinh Minh-ha, 1994, p. 440). Poetic language, like visual and performance art, among other imaginative genres, offers meaning in open, unending ways, "destabilizing thereby the speaking subject and exposing the fiction of all rationalization" (441).

Notes on Painting Ghosts

Poetic language as an artistic endeavor is also transgressive, slicing sharply across convention and expectation. As women, we can never speak outside the patriarchal system of language, but women's relationship to language, and the way in which we work it and it works us, can be explicitly subversive and transgressive. As we have learned to understand research in various and contradictory ways, we are moving from a predominantly "rational," linear approach to inquiry toward a more artistic, or holistic approach, one which allows for recursiveness and for intuitive leaps which defy audit. Doing early qualitative work, for example, I needed to rely on Spradley's (1980) linear and reductive steps for data gathering and analysis. This was not only because I lacked an understanding of the discipline of qualitative research and required direction to "do it right"; it was also a function—and these are connected—of my participation as a woman in the master narratives of social science at the time. I felt neither confident nor authoritative enough to play, to let go, to embrace the ambiguity and the instability of the process of inquiry. The artist in me—the writer, the visual artist—deferred to the external authority. Living the poetry, but not trusting my authority or ability to write it, I reduced poetically-lived experiences to reports, often stripped of flesh and noise, and certainly more prosaic in language.

The rational, logical, cognitive engagement with ideas and numbers which literacy researchers enjoyed in experimental research and in post-positivist qualitative work is making room for the intuitive, exploratory, aesthetic engagement with people and meanings in feminist inquiry. Richardson sees experimental, quantitative work as having the advantage of economy of expression in tables and summaries, while much traditional qualitative work suffers from schooled practice of "writing up" research, rather than writing for discovery. "Almost unthinkingly, qualitative research training validates the mechanistic model of writing, even though that model shuts down the creativity and sensibilities of the individual researcher" (1994, p. 517). Exploring artistic alternatives (poetic, fictional, narrative, dramatic, anecdotal, among others) to writing research, pushes our inquiry as much as it challenges our writing. Stretching our writing stretches our learning: as Greene says (1995, p. 108), "Learning to write is a matter of learning to shatter the silences, of making meaning, of learning to learn."

Eisner (1991), long an advocate of the artistic turn in inquiry, suggests several features about qualitative work which compare with the artistic enterprise: the researcher/artist as instrument, the use of expressive language, the attention to particulars, and the interpretive nature of the work. Oldfather and West (1994) compare the qualitative research process to the art of jazz: "as jazz is collaborative and interdependent, so are the dynamics of qualitative research. As each improvisation is unique, so are the contextually bound findings within each research setting and the peculiar adaptive methodologies of each qualitative inquiry" (1994, p. 23). Collins (1992) claims that research, like art, demands to be understood in its full context. And Stoller (1989) not only recognizes, but promotes the artistic turn in ethnography. Such a turn leads us toward imagination, toward Keats' notion of "negative capability" in which we embrace uncertainty, mystery and doubt, and detours that admit "the origin of reasonings has a spontaneous "instinctive" quality which makes reasonings immediate, sensuous, and poetic" (1989, p. 152).

The difference between the experimental and more traditional, nomothetically-driven qualitative research I conducted and the feminist ethnographic inquiry in which I now participate has become similar to the difference Frederick Franck (1993, p. 108) describes between taking a snapshot and what he calls

Notes on Painting Ghosts

seeing/drawing: "Memory is benumbed by the pseudo-memory of the snapshot.... Seeing/drawing is a total openness to that which meets the eye...to be in touch with the ground of being, inside and outside of oneself" (108). It is a fluid, shifting relationship. Exploratory and expansive words have, for me, overtaken numbers and logical propositional language in their magical power to create both text and trouble. Geertz reminds me that reality does not have an idiom in which it prefers to be described (1988, p. 140), and so, I choose words. Others will continue to argue that "telling stories, concocting symbolisms, and deploying tropes" are not valid approaches, Geertz says, but the argument arises from "a confusion, endemic in the West since Plato, at least, of the imagined with the imaginary, the fictional with the false, making things out with making things up" (1998, p. 140).

Letting go, as we observe, write, talk, and fully attune ourselves to processes of inquiry commonly brings a heightened sensory awareness, similar to the awareness of artists engaged in creative activity. It is a tension between control and capitulation which psychologist Csikszentmihalyi (1990) calls the "flow state," a state in which full absorption in an activity causes us to lose self-consciousness. Buddhist scholars liken the state to a universal consciousness. But it is a consciousness in which the body is in full concert with the mind. My body/mind is, after all, not an isolated organism, but "a cultural process by which the physical body becomes a site of culturally ascribed and disputed meanings, experiences, feelings" (Stanley & Wise, 1993, p. 196). My conviction about a living literacy extends the feminist claim to "embodied" knowing. An artistic perspective on inquiry embraces, dances and cajoles the senses; it does not repress and deny their role in our learning. It is, as activist Dionne Brand writes about poetry, "just here. Something wrestling with how we live, something dangerous, something honest" (1994, p. 183).

277

Knowing Her Place

As a writer, I have learned as much from personal essayists and literary journalists as I have from research colleagues. As academics, we lose a wider audience when we engage in displays of arcane vocabulary to demonstrate what Patai calls, "correctly positioned scholarship" among contestants in the "vocabulary wars" (Patai, 1994, p. 69). Patai claims the most successful word-slingers are members of a class which has time to indulge in "orgies of abstraction" (71) and displays of power using words in the race for political correctness. As writers, we need to think carefully of the audience we want to reach. If we believe that words are used in the service of connection, and if we believe that inquiry processes and products are open to the entire field of education, including classroom teachers, we must learn to use words to support and reach, not to defend and create barriers between select communities.

The essay form is the genre in which science conflates with art. It bridges the traditionally separated domains of literature, art, and culture and the world of science. The essay is an ambiguous genre, as Barthes says, "in which analysis vies with writing" (Barthes in Lopate, 1995, p. xliii). The personal essay, like the best literary journalism, brings the writer into the writing where she must bear witness: the use of "we," the active, the agent, replaces the passive voice so common in traditional scholarly writing. The personal essay invites poetic language, calls for metaphor and detail. Data appear in the form of critical incidents, stories, and anecdotes; and narrative can be linear, in montage, segmented, fractured. The personal essay enters the realm of inquiry because it recognizes that the process of research relies not on "the interview so much as on the shared experience with somebody" (Conover, in Lopate, 1995, p. 13), allowing the participant/observer a knowledge available neither to the participant nor the observer. During the writing of the

278

inquiry the writer is explicitly inside the text; she is both agent and subject.

The personal, or autobiographical essay is not an attempt to say "This is what is"; it is a genre through which the writer can add her particular voice to the collective chorus pursuing understanding ("this is what I/we see"). In the post-modern abandonment of the truth project, such an approach to writing with/about and for others can be considered nihilistic (Rosenau, 1992) and narcissistic: all such individually-expressed truths are equal, and equally self-indulgent. But writing which admits the writer into the experience can also be considered a contribution to what Haraway (1991) has called a "doctrine of embodied objectivity" (188) in which one situated, partial perspective in the endless play of signifiers contributes to a larger feminist project of dismantling agonistic and arrogant hierarchies. The uncomfortable make jokes about the reflexive nature of some feminist research ("let's talk about me for awhile"), and yet, who else, after all, can we speak for but ourselves?

Ironically, the researcher (and the literary journalist, or essayist) who "goes deep" in inquiry and in writing invites charges of arrogance. And yet, it is the work of finding the one telling detail which may result in text that connects, resonates, lingers, and perhaps moves. And it is movement, resonation that often marks the authenticity of the writing, regardless of the genre we use. When my writing fails to connect, it is because it lacks coherence, verisimilitude and interest (Richardson, 1994, p. 521), traits that speak to the issue of authenticity more than accuracy. Like the quality of the stories passed from one generation to another, it is the recognition of the authentically human that assumes importance in memory and in changing human behavior. "Truths" then become the filaments of light and life between us, at once highly individual and deeply universal.

279

Knowing Her Place

Agar (1995) disagrees. He claims that "ethnographic texts are more about making a case out of collected material than they are about creating entertaining art" (127). His concern is that, while an awareness of textuality in research is long overdue, textuality ought not to take more attention than its due. His worries about self-conscious prose and writerly affectation are understandable, but such an argument is another way of pitting art against conventional notions of science, suggesting a separation between content and form and between words and the ideas within which they are woven. Good qualitative research, like good writing, illuminates, inspires, provokes, startles, enchants, and incites. Good research releases the imagination, opens new worlds. It is meant to turns pages, and it means to turn lives. When words are the signs we read and we write, how can we not consider writing research as "doing fieldwork in the land of representation" (Agar, 1995, p. 127).

• • • • •

Artful living, artful writing, connecting with a purpose to help each other transcend and to grow through inquiry. Connection, embodiment, transformation, transcendence. All these expressions tap spiritual chords. A friend cautions me that my words may sound more like they belong in a crystal workshop than in the research community, and he may be right, at least for now. But if inquiry is to transcend the destructive circumstances of our lifeworlds, if its purpose is to make a difference not make a career, we cannot avoid using words such as vision, spirit, humanity, soul. How can we deny the metaphysics of the work we do? Interest in metaphysical perspectives is not new in feminist circles, but it is new in conventional research communities where the intangible, the deeply-disturbing and con-

sciousness-awakening dimensions of life are compartmental-
ized, reserved for Sunday morning at church, for a walk by the
ocean, for the rare meditative times in our lives, if we find them
at all.

But the awareness we know when we live in the eternal
present, that state of heightened understanding of our place in
the universe of teaching and learning, is an awareness full of
tremendous power and, ultimately, hope. Last year, I spent the
afternoon at the art gallery, at a national show of artists' works
representing women's battle against breast cancer, entitled
"Survivors." Of the women represented by the artists' render-
ings, all had since died. What survived—in the grisly video of a
breast being eviscerated of a tumour, of the sound of a heartbeat
in the room, in the intimate accounts of family members, in the
images of idealized, trivialized, desecrated, distorted, butch-
ered, loved, and lost breasts—was the chorus of anger and
optimism that reverberated long after my colleague and I had
left the room. The immediacy and the depth of this experience
touched us in a way that we knew would mark us for life.

Yes, this too was research, we agreed. It is embodied, spiritual, imagined, lived, engendered. And it endures. The science
we have known and have tried to master or emulate has done
little to move me the way the inquiry into the ravages of this
disease has moved me. When we have touched the nerve of
humanity through working with others intimately and respect-
fully, we are moved to action. And it is this depth we crave, this
connection. Bathetic, simplistic, sentimental, cliched represen-
tations can, like so many popular cultural products, bring easy
tears and even easier publications, but these products rarely
endure in their capacity to incite, disturb, and celebrate, and
rarely linger in our communal memory. Work that matters and
endures is daunting in its expectations, ruthless in its demands,

and uncompromising in its humanity. How can we ignore it?

Our research literacies must be both passionate and com-passionate. Much we have done in and out of classrooms is of the nature my colleague, Ann Vibert, calls "the merely urgent," the tasks of the everyday which we typically perform to keep the world we know functioning, to keep paper moving and institu-tions greedy for our time. Many of our research reports are done as "the merely urgent." But the embodied imaginings of many feminist researchers seek to understand the emotion, imaginal contexts, gut feelings, desires, agonies, and fleshy gestures which disappear behind the discursive practices, the texts which write our everyday. I can, for example (and did), produce a research report which describes the gender inequities in the computer room in a high school, complete with theoretical underpinnings and requisite bibliography. But I know, too that behind that report is the living story of Kelly, overweight, overcome with allergies, picking away at the computer keys in the hopes that she can complete the work on her own (for the boys are busy with their screen games, and would ridicule her lack of skill). She must finish in time to prepare dinner for her father, a widower with physical disabilities, and for her younger sisters. Kelly has told me she wants to learn because she wants a job in the information industry. The details of Kelly's story and my responsibility in working with her are diminished when Kelly is data, when her life becomes my report.

Academic scholarship as we have known it needs re-bodying, re- imagining. As Kathleen Rockhill claims, it is "in the mind, in logic, in a form of discourse which totally erases the body, the emotional, the symbolic, the multiplicities and confusions—and all in ways (which) order the chaos of our lived experiences so that we no longer feel their power, their immobilizing conflicts, as we live them" (1987, p. 6). Feminist scholarship is not immune to this erasure of the body, and we, like Miller (1991, p. 25) must "repersonalize" our work in feminism to create a critical fluency that serves as a relay between scholarly ideas and living exigencies. As I sit at the computer writing this, I am not out there doing grassroots work. Scholarship, whether feminist or otherwise, continues to find it easier to hide behind words in an academic journal or at the podium. And, as Sue Middleton says, "one becomes complacent when one lives in one's head" (1993, p. 7).

As a researcher and a writer, my perspectives and my literacies have changed. Everything has changed. As Susan Griffin has said, "something softens in the field. One begins then, in the light of this changed focus, to see a different outline, moving just there, a dot on the horizon. And then suddenly the whole picture has changed. And it is by grace alone that one moves into a new landscape" (1992, p. 231).

Ahead are the work, and the words. And the hope for grace.

References

Agar, M. (1995). Literary journalism as ethnography: Exploring the excluded middle. In Van Maanen, J. (Ed). (1995) *Representation in ethnography*. Thousand Oaks, CA: Sage.

Aisenberg, N., & Harrington, M. (1988). *Women of academe: Outsiders in the sacred grove*. Amherst, MA: University of Massachussetts Press.

Bell, D. (1993). Yes Virginia, there is a feminist ethnography. In Bell, D. et al (eds). *Gendered fields: Women, men and ethnography*. New York: Routledge.

Bell, D., Caplan, P., & Karim, W.J. (Eds). (1993). *Gendered fields: Women, men and ethnography*. New York: Routledge.

Brand, D. (1994). *Bread out of stone*. Toronto, Ontario: Coach House Press.

Carr, W., & Kemmis, S. (1986). *Becoming critical: Education, knowl-*

edge, and action research. London, UK: Falmer Press.

Cixous, H. (1991). *Coming to writing and other essays.* (Edited by Jenson, D.). Cambridge, MA: Harvard University Press.

Campbell, D., & Stanley, J. (1963). *Experimental and quasi-experimental designs for research.* Chicago, IL: Rand McNally.

Collins, E. (1992). Qualitative research as art. *Theory into Practice,* 31 (2): 181-186.

Cranny-Francis, A. (1995). *The body in the text.* Melbourne, Australia: Melbourne University Press.

Csikszentmihalyi, M. (1990). *Flow: The psychology of optimal experience.* New York: Harper & Row.

Denzin, N., & Lincoln, Y. (Eds). (1994) *Handbook of qualitative research.* Thousand Oaks, CA: Sage.

Dillard, A. (1989). *The writing life.* New York: Harper & Row.

Eisner, E. (1991). *The enlightened eye: Qualitative inquiry and the enhancement of educational practice.* New York: Macmillan.

Fine, M. (1992). *Disruptive voices.* Ann Arbor, MI: University of Michigan Press.

Franck, F. (1993). *Zen seeing, zen drawing.* New York: Bantam.

Frank, B. (1995). Everyday masculinities. Occasional paper. Mount Saint Vincent University, November.

Geertz, C. (1988). *Works and lives: The anthropologist as author.* Stanford, CA: Stanford University Press.

Gitlin, A. (ed). (1994). *Power and method: Political activism and educational research.* New York: Routledge.

Gitlin, A. (1990). Educative research, voice and school change. *Harvard Educational Review,* 60 (4): 443-466.

Goetz, J., & LeCompte, M. (1984). *Ethnography and qualitative design in educational research.* New York: Academic Press.

Graham, R. (1991). *Reading and writing the self: Autobiography in education and the curriculum.* New York: Teachers College Press.

Greene, M. (1995). *Releasing the imagination: Essays on education, the arts and social change.* San Francisco, CA: Jossey-Bass.

Griffin, S. (1992). *A chorus of stones.* New York: Anchor Books, Doubleday.

Grumet, M. (1990). On daffodils that come before the swallow dares. In Eisner, E., & Peshkin, A. (Eds), *Qualitative inquiry in education: The continuing debate.* New York: Teachers College Press, 101-120.

Notes on Painting Ghosts

Guba, E.G., & Lincoln, Y.S. (1987). Naturalistic inquiry. In Dunkin, M.J. (Ed), *The international encyclopedia of teaching and teacher education.* Sydney, Australia: Pergamon Press, 147-151.

Guba, E.G., & Lincoln, Y.S. (1981). *Effective evaluation.* San Francisco, CA: Jossey-Bass.

Haraway, D. (1991). *Simians, cyborgs, and women: The reinvention of nature.* New York: Routledge.

Harding, S. (1991). *Whose science? Whose knowledge? Thinking from women's lives.* Ithaca, NY: Cornell University Press.

Heilbrun, C. (1988). *Writing a woman's life.* New York: Ballantine.

Holland, J., & Blair, M. (1995). *Debates and issues in feminist research and pedagogy.* Clevedon, Avon, UK: The Open University.

James, J. (1996). Experience, reflection, judgment and action. In Bell, D., & Klein, R. (Eds), *Radically speaking: Feminism reclaimed.* North Melbourne, Australia: Spinifex Press, 37-44.

Jardine, D. (1994). "Littered with literacy": An ecopedagogical reflection on whole language, pedocentrism, and the necessity of refusal. *Journal of Curriculum Studies,* 26 (5): 509-524).

John-Steiner, V. (1985). *Notebooks of the mind.* Albuquerque, NM: University of New Mexico Press.

Kelly, U. (1993). *Marketing place: cultural politics, regionalism and reading.* Halifax, Nova Scotia: Fernwood Publishing.

Koestler, A. (1964). *The act of creation.* London, UK: Pan Books.

Leggo, C. (1993). Writing the unwritten sentence: Living poetically with teachers and students. Paper presented at Narrative Conference, London, Ontario, October.

Lincoln, Y., & Guba, E. (1985). *Naturalistic inquiry.* Beverly Hills, CA: Sage.

Lopate, P. (1995). *The art of the personal essay.* New York: Anchor Books, Doubleday.

McCarl Nielsen, J. (1990). *Feminist research methods.* Boulder, CO: Westview Press.

Metzger, L. (1994). Modifications of genre. In Higonnet, M. (Ed), *Borderwork: Feminist engagements with comparative literature.* New York: Cornell University Press.

Middleton, S. (1993). *Educating feminists: Life histories and pedagogy.* New York: Teachers College Press.

Mies, M. (1993). Towards a methodology for feminist research. In

Knowing Her Place

Hammersley, M. (Ed.), *Social research: Philosophy, politics, and practice.* London, UK: Sage Publications.

Miller, N. (1991). *Getting personal: Feminist occasions and other autobiographical acts.* New York: Routledge.

Minh-ha, T. (1994). Visualizing theory: "In dialogue." In Taylor, L. (Ed.). (1994). *Visualizing theory: Selected essays from V.A.R. 1990-1994.* New York: Routledge.

Mishler, E. (1979). Meaning in context: is there any other kind? *Harvard Educational Review,* 49: 1-19.

Mishler, E.G. (1990). Validation in inquiry-guided research: The role of exemplars in narrative studies. *Harvard Educational Review,* 60 (4): 415-442.

Morrison, T. (1992). *Playing in the dark.* New York: Vintage Books.

Neilsen, L. (1997). Re-making sense, re-shaping inquiry: Feminist metaphors and a literacy of the possible. In Flood, J., Brice Heath, S., & Lapp, D. (Eds). *Handbook for literacy educators: Research in teaching the communicative and visual arts.* New York: Macmillan.

Neilsen, L., & Clifford, P. (1996). Fantastic transgressions in literacy research. Paper presented at the annual meeting of the National Reading Conference, Charleston, SC.

Neilsen, L. (1993a). Exploring reading: Mapping the personal text. In Straw, S., & Bogdan, D. (Eds.), *Teaching Beyond Communication.* Portsmouth, NH: Boynton-Cook/Heinemann.

Neilsen, L. (1993b). Women, literacy, and agency: Beyond the master narratives. *Atlantis,* 18 (1 & 2): 177-189.

Neilsen, L. (1993c). Authoring the questions: Research as an ethical enterprise (A response to Ridgeway, D., & Quian). *Reading Research Quarterly,* 28 (4): 350-353.

Neilsen, L. (1990). When writing goes to work: Voice, power and the culture of the workplace. Occasional paper. McGill University Faculty of Education.

Neilsen, L. (1989). *Literacy and living: The literate lives of three adults.* Portsmouth, NH: Heinemann Educational Books.

Neilsen, L., & Piche, G. (1981). The influence of headed nominal complexity and lexical choice on teachers' evaluation of writing. *Research in the Teaching of English,* 15 (1): 65-73.

Oldfather, P., & West, J. (1994). Qualitative research as jazz. *Educational Researcher,* 21 (8): 22-26.

Notes on Painting Ghosts

Opie, A. (1992). Qualitative research, appropriation of the 'other' and empowerment. *Feminist Review,* 40 (Spring): 53-69.

Patai, D. (1994). When method becomes power. In Gitlin, A. (ed.), *Power and method: Political activism and educational research.* New York: Routledge.

Pinar, W.F. (1994). *Autobiography, politics and sexuality.* New York: Peter Lang.

Purdy, A. (1994). *Naked with summer in your mouth.* Toronto, Ontario: Macmillan.

Rasberry, G. (1995). Who hears the freezing music: An investigation into the writing lives of preservice teachers. PhD prospectus. University of British Columbia.

Richardson, L. (1994). Writing: A method of inquiry. In Denzin, N., & Lincoln, Y. (Eds.), *Handbook of qualitative research.* Thousand Oaks, CA: Sage.

Rockhill, K. (1987). The chaos of subjectivity in the ordered halls of academe. *Canadian Woman Studies,* 8 (4), Winter.

Rosenau, P.M. (1992). *Post-modernism and the social sciences: Insights, inroads, and intrusions.* Princeton, NJ: Princeton University Press.

Schatzman, L., & Strauss, A. (1973). *Field research: Strategies for a natural sociology.* Englewood Cliffs, NJ: Prentice-Hall.

Sims, N., & Kramer, M. (Eds.). (1995). *Literary journalism.* New York: Ballantine Books.

Spradley, J. (1980). *Participant observation.* New York: Holt, Rinehart & Winston.

Stanley, L., & Wise, S. (1993). *Breaking out again: Feminist ontology and epistemology.* New York: Routledge.

Stoller, P. (1989) *The taste of ethnographic things.* Philadelphia, PA: University of Pennsylvania Press.

Yaeger, P. (1991). Afterward. In Bauer, D.M., & McKinstry, S.J. (Eds.). (1991). *Feminism, Bakhtin and the dialogic.* Albany, NY: State University of New York Press.

About the Author

Lorri Neilsen teaches courses in literacy, gender, and research at Mount Saint Vincent University in Halifax, Nova Scotia, Canada. As a scholar, essayist, poet, and reviewer, Nielsen has published widely in academic circles and the popular press. In her research and teaching, she explores literacies for learning, the art of inquiry (and the arts in inquiry), and writing as research.

Permission has been received to use the following essays in their original and revised forms:

"Exploring reading: Mapping the personal text" was originally published in Straw, S., & Bogdan, D. (Eds.). (1993). *Constructive reading: Teaching beyond communication*. Portsmouth, NH: Boynton-Cook.

A version of "Women, literacy, and agency: Beyond the master narratives" was published in *Atlantis: A Women's Studies Journal*, Volume 18 (No. 1 & 2), 1993, Institute for the Study of Women, Halifax, Nova Scotia, Canada.

"Literacy of the invisible" was published in another form in Woodrow, H., & McGrath, C. (Eds.). (1998). *Wayfaring*. St. John's, Newfoundland, Canada: Harrish Press.

"Re-making sense, re-shaping inquiry: Feminist metaphors and a literacy of the possible" is reprinted with permission of Macmillan Library Reference USA, a Simon & Schuster Macmillan Company, from Flood, J., Heath, S.B., & Lapp, D. (Eds). (1997). *Handbook of research on teaching literacy through the communicative and visual arts*.

"Playing for real: Performative texts and adolescent identities" was published in Alverman, D., Hinchman, K., Moore, D., Phelps, S., & Waff, D. (Eds). (1998). *Reconceptualizing the literacies in adolescents' lives*. Mahwah, NJ: Lawrence Erlbaum Associates.